D1291654

EVIDENTIAL
DOCUMENTS

A Monograph in
THE POLICE SCIENCE SERIES

Edited by
V. A. LEONARD
Professor of Police Administration
The State College of Washington
Pullman, Washington

Third Printing

EVIDENTIAL
DOCUMENTS

By

JAMES V. P. CONWAY

Examiner of Questioned Documents
San Francisco, California
Postal Inspector
in charge
San Francisco Identification Laboratory
U. S. Postal Inspection Service

Police Science Series

CHARLES C THOMAS • PUBLISHER
Springfield • Illinois • U.S.A.

Published and Distributed Throughout the World by
CHARLES C THOMAS • PUBLISHER
Bannerstone House
301-327 East Lawrence Avenue, Springfield, Illinois, U.S.A.

ISBN 0-398-00342-4

Library of Congress Catalog Card Number: 58-12151

First Printing, 1959
Second Printing, 1972
Third Printing, 1978

With THOMAS BOOKS careful attention is given to all details of manufacturing and design. It is the Publisher's desire to present books that are satisfactory as to their physical qualities and artistic possibilities and appropriate for their particular use. THOMAS BOOKS will be true to those laws of quality that assure a good name and good will.

Printed in the United States of America
00-2

DEDICATED
to the
UNITED STATES POSTAL INSPECTOR
Devoted Servant
of the
DIVINE LAW OF JUSTICE

INTRODUCTION

Society has evolved today into literally a world of documents. Whether one's interests and pursuits be commercial, social, educational, governmental, military, scientific, legal, investigative, or criminal, one needs, prepares, acts upon, is obstructed by, and complains about existent and non-existent documents.

It is the President's signature on the engrossed bill which consummates his official sanction of law of the land. It is one's signature which directs and approves the withdrawal of funds from his bank account. One's signature is intimately identified with virtually his every consequential act. And it is the forger's, the extortioner's, and the confidence man's documentary handiwork which diverts millions annually from the unwary victim to the hand of the document fabricator.

One's birth certificate, baptismal record, high school transcript, college diploma, medical records, automobile operator's permit, draft board notice, marriage certificate, checks, insurance policies, stock certificates, notes, contracts, citizenship certificate, passport, correspondence, even liquor permit, and finally his last will and testament document him through life. Usually man's documents are not put to rest until long after he has been so reposed, accompanied, of course, by a duly executed death certificate. Or was it duly executed?

To this ticker tape world of documents, handwritten and typewritten, important and inconsequential, genuine and spurious, we have arrived in a relatively short span. Fifty years ago, many households in the United States contained no one who could read and write. Twenty-five years ago, the check had not supplanted gold, silver, and greenbacks in most important commercial transactions. Goods formerly were bought and sold sans today's routine invoices and receipts.

Until a few years ago, one could just about prove he had been born without producing a birth certificate. And he might

vii

secure employment without being processed to the cacophony of a seemingly never ending batch of papers in the "personnel department." We only recently reached the dizzy stage when one must "confirm by letter," perhaps addressed to an office across the hall, statements solemnly presented and witnessed by a dozen people, tried and true.

The purpose of "Evidential Documents" is to lead the reader to take some stock of our present state of documentary affairs, as it affects those concerned with the enforcement of our civil and criminal statutes, especially the latter. As does his brother in legitimate pursuits, the criminal leans on a scrap of paper in the commission of many crimes, in fact most of them. He has found that it is more in keeping with the times to "hold up" a bank with a fountain pen or even its little ballpen cousin, than with a .45 caliber automatic.

In this author's view, the criminal and the civil deceiver will be identified and exposed in more and more cases, if his "scrap of paper" is recognized, questioned, and caused to tell truly by whom it was spawned and whence it came. There is no room in efficient law enforcement today for any reluctance to recognize that proof through the proper interpretation of evidential documents is a necessary, potent, and reliable arm of investigation.

It is the endeavor of the following pages (a) to emphasize the necessity for greater document consciousness in the field of law enforcement, (b) to point up the inadequacy of perfunctory, prima facie acceptance of consequential documents, (c) to advance fundamentals which experience has shown to be effective in the investigative approach to and the technical development of typical document issues, with especial emphasis being accorded to questions involving handwriting because they represent the most common problem, (d) to develop some of the considerations and thinking which are relevant to effective and productive cooperation among the investigator, the attorney, and the examiner of questioned documents, and (e) to be of some assistance to administrative officials who must determine whether their organizations are efficiently exploiting the evidentiary possibilities of documents.

Complementary to these objectives is this writer's hope that the hereinafter data will stimulate those now in the novitiate of the questioned document field, and awaken aspirations in even one additional qualified student to follow in the paths of those men of integrity and objectivity who are promoting justice through the application of scientific principles to suspect and disputed documents.

PREFACE

As expressed introductorily, our modern civilization routinely attests by its daily practices to the individuality, the utility, the efficacy, and the indispensability of documents—as legal and commercial media, as personal emissaries, and as the instruments of crime. Concurrently, there has scarcely been developed an adequate awareness of the availability of proof through evidential documents and a determination by every area of law enforcement to embrace unreservedly these treasurehouses of evidence.

In a close and daily association of nearly twenty years with hundreds of law enforcement officials, civil investigators, attorneys, and administrative personnel from a wide variety of agencies, throughout the United States and a number of foreign countries, in public and in private service, the author has too frequently noted a casual, helter-skelter, unsystematic, and occasionally a downright incompetent appraisal of evidential documents. Conversely, one observes that those officers, those prosecutors, those administrators who exhibit an acute comprehension of the evidential possibilities of documents contemporaneously demonstrate proficiency in their companion responsibilities.

Some encouragement and a lesson or two may be derived from the history of our utilization of the fingerprint. Only fifty odd years ago, society and law enforcement had begun to acknowledge that the fingerprint was a vital arm of investigation and identification. Proceeding from such recognition has been the development of trained personnel and facilities for recording, classifying, filing, investigating, developing, analyzing, and testifying in respect to fingerprints.

Society, the legal profession, the law enforcement profession —they are properly proud of their achievements in the field of fingerprint evidence. At the same time, the facts must not remain obscured that while the fingerprint system is supreme for purposes of direct personal identification, for every single civil and criminal case which is solved via fingerprints, there are thousands wherein the truth lies in documents—documents, those deponents which are not subject to the vagaries of the direct witness' recollection, even when that witness endeavors to bespeak the truth.

It is not in any sense intended to disparage our accomplishments in respect to fingerprint evidence. Neither is it sought to belittle our past and continuing progress in the effective utilization of documents as evidence. These very worthwhile advancements, only part of the broad front on which law enforcement procedures and techniques have progressed within a single generation, light the road ahead. However, it is desired to emphasize that if law enforcement generally will but direct all its *reasoning* powers to evidential documents, the development of greater technical skills respecting them will follow with needful acceleration.

No pretension is embraced that this or any book can or even should try to suggest everything which should be considered in respect to every evidential document case. Rather it is hoped that a discussion of some of the things which should be considered in some cases will help the reader to consider more of the things which should be considered in more cases.

In this brief effort, emphasis seems inexorably drawn to document problems which are intimate to or represent the corpus delecti in general and in cited case situations. It is especially hoped that the reader by acquiring an appreciation of these major document problems may become alert in developing minor and collateral documents to assist in proof of facts, which do not per se hinge on any document.

Finally, it is not intended to suggest that there is a lay substitute for the experienced, qualified examiner of questioned documents who devotes full time to the practice of this new profession, or to relate the what, the how, and the why of every consideration he must explore in his laboratory. It is hoped to stimulate recognition of the existence of rewarding document questions, to expose some of those questions which the law enforcement officer can himself answer, those in which the general criminalist or general identification specialist can be of assistance, and those which merit the thorough laboratory study by the expert examiner of questioned documents.

The chapter specifically relating to the procurement of handwriting exemplars or standards of comparison, has been intentionally positioned subsequent to earlier chapters on the common basic document problems, namely those involving signatures, handwriting, handprinting, and numerals. It is felt that the psychology and mechanics of exemplar procurement will be much more readily apprehended, if the reader will have previously acquired some familiarity with the problems which exemplars are intended to solve.

References and citations to illustrations have been avoided throughout the text to promote continuity, although illustrations generally are proximate to textual matter which they are designed to demonstrate.

Names, words, and signatures appearing in illustrations have been selected to portray technical data only. Some of the signatures have at some time been forged and some of the names have been used as aliases. Others became available incident to research or were graciously supplied by persons cooperating in experimental studies. No unfavorable inference or reference is intended to any person using any of these names legitimately.

Grateful acknowledgment is extended to Messrs. George G. Swett and Francis X. LaTulipe, Examiners of Questioned Documents, Saint Louis, Missouri, and San Francisco, California, respectively, for their valuable assistance in providing a number of illustrations from their extensive casework experiences for use in this volume.

J. V. P. C.

San Francisco, California

CONTENTS

EVIDENTIAL
DOCUMENTS

DOCUMENT CONSCIOUSNESS

Documents depict man, his motives, his words, and his works. Evidential documents encompass all documents, writings, type-writings, printings, and marks intended to prove, or capable of proving, any principal or collateral fact of investigative or legal interest.

Evidential documents are competent witnesses as surely as are their authors. Though silent, they need not remain inarticulate. Because inanimate, they need enjoy no immunity from question. Documents are personal word pictures, intimate brain-children of their authors. Like their authors, they are in turn virtuous and authentic, then evil and spurious. Unless questioned, they some-times mislead, lie, cheat, and travel incognito. If questioned, they usually will tell the truth of their authorship and history.

Frequently, evidential documents are misapprehended simply because they have remained totally unquestioned. Intermittently, they are ignored when they fairly shriek for a hearing. Too often, they are forced to stand mute when they have much to tell. Occasionally, they are misinterpreted by unskilled and bungling questions. But unswervingly they stand ready to unmask the guilty, to exonerate the falsely accused, and to uphold the truth because their very inanimacy does not permit them partisanship or dishonor.

In this enlightened age, evidential documents can be caused consistently to reveal the truth of their authorship and their gen-uine import by the intelligent, reasoning intercooperation of investigator, document examiner, attorney, and judge. The reve-lation of the truth from evidential documents is the logical out-growth of a practical, realistic, inquiring attitude. Treat docu-ments like people. Accept them for what they are, but be sure they are what they say they are. The right of reasonable inter-rogation and cross-examination is inherent in our way of life as to verbal evidence. So should it be with documents. Corroboration

1

is sought in weighty matters even for the testimony of the recognized man of high repute. This too should apply to documents. They should be routinely subjected to inquiry, searching but not unreasonably suspicious, thorough but not unreasonably overdrawn, and subjective but including the objective impact of everything surrounding them.

In considering the proper basic approach to evidential documents, it is appropos to contrast the variety of unrealistic attitudes which one encounters in the law enforcement, legal, and judicial professions. We see the detective or attorney who contends "Why should I be expected to know anything about handwriting or this so-called questioned document business?" He makes his own job difficult and unproductive because his non-recognition of the realties of the day causes him to attempt conclusions without the important facts documents alone can reveal. Paradoxically, this sort frequently will allow that he is considered somewhat of an authority on "evidence."

Then there is the investigator who cannot shoulder responsibility. He would not presume to look searchingly on a questioned document because he fears he might fail to see or interpret correctly an important evidential fact therein, and his own limitations would be exposed. He protests "I know absolutely nothing about handwriting, about documents," and hopes that by avoiding his document problems, they will solve themselves. When that fails, he stumbles belatedly to the most convenient document examiner to sublet his problem. Even at this point, he would not presume to inquire or evaluate whether he has consulted a good, bad, or indifferent document examiner, or has compiled adequate or inadequate documentary data.

Quite different is the superscientific police chief or special agent perhaps, who indulges a calculated risk that his superiors do not review critically his results. He ambitiously reckons to demonstrate his competency and scientific objectivity by consulting criminalists, document experts, chemists, and all manner of specialists, on the slightest provocation. This boy, and not necessarily in years, is not too sure exactly what he is accomplishing but he stages an impressive show and the line of least resistance on the part of his superiors seems to be to go along with him rather than to risk criticism for failing to be "modern" and "scientific."

An opposite number whom we occasionally brush against is the independent, negative-minded sort, perhaps a government executive, a trust officer, a "I came up the hard way" police official, or even a jurist. Although not necessarily old in years, he is rather opposed to all things new, unless he originated them himself. This type tends to resent the assistance of specialists as an intrusion into his sphere of responsibility. Even when his arms seem to become too short for the fine printing in the telephone book, he is reluctant to concede that a document examiner with sound photographic illustrations can help him arrive at the truth concerning evidential documents. And he tries to silence his gnawing conscience by insisting that his intuition is superior to any so-called scientific evidence.

The unimaginative, self-satisfied probate lawyer, tax investigator, or personnel officer presents a further variety. True, he has heard about forgeries and that sort of thing, but such incidents are remote, he keeps telling himself, and they certainly could not happen in his organization. He would be shaken to learn how many times his attitude had blinded him to backdated deeds, altered notes, fictitious transfers, fraudulent invoices, and forged references.

The egotist who virtually dares the specialist to develop conclusions from inefficiently assembled and inadequate documents is becoming scarcer but he is not extinct. He is the patient who withholds symptoms and then criticizes the doctor's diagnosis. The demise and burial of an unsolved questioned document problem does not disturb him.

The pushing, partisan advocate is ever present—perhaps the prosecutor who is disposed to ignore documents which do not coincide with the prosecution's theory. He may be the attorney for the defendant forger who is "form blind" to agreements but "sees" differences galore in his client's typewriting as compared with a fabricated document. Or the testy investigator who cannot comprehend why the document examiner cannot identify the skimpy seven-letter forged endorsement because "After all, the storekeeper who cashed the check has made a personal identification, hasn't he?" Or perhaps the chief of inspectors who always sees similarities, never differences, when he compares embarrassingly unsolved forgeries with the writings of suspects. Or the bureau chief who insists that the document expert certainly ought to be able to determine whether an ink writing is three years, nine months, four days, seven hours, and twelve minutes old.

Whatever one's past attitude, several realities should be faced squarely. Every person who can read and write does know "something" about handwriting, about typewriting, about ink, about pens, about pencils, and about documents in general. Each literate member of society has enjoyed some training in the preparation and execution of documents and experience in their uses. And he who embraces the responsibility to draw inferences and conclusions from evidence must ever seek to learn more about evidential documents, with their fortes and their foibles, because documents hold the inevitable plurality in our evidential media. Whether he approves or not, each officer, each attorney, and each judge must recognize that documents are going to characterize virtually everything he does and encounters in his professional life. Those who assume from the whole of society the obligations of investigating, presenting, accepting, ruling upon, and acting on important documents must be document conscious if they are to discharge properly their respective and collective responsibilities.

Fortunately with every passing day, the objective, orderly, accurate evaluator of men and their documents slowly but surely becomes more in the majority. He is found in our law enforcement agencies and courtrooms in ever increasing numbers. He is characterized first of all by his practical common sense. He understands, forthrightly, that every art and science is his ready ally in the discovery of the truth and the unmasking of error. He is document conscious because he knows well that documents surround our every act and that no law enforcement officer, attorney, or judge can be completely efficient and effective without a thoughtful discerning approach to every evidential document. He comprehends fully that document evidence is intrinsically the same as other evidence, in that it should be accepted or rejected, it should stand or fall, on its reasonableness and inherent convincingness.

There follow a few general questions pertinent to every document and a number of specific questions relevant to a few documents. It has been observed repeatedly that the most frequently overlooked of these inquiries are those which should be the most obvious. These questions are in no sense all inclusive of considerations which merit study but they provide a basis for the thoughtful, reasoning approach to evidential documents. The applicability of these and other questions will be elaborated in the ensuing pages.

1. When and where did the document, say a check, deed, or note first appear?
2. By whom was it presented? What is his interest? His reputation?
3. Is the document's very existence suspicious? Doth it protest too much the cause it was designed to serve?
4. What did the presentor say about the document at the time he presented it? Later? Why discrepancies, if there be such?
5. Is the document in the same condition now as when it was first presented? Have you so assumed or do you really know?
6. By whom does the document purport to have been drawn or prepared?
7. Have you erroneously assumed that the date, body, and signature were written by the same person?
8. If an endorsement, have you assumed that the signature and address were written by the same person? Can you establish the correctness of your assumption?
9. What do the executors of the document have to say about their participation? Did they indulge complete details or were they glossed over? Did you err by permitting a collaborated story to be given by several interested parties?

10. Is the date of the document logical to its content? If a letter, did the author betray himself by improper tense of verbs or the "forecasting" of events inconsistent with the document's date?

11. Is the date of the document consistent with the movements of the principal? Have you considered hospitalization, injuries, vacations, business trips?

12. Was the document presented timely in the light of its date? If not, where has it been, and why?

13. Are the writing media, pen, pencil, paper, and ink, consistent with the document's date and the representations made for it by its proponents? With the habits of its purported author at the time in question? With his physical and mental condition at that time?

14. Have you identified the author and signer through his or their handwriting or have you merely assumed writing authenticity? Have you acquired technically adequate, provable, and legally admissible exemplars?

15. Have you examined companion documents of proper vintage to ascertain their agreement or otherwise with the habits reflected in the evidential documents?

16. Do you recognize that authentic companion documents provide a much more reliable mode of proof than self-serving, accusatory, or otherwise partisan statements by interested principles?

17. Have you reconciled disagreements between the evidential document and companion documents? Is your reconciliation reasonable in itself and consistent with the representations made by the proponents of the document?

18. Are there witnesses to the preparation, execution, or presentation of the document? What is his or their interest? Reputation?

19. Have the witnesses supplied complete details as to time, place, and circumstances? If not, why not? Do they remember not wisely but too well all the self-serving details?

20. Are the witnesses certain they could not be confused about a similar document? A similar transaction? Was your consideration of these points cursory? Partisan? Presumptive?

21. Does the document, for example a check, have a number? Should it have one in view of the habits of its purported author?

22. Is the number of the document, say a check or invoice, in proper sequence by comparison with companion documents of the same vintage, or has it clearly been postdated or antedated?

23. Have you too readily accepted a hotel or motel registration as an alibi? Does its time and does its number coincide with other registrations of the same date? Is it supported by correct accounting records? Is its format, including printing, in agreement with companion registrations?

24. Does the document bear any indication or suggestion of an erasure or alteration? Is the suspect area contiguous to or does it embody a key part of the document?

25. If a photostat, where is the original? Is presentation of the photostat rather than the original suspicious in itself?

26. If a photostat, why is the original unavailable to you, if it is? If a court order or permission of a third party is necessary for inspection of the original, have you ascertained complete details for timely action?

27. Have you considered and accounted for ALL the handwriting, initials, addresses, telephone numbers, identification data, stamped impressions, etc., on the questioned check?

28. Have you been wasting your time, or do you have men on your staff who have been dissipating their time, comparing check endorsements with the writing of suspected forgers, without first ascertaining that parts of these endorsements were not written by the forger at all, but represent the handwriting of the second endorser or his agent?

29. Have you dissipated hours of investigative time, reached erroneous conclusions, and perhaps confused your document examiner, by comparing the signatures or issuing particulars on forged checks, when your problem involved *tracings and simulations?*

30. Have you issued circulars which advertised all too clearly that your department did not understand how responsibility must be established in cases involving *tracings and studied simulations?*

31. Does the document purport to have been written or signed with a ball point pen prior to 1945?

32. Does the document purport to have been written or signed with a liquid lead pencil prior to 1955?

33. Does the typewritten document contain a short center "W" or "w" and is it dated prior to 1935?

34. Is the document, perhaps a will, hiding behind deceased witnesses? Have you examined their signatures of comparable date, or have you assumed somewhat automatically that the witnesses' signatures are authentic?

35. Is the document ceremoniously hiding behind a notarial or other seal of no real identifying value?

36. Have you established that the notary or other public official physically witnessed execution of a document, so purporting? If so, did he correctly identify the signer?

37. Is the seal on the document legible and authentic? Have you compared it with admittedly authentic seals?

38. Have you assumed that the signature of the notary or other public official was authentic? Have you compared companion signatures? Are the latter and related records for the date in issue maintained with similar pen and ink?

39. If a printed form, have you checked its origin? Have you compared similar and companion forms of corresponding date?

40. Is the location of an obliterated or eradicated area of the document highly suspicious in itself? Have you sought specialized assistance to develop the original writing?

41. If the document is folded, is this condition consistent with its alleged origin and later repositories?

42. If the document contains creases and folds, allegedly because it was carried about in a pocket or wallet, is the document's condition in respect to soiling consistent with this alleged history? Is the document clean where it should be soiled and vice versa? Do the folds fail to reduce the document small enough to fit the wallet or pocket in which it allegedly was placed?

43. Does the document fit the envelope in which it was allegedly received? Do depressions and impressions correspond? Ink and pencil smudges?

44. If a mailed inclosure, does it bear a latent postmark inconsistent with the visible postmark on the envelope in which it was allegedly inclosed?

45. Does the document bear a watermark consistent with its date?

46. Have you studied both the apparent and latent thought content of the document, for example, an anonymous letter, for evidences of authorship?

47. Have you catalogued the individualities of word choice, colloquialisms, spelling, arrangement, capitalization, and mode of expression for evidences of authorship? Have you delineated the individualities of letter conformation and letter connections?

48. Does the document have a foreign script or language influence even though its alleged author was born and educated in the United States? Or does it have unmistakable "United States" script and language despite the allegation that its author was born and educated in Europe?

49. Are you satisfied that you have scrutinized the document thoroughly from top to bottom, front and back, and accounted for all writing, typewriting, printing, job numbers, marks, holes, discolorations, odors, erasures, folds, creases, seals, bindings, fasteners, indentations, depres-

sions, and what have you, therein and thereon? Have your aggregate inferences supported the representations made by the proponents of the document? Have your aggregate inferences clearly established the document's true origin and subsequent history?

50. Have you consulted a qualified document examiner? Should you now?

Of more than passing note is what seems to be a proclivity of our age, namely, to assume a great deal simply because a particular document exists, has a particular name on it, and rests in a particular place. It cannot be emphasized too strongly that the proponent of every consequential document should, by casual but incisive questioning, be caused timely to take a definite position about every facet of that document. What the proponent initially has to say about the origin, preparation, signing, and handling of his document furnishes a yardstick by which such document may be measured.

At the time a document is first presented, its proponent wears the burden of explaining it, of justifying it. He should be caused to exercise fully this responsibility at that time, before he shifts the weight of his responsibility or evades it entirely. Later revisions in his explanation or justification concerning the document will provide media of testing his credibility and the document's reliability. It should not be overlooked that the presentor of a fraudulent document in many cases is later permitted to "fashion" a defensible position concerning a document's discrepancies simply because he was not pinned down to definite, detailed statements about the document's origin, preparation, signing, and handling, when he first presented it. Physical irregularities in a document provide definite evidence of fraud, if they are in direct conflict with material statements made by the presentor of the document. However, such irregularities are explained away on occasion by fabricators who were not required to furnish detailed statements prior to disclosure of the document's irregularities.

Similarly, the authors of incriminating documents on occasion elude identification because of the failure of investigators to obtain timely and demonstrative exemplars. The individualities of a questioned document provide evidence of authorship. However, these individualities can demonstrate authorship only when fully linked to companion exemplars, independently identified with their author. Thoroughness in the development of background data concerning evidential documents, thoroughness in the compilation of all representations made for evidential documents by their presentors, thoroughness in the procurement of companion documents as exemplars, and thoroughness in evaluating every identifying characteristic of evidential documents, together provide a solid foundation for sound conclusions.

It is suggested that a searching appraisal of one's past practices in the light of even the fifty sets of questions hereinbefore listed, and others which will prompt themselves thereafter, will stimulate proper future approaches to documents which are presented as support for evidential facts, motives, and circumstances. The most minute detail of a document, even a little staple hole, may be the beacon which will light up the truth concerning that document.

EVIDENTIAL SIGNATURES

Webster would define a signature as one's name written by himself on a document as a sign of acknowledgment. Investigators of evidential signatures should not succumb to the simplicity of this intrinsically correct definition.

Most writers have at least three classes of signatures: the formal, complete, correct signature for an important document

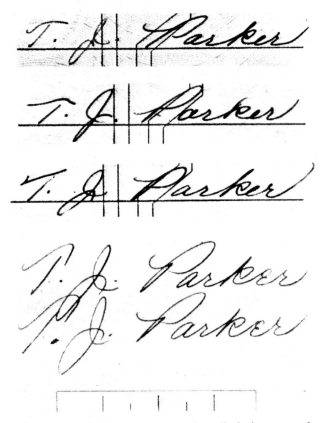

Figure 1. Signatures of above average writer disclosing normal variations in initial and terminal strokes and optional letter designs.

such as a will; the informal, cursory signature for routine documents and personal correspondence; and the careless scribble for the mail carrier, delivery boy, and perchance the autograph collector.

Many writers, conscious of possible forgery, inject a "secret" personal ingredient into their signatures on checks or important business correspondence which would not be employed in their signatures on a different class of documents of a more personal character. Some writers intentionally alter their business and check signatures from time to time. Others vary considerably with the type of instrument used—fountain pen, steel pen with holder, ball pen, pencil, marking crayon.

The events immediately preceding the execution of a signature may have a material bearing on its fluency or otherwise. Have you noticed, for example, that grotesque scrawl your strained hand recorded on the hotel register immediately after you dropped your heavy luggage? Or the scribble the telegram messenger received from your frigid hand as the snow fell in January? Or the self-satisfied, rhythmic signature you endorsed on the first check which marked your largest salary increase?

All writers are affected in lesser or in greater degree by injuries to their writing member, illness, advancing age, radical changes in writing incidence, excitement, hurry, unusual writing positions, unaccustomed writing implements, missing spectacles, intoxication, irritability, heavy medication, and intentional deception. These ramifications of signatures at times will impede but they will not mislead the investigator who insures that such ramifications routinely receive intelligent, thorough consideration.

The thorough investigator will weigh carefully the circumstances which attended the signing of any evidential document and he will apply those circumstances to the evidential signature continuously in his appraisal of it and in his comparisons thereof with admitted and proved signatures. When the precise circumstances are unknown or partially unknown, the diligent inquirer for the truth will compose a reasonable hypothesis of the probable and possible surrounding circumstances. An evidential signature is not simply a signature—it is a signature, signed at a particular

Figure 2. Signatures by average writer embodying normal variations in letter size, spacing, and flourishes.

time and place, under particular conditions, while the signer was at a particular age, in a particular physical and mental condition, using particular implements, and with a particular reason and purpose for recording his name. These circumstances must follow the evidential signature. They are as integral a part of it as the letters which comprise it.

QUESTIONED

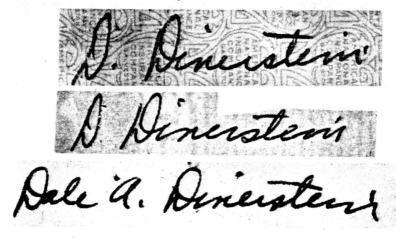

EXEMPLARS

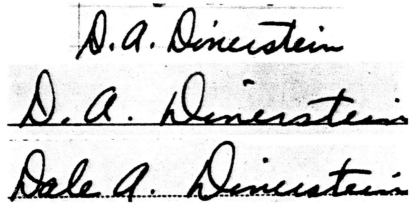

Figure 3. Signatures by somewhat below average writer revealing limited variation and limited individuality.

It should be understood that no conclusion in respect to the genuineness of any signature is in order without comparing such signature with other signatures which have been proved to be authentic. However, genuine signatures per se embody certain characteristics of their legitimacy. Studied attention to the writing process is a necessity for the forger as a general rule. Conversely, lack of attention to the writing operation is a concomitant of the signer of his own name as a general rule. The genuine writer need inject no guile and deception. He has no fear of the sort which might engulf him in attempting to adopt the writing personality of another. Uncertainty and unfamiliarity with the name do not plague his efforts. The authentic signer knows his own writing operation fully. Remember he has been writing his signature for years, over and over again, and he suffers no trepidation about why and how he should sign his own name. His mind provides only the general impulse—his hand knows his signature well. He may begin with a freewheeling start, with the pen motion preceding the actual spot where the pen comes into contact with the paper. He may write quite rapidly if he is that sort of an individual, or he will write slowly if he is a more deliberate fellow, but his writing mien is natural and consistent within itself.

The signer of his own name may indulge careless, slam-bang "i" dots, "t" crosses and punctuation. He may form some very delicate strokes and again shaded pressurized strokes. He may conform some letters much differently than anyone else or at least give uniqueness a good try in his letter designs. He will probably inject a bit of variety in the design of the *same* letter, depending on its preceding and ensuing letters. He may finish with a flourish if he feels that way. He may exhibit laboriousness if he has never learned to write with facility, or he may have reached the labor of age or illness. *But he will be natural and consistent withal.* And when he blunders in his signature, he need not surreptitiously hide his patching or correcting strokes. After all, who has a better right to correct it, he says, it is his own name and nobody else's, isn't it?

In brief, and reiterating always that no conclusion as to genuineness is warranted in advance of a comparison with proved au-

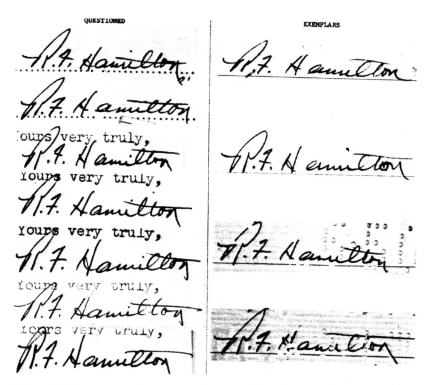

Figure 4. Signatures of average writer revealing individuality in vigorous, rhythmic execution, capital letter proportions, initial movement of *a*, final stroke of *n*, and *t* crossing.

thentic signatures of proper vintage, it should be recognized that a genuine signature expresses a combination of characteristics which are completely consistent with the natural conditions surrounding the signing of a document by its rightful owner, a combination of characteristics which are incompatible with the states of mind and hand which produce forgery.

TRACED SIGNATURES

One of the incomprehensions which the document examiner experiences not infrequently in consultations with those who utilize his services is the lack of understanding of, first, precisely what a traced forgery is and, secondly, what may be adduced from

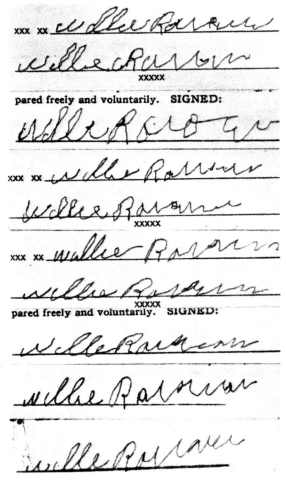

Figure 5. Signatures "Willie Robinson" by illiterate showing wide variation in pen control and contrasting legibility between capital and small
letters, typical of many writers of this class.

analysis of a traced forgery. Some law enforcement officers express
surprise and annoyance when they are told that it is pointless and
a waste of time to compare the writing of a suspected forger with
check endorsements, for example, which have been established to
be traced forgeries of the signature of the check's true payee.
They might even adopt the attitude: "A fine expert you are if

you cannot determine whether this suspect did or did not write this forged endorsement. What difference does it make if it is a tracing, as you say?"

Or in the courtroom, one may hear the defense advocate, with perhaps a slight nod of approval from the judge, pose to the jury: "Why should we believe the expert when he says this signature is a traced forgery, when he himself admits he cannot tell us whether my client did or did not write it?" One feels certain that in a murder case, this same advocate would scarcely dispute the lifelessness of the corpse because the medical examiner admitted in good faith that he could not identify or eliminate the defendant as the murderer.

To understand clearly what a tracing is, it is appropriate to preconsider what a tracing is not. A tracing, properly so-called is not a writing, as such. Tracings are accomplished in a manner foreign to the writing processes. Consequently, the identifying data which exist in writings and by which they are identified are not present in tracings.

Let us review how tracings are perpetrated. One common method is usually referred to as the carbon process. Here the forger places the document to be forged on the bottom, interleaves a piece of carbon paper, and places on top a document containing a genuine signature. The forger then traces over the genuine signature with a pencil, pen, stylus, or other sharp pointed instrument. Even a strong toothpick, a paper clip, or a hair pin has been employed. The pressure of this overtracing against the carbon paper imprints the signature outline in carbon on the bottom document. If a piece of blue carbon paper has been used, the signature outline will grossly approximate the line of a blue pencil. When a black carbon paper is used, the signature outline will grossly resemble the work of a soft lead pencil.

The forger may attempt to pass off this outline or tracing as a genuine signature without further treatment. In most instances, however, he will endeavor to "improve" the appearance of the outline by retouching it with pen and ink or with pencil. Carbon process tracings are usually readily cognizable as such by the carbon traces, slow irregular drawing execution and, in the latter

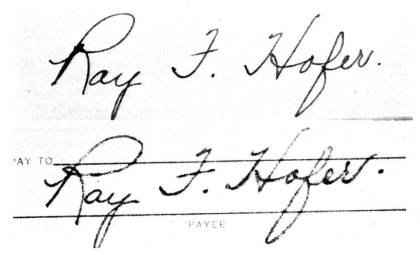

Figures 6. Natural execution of upper authentic signature readily distinguishes it from lower traced forgery, containing irregular movement impulses, carbon traces, and double tracks of ink overwriting and carbon outline.

type, by the double tracks of the carbon outline and the ink or pencil retouching strokes.

A second method of traced forgery is similar to the carbon process, except that the carbon paper is not interjected. The document containing the authentic signature is placed on top of the spurious document being forged. The forger traces, usually with considerable pressure, over the genuine signature, using a pencil, pen, stylus, or similar instrument and creates an indented signature outline on the document being forged. This indentation or depression outline is thereafter overwritten, using pencil or pen and ink. This sort of traced forgery likewise is usually readily apprehended because of its slow unnatural execution, the presence of indentations and depressions, and a lack of precise coincidence between the indented signature outline and its overwritten counterpart.

A further mode of forgery by tracing involves the use of transmitted light. The document to be forged is placed on top of the document containing the genuine signature. In registration, the two documents are superimposed over a light source and a flat surface. The ever available window, a photographic printer, or the draftsman's tracing easel might be utilized. The forger traces a signature outline with pencil or pen and ink, following the design of the genuine signature, made visible by the light in back of it. Among trademarks of this manner of tracing are sluggish, unnatural execution, heavy and irregular pressure, blunt ending strikes, a lack of rhythm, and uncertainty.

Variations of the foregoing processes are attempted at times. For example, when transmitted light is employed, a light pencil outline may first be drawn, to be overwritten later with pen and ink. Whatever method of tracing is used, its very essence debars individuality and writing personality. Tracings will not pass muster as genuine when they are examined searchingly and intelligently, and compared with authentic signatures. They wear the chains of slow, unnatural, drawing movement, artificial studied attention to overall form of the letters, carbon traces, indentations and depressions, pencil traces, mixture of carbon outline and pencil or ink overwriting, "improving and correcting" strokes, faulty adherence to the line of writing caused by movement of the paper. When several traced forgeries are made from the same model signature, they inevitably are characterized by stultifying common faults among them.

The diligent gathering of authentic signatures for comparison with traced forgeries may produce the exact model or models from which they were produced. A precise agreement in the form of two signatures establishes that one is a tracing of the other. And the freely written model will testify against its unnatural, traced, illegitimate offspring.

It is highly important to note that every tracing grossly approximates the form of the authentic model signature from which it was traced. Accordingly, it follows that a general resemblance between the form of an authentic and a questioned signature provides basis *only* for a further study to determine the significance of such general overall resemblance. No thinking examiner of evidential signatures will base an ultimate conclusion on general form resemblance between two signatures. If he did so, he would label every traced forgery to be genuine.

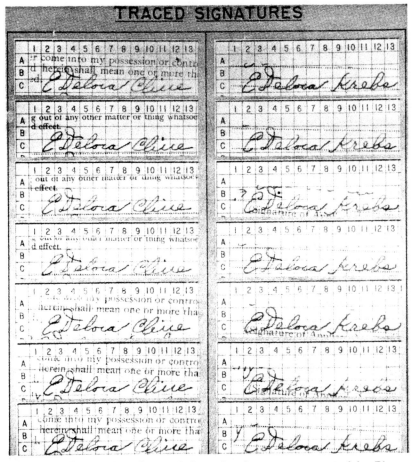

Figure 7. Two series of traced forgeries from common models. Photographed under ruled squares, stultifying adherence to the form of the master models as well as unnatural execution are apparent.

The question: "Can the author of a traced forgery be identified by comparing the forger's handwriting with the traced forgery?" can only be answered in the negative. And it might be added that it would be well to have a long look at any pedant who equivocates at this negative answer. It is unreasonable and incompatible with experiment and experience to expect to find one's *writing* characteristics, and in sufficient number and kind to identify him, in a *traced drawing* of the signature of another.

SIMULATED SIGNATURES

Simulated signatures are freehand drawings in imitation of a model signature. There are two basic classes of simulations. The more common involves the use of an actual model document. This model is placed in proximity to the document to be forged, and the forger copies with pen or pencil his conception of the form of the genuine signature model, in the manner of the artist sketching from a live model.

A studied simulation from a master model signature usually embodies a slow drawing movement, unnatural starts and stops, a lack of rhythm, and uncertainty of letter conformations. Touch-up strokes and patchings are common also because the forger by simulation, like the artist, is his own severest critic. He is rarely content with his efforts without adding a few "improving" and "correcting" touches.

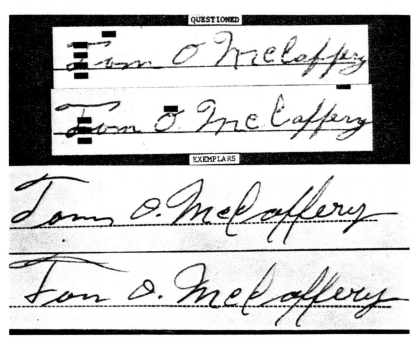

Figure 8. Upper signatures are simulated forgeries of lower authentic signatures. Compare uncertainty of forgeries with naturalness of genuine signatures, despite lack of writing skill in latter.

Test yourself. Even with the serene conscience and steady hand of the experimenter for the truth, you will not find it possible to *copy* closely the signature of another and, at the same time, retain your natural, rhythmic *writing* movements.

A second class of forgery by simulation finds the forger without an actual model document at hand. The forger must rely for inspiration on his recollection from past observation of the genuine signature he proposes to imitate. If such a forger has a unique photographic memory, he may be able to compose a simulation from his mental image about as readily as if he were copying from an actual model signature. Usually, however, simulations from memory are grossly inaccurate in some particulars of form which the forger is unable to recall with precision. The stigmata of this second class of simulation correspond generally with those cited in the preceding paragraphs, with the additional probability of greater variation from the letter formations of the signature being imitated, due to lapses in memory.

Here again, the reader is urged to experiment. Nothing complex need be involved. Simply reproduce your recollection of a signature of a relative or associate. Thereafter compare your handiwork with several authentic signatures of that individual. How well does your "forgery" approximate the form of the authentic signatures? To what degree did you have to inject your own *writing* habits because of your incomplete recollection of the form of the signature which you were imitating?

From the foregoing, it should be apparent that in forgeries produced by simulation from a visible model, as in a tracing, the forger is enslaved to his model and is not writing with his personal writing resources. Within the limits of his capabilities, he is manufacturing, he is drawing the form and general appearance of the writing of a second person. He is not indulging the act of writing as it is familiarly practiced. He has no impetus to incorporate his own *writing* habits in such forgeries.

The drawing process of copying from a visible model by its very nature disallows writing individuality and excludes the personal writing inclinations of the forger. A hundred simulations from visible model signatures of John Smith by a hundred different forgers would rarely be distinguishable, let alone identifiable with their authors.

In the process of simulation from a mental signature image, the forger must revert to his own writing habits to supplant incomplete recollection of the form of the signature being copied or imitated. For example, the forger of the signature "John Smith" may have a clear recollection of the appearance of "John" and the capital "S" but be very hazy when he approaches "mith." In this predicament he is impelled to rely in the latter sequence to some degree on his own writing fundamentals. If he is tackling the much longer signature, "Alexander Pierpont Greathouse, III," the resources in his memory are apt to be sketchy and necessarily augmented in considerable degree by insertion of his own writing habits and impulses.

Figure 9. Upper signature is authentic, middle signature is simulated forgery, and bottom signature is exemplar of confessed forger. Consider gross form agreement between authentic signature and forgery, in comparison with form disagreement between forgery and writing of admitted forger.

Figure 10. Left column contains authentic signatures, center column illustrates simulated forgeries, and right column shows exemplars of admitted forger. Copying process of simulations served to exclude forger's writing habits.

It follows that simulations from memory are usually combinations of drawing and writing. In such proportion as this type of simulation embodies the *writing* habits of its author-forger, it is distinguishable as his work. As a practical matter, undue optimism is definitely unwarranted looking to the definite identification of the forger via an adduction of his writing habits from a single simulated forgery. The situation is somewhat more encouraging when series of simulations are involved, as the forger may lapse progressively at various points within the forgeries, permitting an ultimately complete pattern of his writing habits to be catalogued. At best, the identification of the author of simulated forgeries through handwriting comparisons might well be viewed by the investigator as a possibility rather than a probability, and a question which should be reserved for the experienced document examiner.

A particular note of caution should also be recorded respecting the elimination of suspected authors of simulated forgeries through handwriting comparisons. Form differences between the normal writing of a suspected forger and simulated writings lend no weight of themselves to a conclusion of the suspect's innocence. This is a truism which seems extremely difficult for many intelligent investigators and attorneys to recognize. Nevertheless, each can readily demonstrate it for himself. (1) Write the name of an associate in your normal handwriting without any reference to his signature. (2) Carefully simulate the signature of this associate. (3) Compare your writing with your imitation. Certainly, there are many form differences in your writing of your associate's name as compared with your drawing of his signature. So there is in the *writing* of any suspect as compared with *drawings* for which he is responsible. Simulations must be properly reckoned as special purpose copies in which neither differences nor similarities to the writings of suspects merit any significance, unless they are truly divorced from the drawing process and truly reflect writing injections therein.

SIMPLE FORGERIES

A simple forgery is defined as the fraudulent writing of the signature of another in the natural or disguised writing of the forger, the latter exerting no effort to effect a resemblance between the forgery and the genuine signature of the individual whose signature is being forged. In such forgeries, the forger simply writes the name in question with no unnatural attention disturbing his usual writing processes, or he endeavors to alter the appearance of his usual writing by adopting a camouflage, commonly referred to as a disguise or distortion.

Contrary to some popular impressions, simple forgeries represent the most common class of forged signatures encountered in law enforcement. The carefully planned forgery of a consequential will, deed, contract, or note usually results in a simulated forgery. The forger expects that such documents will be carefully scrutinized. It is essential to the attainment of his ends that such forgeries pass a more than perfunctory inspection by individuals who are familiar with not only the authentic signature of the purported signer but also his habits, interests, and wishes. Conversely, the single or multiple forger of checks, drafts, money orders, bonds, savings account withdrawals, credit purchase orders, etc., has some assurance that his handiwork will not be uniformly examined either with care or proficiency at the point of negotiation. It must be conceded that the volume of commercial transactions, the caliber of personnel who handle these transactions, and the limited information which is within the purview of the banker and the merchant when he must decide whether to accept most commercial instruments tend to place an advantage in the hands of the forger of commercial paper. The forger is well aware of this. He recognizes that however transparent his forgeries may be in the questioned document laboratory, that the thousands of authentic documents placed in circulation daily by honest people tend to shield his spurious instruments from prompt detection at the time of their negotiation.

Many forgers who prey on banks and retail establishments utilize fictitious names entirely which could involve no element of tracing or simulation. Others who forge the names of actual persons do not have access to model signatures from which to fabricate forgeries by tracing or simulation. Documents such as checks, endorsement of which is customarily witnessed or should be witnessed, are not amenable to tracing or simulation when their execution is so witnessed. Finally and perhaps most significantly, many forgers, driven by greed and indolence and with the knowledge that their apprehension, however indefinite as to time, is ultimately inevitable, subordinate the rudiments of skilled, planned, imitated forgeries and even efficient disguise of their normal handwriting in the interests of rapid, if evil, dollars.

Simple forgeries are readily cognizable as such by comparison with the form of the genuine signature they purport to be. The prospects of developing the simple forger's writing habits, and thereby definitely identifying him through handwriting comparisons, are good, but subject to the conditions which are particularized in the following chapter entitled *The Identification of Handwriting.*

Especial emphasis needs to be directed in very positive fashion by everyone concerned with evidential signatures of all classes to increasing their identification bases. A valuable and highly recommended method of so doing requires the signer of a document to write concurrently his street address, city, state, and telephone number, *within the observation of the prospective acceptor of the document.* Further, when identification papers attend the presentation of a document, the signer should himself be requested to make note of them in his own handwriting on the instrument being presented, for subsequent verification by the acceptor, such as the bank teller or retail salesclerk. The writing of the identification data should also be specifically witnessed by the acceptor. These simple requirements provide two or three or four or five times the quantity of writing which is in a signature standing alone. Qualitatively they do far more. They assist to unmask the forger, to expose the false claimant, and specifically to protect the innocent victim whose signature is traced or copied.

The forger by tracing or simulation will be hard pressed to carry his deception through an address and telephone number, in the presence of a witness, even if he has or had models of the correct address and telephone number in the handwriting of the individual whose signature is being forged. The forger will be forced to inject his own handwriting habits. And incidentally, if the forger should have model handwritings of the address and telephone number, that circumstance alone will definitely limit the number of forgery suspects to be investigated. The forger may camouflage his normal habits to a considerable degree in a short signature. The walls of his disguise will surely crumble when he is caused to add the numerals, punctuation, and additional words of an address, telephone number, and identification details. The on-the-spot necessity of performing these writings may result in the immediate discovery of fraud by way of differences between the on-the-spot writings and a carefully prepared signature forgery which was drawn prior to the presentation of the instrument. Psychologically the additional witnessed writings shake the forger from his perch. He may be somewhat poised and undoubtedly he will be rather posed for the signature forgery alone. But rarely is he prepared for the added requirements of address, telephone number, and identifying data in his own handwriting. These written additions to the forged signature force the forger to unfamiliar, unfavorable terrain where he did not reckon to do battle—where his identity certainly will be adducible from the work of his own hand.

THE IDENTIFICATION OF HANDWRITING

Every handwriting can be identified with its author provided it contains the writing habits, the individualities, the characteristics of its author in adequate kind and number, and provided further that such writing is subjected to adequate evaluation and comparison with adequate exemplars of the handwriting of its author. No handwriting is susceptible of identification if it is not truly representative of its source. Neither may it be identified if its individualities remain unrecognized. In this chapter, from the standpoint of the investigator of evidential documents, it will be endeavored to cast some light on what constitutes adequacy in handwriting habits, individualities, and characteristics and adequacy in their evaluation.

To the intelligent inquirer for the truth, adequacy is never a mysterious stranger to be unknown, unsung, and altogether avoided. Adequacy of habits, individualities, and characteristics measures and controls the recognition of man and all his creatures. Man is identified by his date of birth, height, weight, eyes, hair, complexion, build, walk, talk, scars, mannerisms, intelligence, occupation, skills, parents, associates, and dozens of other personal and collateral characteristics. Man, his automobile, his wine, his cake, his fingerprints, his handwriting, his everything—they are all identified positively, partially, or not at all in such proportion as they adequately contain recognizable characteristics rendering them distinct from all other men, automobiles, wines, cakes, fingerprints, handwritings, ad infinitum.

None would be so foolish as to attempt the identification of a man from the color of his eyes and his height alone. Many of God's children are five feet, six inches tall and have blue eyes, or are six feet, one inch in height and have brown eyes. More characteristics are needed. One hesitates to identify the face, whose individualities are not adequately and clearly in his memory. We smile with the automobile mechanic when the college professor cannot distinguish his blue Chevrolet from the juxtaposed Ford, equally blue. And heaven help him, had they both been Chevrolets. The professor speaks authoritatively on zoology perhaps but he knows not adequately his Chevrolet's characteristics because he has not adequately considered their existence. It is the mechanic who looks on automobiles with authority. He understands the styles and lines which differentiate the various makes of automobiles as well as the evidences of wear, scratches, dents, misalignments, and repairs which identify the individual automobile.

The wine chemist promptly recognizes the domestic simulation of the expensive imported cognac. One would not even have to be a connoisseur to detect the imitation if he had adequate exemplars of the real thing for sampling and comparison, although some imitations are so poor one hardly needs to make comparisons. True, it would be difficult to detect the manufacturer from the imitation alone. Many imitators of the same cognac would be apt to imitate it in the same clumsy way. Even the housewife has no difficulty in differentiating her angel food from that baked by her daughters using their mother's recipe. To say which daughter would not be easy—still if several cakes could be tested, mother might distinguish Mary's copy from Martha's. The fingerprint expert does not identify the fingerprint so smudged its ridge formations are indiscernible. It has not adequate characteristics. But a smudged fingerprint does not destroy the science of fingerprint identification, firmly established through thousands of definite identifications of adequate fingerprints.

Similar general thinking should embrace handwriting. Sometimes what passes for handwriting is not really handwriting at all but a copy by tracing or simulation and it therefore is unidentifiable. In other instances, a handwriting is "smudged" because of skilled disguise or its minimal quantity and it fails of identification. Occasionally, a handwriting contains only one or two characteristics and escapes positive identification. Infrequently, handwriting is misapprehended because one having less than a thorough acquaintance with handwriting individualities hazards an educated or even an uneducated guess under the guise of an "expert" conclusion. Intermittently, handwriting which embodies an impressive combination of individualities is not identifiable because inter-related exemplars, standards of comparison, are inadequate from which to ascertain whether they too contain the same individualities in combination. In many, many more cases, however, a handwriting under investigation contains adequate combinations of characteristics which are verified competently in adequate exemplars and serves to identify one person and one person alone as its author.

In approaching the basis and method of handwriting identification, it is essential that some consideration be directed to the beginning and evolution of one's handwriting. Writing is commonly learned in elementary schools from published systems of letter designs and methods of instruction. In the schools of this country and its territorial possessions, The Palmer Method and the Zaner-Bloser System are most frequently encountered. These systems were initiated prior to the turn of the twentieth century when the commercial system of handwriting had its inception. Other systems in current or recent use include Cavanaugh-Myers, Courtis-Shaw, Creamer, Economy, Freeman, Goodfellow, Graves, Graves-Prewit, Hausam, Hall-Savage, Kelly-Morris, Kittle, Kirk-Freeman, Lister, Locker, New Laurel, Peed, Putnam-Mills, Rice, Rinehart, Stone-Smalley, and Tamblyn.

For a number of years in the majority of schools, the teaching procedure has been to present manuscript writing to the pupils in their first two elementary grades. Manuscript writing has been mislabeled by some critics as a passing fad. There now seems no doubt that the teaching of manuscript especially in the lower elementary grades is and will continue to be an established practice. Several surveys undertaken in 1946 indicate that from eighty to ninety percent of the elementary school systems begin handwriting instruction with manuscript writing and convert to cursive writing in grade three. A few schools teach manuscript through the elementary grade levels but the usual changeover to cursive writing is effected gradually in the majority of school systems during the third grade.

Early school training for obvious reasons is standardized. It strives to teach all the students of a particular system to achieve

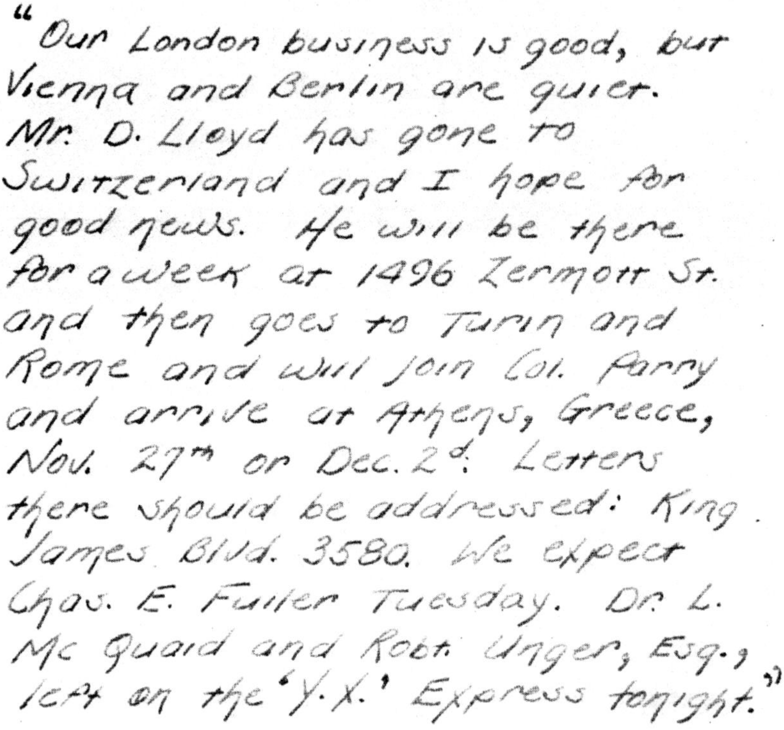

"Our London business is good, but Vienna and Berlin are quiet. Mr. D. Lloyd has gone to Switzerland and I hope for good news. He will be there for a week at 1496 Zermott St. and then goes to Turin and Rome and will join Col. Parry and arrive at Athens, Greece, Nov. 27th or Dec. 2d. Letters there should be addressed: King James Blvd. 3580. We expect Chas. E. Fuller Tuesday. Dr. L. Mc Quaid and Robt. Unger, Esq., left on the "Y. X." Express tonight."

Figure 11. Manuscript writing by adult writer who retained manuscript as predominant style. This and similar paragraphs which embody all letters and numerals are useful in obtaining request exemplars. (Paragraph suggested by Osborn: *Questioned Documents*, 2nd Ed. Albany, Boyd, 1929.)

general uniformity in correct writing posture, grasp of the writing instrument, writing movements, and letter forms. The embryonic writer of the first grade directs his efforts to writing exactly like the copy before him. In effect, he and all his little contemporaries simulate Mr. Palmer or Messrs. Zaner-Bloser, subject to the specific influences of their individual teachers. Even from the outset of school training, some writing individuality creeps in because all the little, six-year-old dears do not have the same sized fingers, the same muscular control, the same eyesight, the same artistic appreciation of letter forms, the same attentiveness and concentration, the same desire for achievement, and the same mental-manual coordination. But in these early stages of handwriting development, which emphasize imitation, each writer necessarily is heavily dependent upon and conforms to his writing system. With studied effort attending his writing movements, he endeavors to produce letters corresponding to the master letter formations on which his system is based. As the young writer acquires more skill, he is less and less dependent on the system and his hand is not in constant need of specific mental direction for his every writing impulse.

As there is variation in individual acceptance of basic handwriting training, there is likewise variation in individual implementation of that instruction. Nevertheless, the constant compulsion to write, which is inherent in the daily lessons and tasks, prods each young writer, rarely to writing excellence, but indispensably to a personal legibility which will finally become his individual handwriting and his alone.

While each writer works out his own handwriting destiny according to his capacities, needs, tastes, and flair for individuality, the school system and training provide the basic pattern from which each writer reaches for writing maturity. Initially, one's writing is exclusively motivated by the school system and training. Gradually, his writing proceeds through an intermediate amalgamation composed in major part of the writing system and in minor proportion of the writer's own personal limitations and inclinations. Ultimately, one's writing completely evolves from the consciousness of the training and system to the composite of each

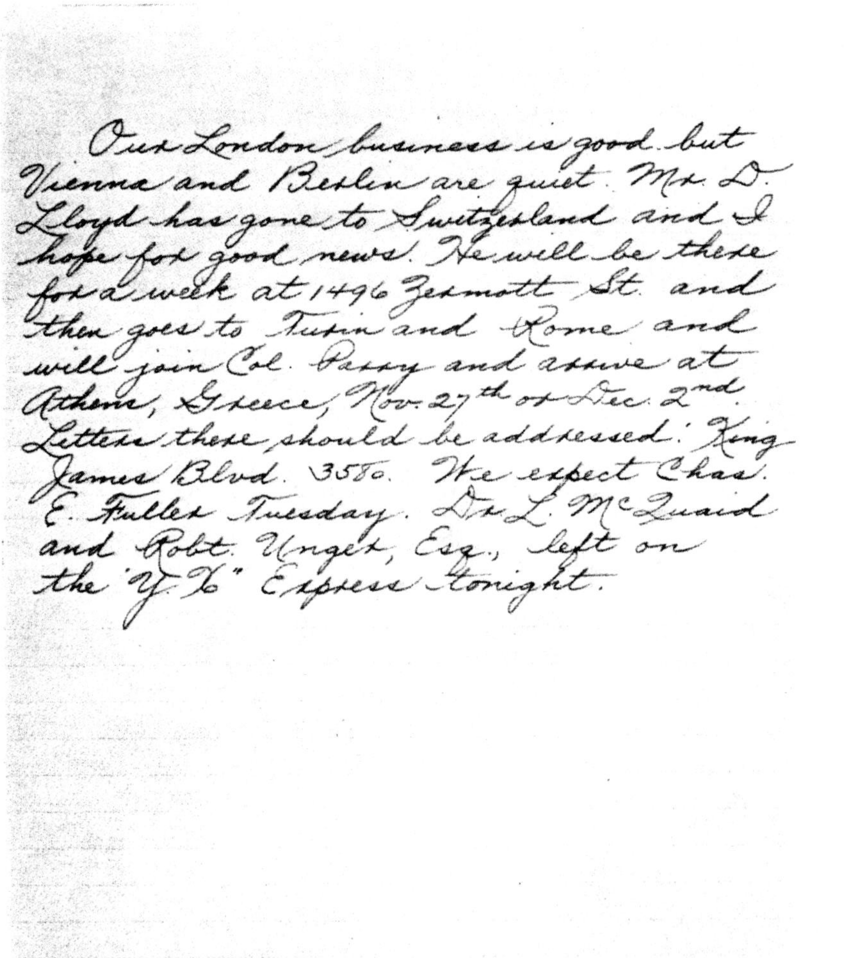

Figure 12. Exemplar by adult writer retaining Palmer Method letter
forms.

writer's personal peculiarities and habits which emerge and assert
themselves unconsciously in his handwriting. As the basic instruction provides the impetus to first labored, imitative writing, as
the necessity to write sparks the progression to personal legibility,
the continued handwriting usage in our daily pursuits is the
developer and maturer of each writer's personal characteristics—
the trademarks, the aggregate identifier of his handwriting.

Writing changes are usually numerous and quite pronounced as the student writer progresses through elementary and high schools. The school writer appropriates and discards letter designs, slants, sizes, for a variety of reasons which are neither accurately measurable nor predictable. For example, Jack Smith may radi-

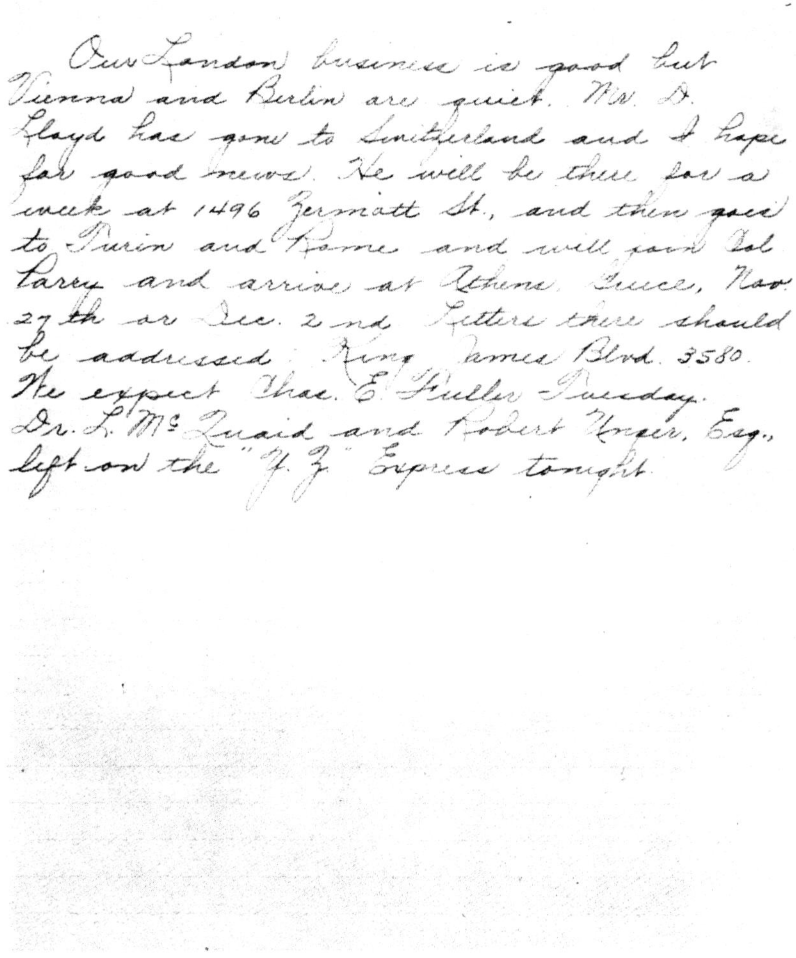
Our London business is good but
Vienna and Berlin are quiet. Mr. D.
Floyd has gone to Switzerland and I hope
for good news. He will be there for a
week at 1496 Zermatt St., and then goes
to Turin and Rome and will join Col.
Larry and arrive at Athens, Greece, Nov.
27th or Dec. 2nd. Letters there should
be addressed: King James Blvd. 3580.
We expect Chas. E. Fuller Tuesday.
Dr. L. McQuaid and Robert Unger, Esq.,
left on the "Y. Z." Express tonight.

Figure 13. Exemplar by adult writer disclosing influences of Zaner-Bloser System.

cally alter the style of his "J" to resemble the "J" written by his dreamy new English teacher and then resolve never to write such a style again when he fails to receive a passing grade on his first theme. Or Jill Smith may find it sophisticatedly necessary to adopt a backhand slant about the time she dons her first pair of high heels and struggle with this slant for a few months until she surrenders to the circumstance that her writing has been slowed down to a crawl and possibly a scrawl. Reversion to manuscript writing for one, a few, or all of the letter forms is not uncommon from the fifth to the twelfth grade levels.

About the time the average writer graduates from high school, his writing individualities have stabilized to a considerable extent. Writing maturity is usually reached within a few years of high school graduation. This does not preclude subsequent changes and revisions in one's handwriting repertory. Handwriting changes are more properly regarded as handwriting development, the result of training, personal, and occupational experiences. This development earmarks each writer through life.

An awareness of handwriting development should lead the investigator of evidential handwritings in his evaluations to make certain of the vintage of writings which he examines and compares. Handwriting changes are not tolled merely by closing one's eyes to them. The gentleman with the glistening pate is not less bald at forty-five because he had curly locks on his high school graduation. His handwriting too has probably changed and possibly just as radically. When evaluating and comparing writings of any class, it should always be considered carefully whether they are contemporaneous and represent the same stage of handwriting development for the particular author who is under inquiry.

Similarly, it must be recognized that groups of writers who were subjected to the same or similar training and systems of letter forms spring from a common initial writing impetus. Accordingly, the particulars of a given handwriting which are an integral ingredient of a system of writing do not assist in identifying the individual writers of that system. System particulars aid in distinguishing the writer as belonging to a particular group of writers or in differentiating him from writers of other systems.

Figure 14. Signatures written over thirty year period disclosing above average uniformity for that time period.

An analogy exists in the examination of fingerprints. Because two fingerprint impressions are both loops, it does not follow that they represent the fingerprint of one and the same person. This circumstance merely shows that they are fingerprints of the same pattern, and a further study must be conducted to determine whether individual points of agreement exist within the patterns, thereby identifying the prints as those of one and the same person. However, if one fingerprint impression is a loop and a second is a whorl, they are clearly of different origin.

The influence of writing systems need not hopelessly mislead the investigator. Even though he may not be a specialist in The Palmer Method or the Zaner-Bloser System or the various other published systems of writing, the investigator can direct himself to a workmanlike appreciation of copybook letter forms, school letter forms, and system letter forms. His own handwriting training and his own handwriting experience will warn him almost unerringly, if he will but let them, when he is confronted with a letter design which has been lifted bodily from one of the commonly taught writing systems. Letter designs, letter connections, proportions and sizes, slant, and movement which are the direct product of a writing system should be accepted for just what they are—indications of class and group rather than of the individual writer. Characteristics to be of significant value in identifying the indi-

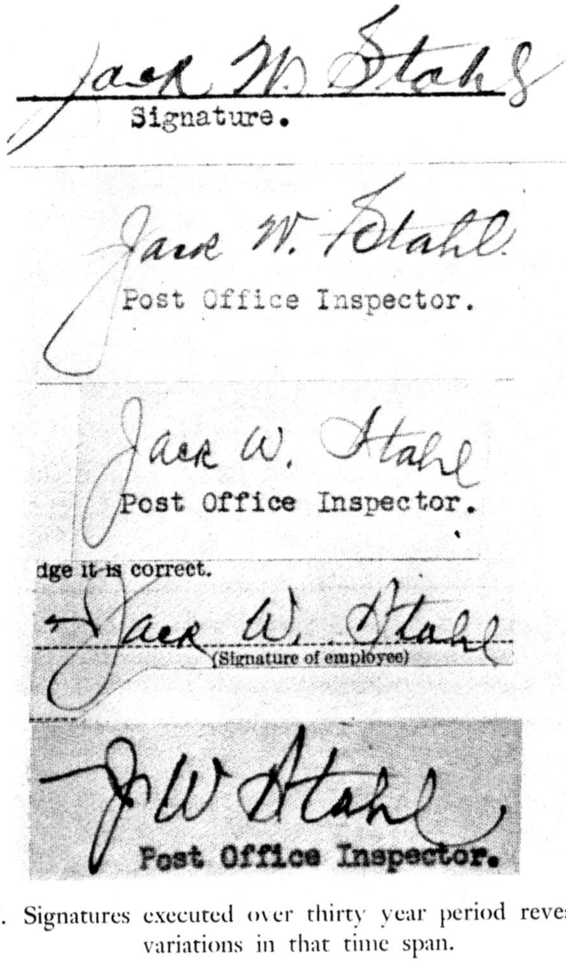

Figure 15. Signatures executed over thirty year period revealing normal variations in that time span.

vidual writer must be pinpointed as springing from the individual—his individualities, which are distinct from the general system or group influences affecting all the writers of that system or group.

Present day handwriting instruction, while based on standardized systems of letter forms and methods of execution, definitely does not suppress individuality. Even the very young student enjoys considerable latitude both in his general method of writing and his selection of letter forms. Gone are the long hours of practicing ovals and push-pulls with perhaps a copper striving to cling to the back of the pupil's struggling hand. Stern lectures and reprimands no longer are occasioned by the slightest deviation from the precise letter forms and methods of the system being taught. Today emphasis is on legibility and utility accompanied by less than punctilious attention to each and every detail of writing posture, writing implements, position of the hand and forearm, and precise letter forms.

Formal handwriting instruction ceases in many schools about the fifth or sixth grade levels and thereafter instruction tends to be confined to remedial criticism by the teacher of undecipherable efforts by individual students. The expert penman of yesteryear might contend that "Johnny can't write today" but he would have to concede that Johnny's written efforts abound with individualities. He would necessarily be impressed also by the fact that millions of Johnnys, rather than the thousands of his generation, employ handwriting as an ever ready tool in every facet of their daily existence. The simple truths are that handwriting is more individual than ever before, and that evidential handwritings provide more fruitful avenues of investigation than ever before.

An extortion letter was received for investigation which contained some thirty words. A study of the handwriting quality indicated an immature writer probably in the higher elementary grades. Questioned in the light of this intelligence, the intended victim voiced the suspicion that any of the sixth grade students in a local school might be the author-culprit. This particular class comprised about seventy students, ranging from eleven to thirteen years of age. The investigator was advised of six key points of individuality—habits reflected in the extortion letter which were

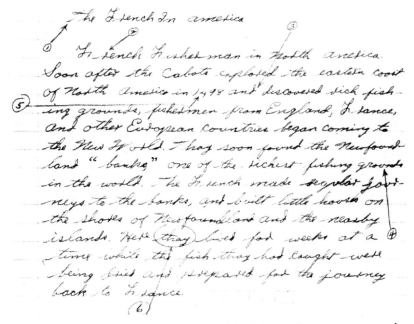

Figure 16. Worksheet showing six individualities used to screen extortion
letter writer from among seventy elementary school students.

not the product of or intimately related to the handwriting instruction of these seventy students, and which were therefore personal
to the would-be extortioner.

Through the cooperation of the school authorities, the investigator obtained handwriting exemplars from each of the seventy
pupils. Not just any handwriting—a routine school assignment
designed to elicit the words and word combinations of the extortion letter in the normal handwriting of each of the seventy
possible suspects. It might be noted that this method of acquiring
exemplars protects the innocent from improper suspicion, elim-
inates the questioning of the innocent, and permits timely confrontation of the guilty. The author of the extortion letter was readily
identified by the investigator as the only one of the students whose
writing revealed the six key individualities. Confirmation was
promptly obtained from the document laboratory, where numerous other individualities were also found to coexist in the ques-

tioned letter and known exemplar. Interestingly enough, only one of the key individualities was found to exist in any of the sixty-nine innocent. A confession was immediately forthcoming in this case.

In another case, a series of highly obscene letters was reported emanating from a military base having a complement of some twenty thousand men. Most of these men were recruits who had reached writing maturity only recently or were approaching writing maturity. A study was conducted of these letters and their outstanding individualities were isolated. The field investigator skillfully designed a questionnaire which, with the cooperation of the military authorities, was assigned for completion by all personnel as a routine duty. The questionnaire was competently arranged by the investigator and cooperating military authorities to require the use of printed letters, letter combinations, words, numerals, punctuation, and phrases corresponding with those which were distinctive in the series of lewd letters. The guilty psychoneurotic writer was identified by a mere rapid scanning of the questionnaires. He abjectly confessed his authorship in obvious amazement at his detection from among twenty thousand young men.

Within the past few months, kidnap-murderer Angelo La-Marca was apprehended and convicted in New York. His detection was the result of efficient appraisal of the individualities in his extortion letter in comparison with the handwriting of an estimated two million persons in the New York area, a noteworthy exemplification of the skilled use of handwriting individualities to identify the individual.

A short time ago a series of highly objectionable communications was reported by a wide variety of highly placed personalities in public and private life. These abusive epistles, the work of a highly prolific writer, emanated from a metropolitan area of five million people. A diligent investigator pinpointed eight individualities in the addresses of this series of letters. He distributed photocopies of a typical address, with the key individualities marked for ready recognition, to mailing units in the metropolitan area. An alert distribution clerk recognized a letter in transit containing a return address as having the identical individualities of the objec-

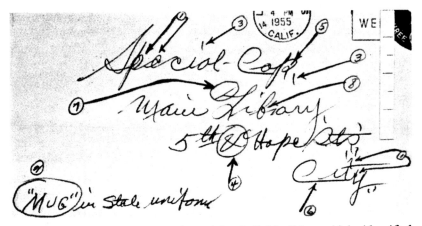

Figure 17. Worksheet illustrating eight individualities which identified anonymous letter writer in area of five million people.

tionable series under investigation. The offender was promptly apprehended and confessed in astonishment that he had been uncovered from among five million people.

The investigative approach to these successful handwriting identifications and case solutions was basically the same and it typifies the thinking which leads to sound conclusions. Whether the number of suspects was seventy children, twenty thousand young men, two million men, or five million men and women, the investigators catalogued themselves or were furnished by document specialists a list of key individualities, outstanding habits, recognizable characteristics of the evidential writings under inquiry. They then concentrated on these individualities in their comparisons with the known material of suspects. Vague comparisons of handwriting produce vague results. Concerted efforts based on established combinations of individualities promise success.

If the investigator cannot himself compile a list of key individualities from a questioned writing, he needs assistance from the outset. Otherwise he has nothing to evaluate and compare. In such event, he should consult a document examiner or supervising investigator for advice. He may ascertain that the evidential writing in a particular case is so limited in individuality that an identification will necessarily lie in a medium other than the handwriting itself. Should this be the case, it is essential that such be determined early in an investigation so that investigative time and effort will not be dissipated along unproductive lines.

Occasionally, an investigator studiously and honestly attacking this initial phase of a questioned handwriting problem will realize that he is attempting what for him is impossible. He should not hesitate to seek other types of assignments if he cannot "see" handwriting individualities, even after they have been delineated to him by others. Obviously, one who cannot "see" individualities cannot interpret or locate them in the handwriting of a guilty suspect. Administrative supervisors have a responsibility to insure that investigators assigned to casework involving a material percentage of evidential handwriting and typewriting have acute form perception. Check frauds, for example, are not proper assignments for one who has any tendency to "form blindness." Aptitude tests are readily obtainable to determine the ability to differentiate forms, sizes, shapes, letter conformations, designs, and angles. They should be utilized to the end that only those with critical

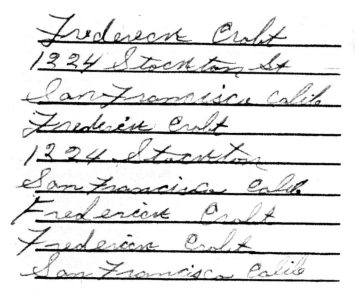

Figure 18. Below average writer with self-invented letter forms having high individuality—C, f, and k.

form perception are regularly assigned to matters requiring this faculty.

How should the investigator proceed to recognize individualities of significant value for identification purposes? Understandably, he will devote most of his attention to letter forms and delegate most of the fine points of analysis to the document expert and his laboratory facilities. However, the investigator should be aware of the foremost considerations which should guide his efforts. These are: Is the handwriting under investigation the usual, the normal, the unconsciously executed writing of its author? Or is it a consciously disguised, a consciously distorted handwriting? Is it a studied tracing? Is it an imitation or a copy of the writing of a second person? These basic considerations overshadow the entire evaluation of a handwriting. When a handwriting is normally executed, its singular manifestations may be accepted readily as the identifying individualities of its author. When a handwriting is abnormally accomplished, its every aspect must be weighed carefully in the light of its abnormal, special purpose.

A like situation may be seen in the evaluation of the individualities of the person. When he is his usual self, normally attired and undisguised, his identifying individualities may readily be catalogued. But when he is disguised, the false eyebrows, the wig, the molded nose, the padded shoulders, the tinted cosmetics, the pitched voice, the elevated heels, the false gait must be subtracted to pierce the disguise. A correct interpretation of the camouflage can reveal the true individual beneath it. *Even the disguises of the person are of value in identifying him should he adopt the same camouflage again.* Some disguises of the person are so skillful that they would virtually defy penetration on a single examination. If repeated often enough, these poses usually fail. A proper consideration of the individualities of a person necessitates a strict, analytical compartmentization of what is the real person, what may have been adopted for the special purpose of disguise, what may have been put on for the special purpose of posing as a second person, and what may be the result of the special influences of the situation in which the person is at the time. Handwriting should be similarly viewed.

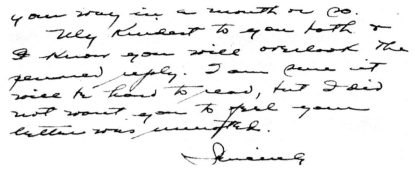

Figure 19. Skilled writer having numerous significant individualities—speed of execution, long initial strokes, eyeleted *y* followed by hiatus, *be* combination, initial *p*, terminal *d*, elongated *f*, et al.

With these prime considerations guiding his efforts, the investigator may then direct his attention to the following features: Writing skill—expert, good, average, mediocre; if the writing is barely legible, is this due to limited ability, haste, carelessness, deception? Writing speed and freedom of movement—very rapid and rhythmic, average, slow and laborious. Are the speed and movement uniform or irregular? What particular letters or combinations are involved in any departures from uniformity? Letter sizes—large, average, small. Are the letter sizes uniform or irregular according to the class of letter? What particular letters or letter combinations are involved in any departures from uniformity, according to the class of letter, for example, capital, upper loop letter, lower loop letter, small letter?

Are the writing strokes of uniform width and intensity? Do they vary from light to heavy pressure? Are they heavy on the upstroke and light on the downstroke or vice versa? Are the beginning and ending strokes blunt, abruptly formed strokes, or are they thin flowing strokes, accomplished with freedom and facility?

Are all the letters connected or does the writer frequently lift the writing instrument from the paper? Which letters consistently precede or follow these breaks in continuity? Is there a class relationship in breaks in continuity, for example, if a lift of

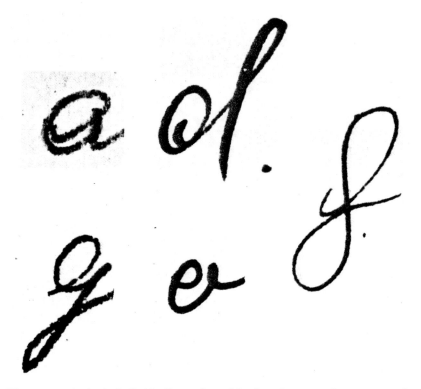

Figure 20. A single individuality reflected in four letters and one numeral, significance of which should not be pyramided.

the writing instrument precedes the "a," the letters "d," "g," "q," "c," and "o" should be examined for similar traits.

Which letter appears most frequently in the writing under investigation? At first examine this letter where it is the beginning letter of words. Then consider this letter where it is an intermediate letter, that is, connected to preceding and ensuing letters. Finally consider this letter as it ends various words as the terminal letter. Letters are affected by the exact writing situation in which they appear. A writer may have one form of "e" following the letters "u," "v," and "w" as in "hue," "have," and "we," and a materially varied form following the letters "h," "r" and "m" as in "he," "there" and "element." One's "y" in "you" may vary substantially from his "y" in "everything" and "continually." A writing should

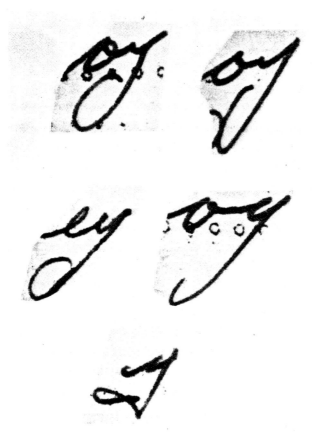

Figure 21. Five individualities in a single letter, significance of which should not be underevaluated.

be considered in this light as it may disclose a variety of forms of the same letter and its sequence—initial, intermediate, or terminal—has a material bearing on form usage.

What, if anything, is consistently unusual about the most frequent letter? Which features of this letter are fixed each time it appears? Which characteristics of this letter appear only occasionally, in perhaps one out of three? Which habits are rare, appearing in perhaps one out of twenty? Do one or two or more forms of this letter vary substantially from its customary design?

Do these letter formations or any aspects of this letter impress you as accidental departures from the writer's normal method or are they the result of intentional distortion?

Then apply these same considerations to the second most recurrent letter and so on through the various letters appearing in the questioned writing. What impresses you as the most unusual feature of the entire writing? Perhaps the writing contains forms of letters or letter connections which are much different than anything you have ever observed previously. Does the writing contain any errors or mistakes? Do they impress you as natural errors or does it appear that the writer intentionally injected these "errors"?

Is your ultimate judgment that the writing under consideration actually contains individualities which will reliably lead to their author? If not, consultation with a document examiner is in order either to confirm the absence of individualities or to delineate those which do exist. If so, prepare a separate drawing of those features of the writing which impress you as having the greatest individuality, those which you consider the most singular. If you are incapable of accurately accomplishing such drawings, prepare a photostat or photograph of the writing. Then cut out and mount on a sheet of paper or cardboard all the particulars of the

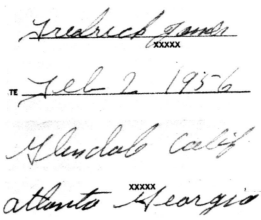

Figure 22. Writing personalized by incomplete strokes and movements, exemplified in *F, a, e, f, i, k, s,* and punctuation.

writing which you have reckoned to contain identifying value. Arrange these various characteristics in the order of their singularity, that is, arrange first those individualities which you feel would be found in the handwriting of perhaps only one person in a hundred thousand or in fifty thousand. In descending sequence arrange those characteristics which you believe would be found in the writing of one person in ten thousand or in one thousand. Proceed until you have considered those characteristics which you would reckon to be found in the writing of every fiftieth or every twenty-fifth person. In the interests of conservatism, omit from your compilation those characteristics which you feel might be found in the writing of every fifth person.

Such list of individualities, assembled from a careful study of the questioned writing should be the basis for your evaluation of the writing of any suspect. If you have followed the various propositions previously outlined and you still have a nebulous conception of exactly what, if anything, is individual in the questioned writing, you are obviously in no position to seek out the writing of the author. Investigators who indulge this absurd practice should realize that their actions are comparable to an attempt to locate a man in a crowd without knowing his description and physical characteristics, without knowing "what he looks like." An ordered study of a questioned writing is prerequisite to identifying its author.

In considering the writing of any suspect, you should determine whether his writing contains the same individualities which have been previously isolated in the writing which is under investigation. Remember well that it is unreasonable to explain away a difference as a disguise unless you have independently so classified the particular letter or letter combination incident to compiling your list of individualities in each unit of writing. Further, it is unsound to attach great significance to similarities in two writings unless you previously adjudged that these points embodied singularity in the separate units of writing. A common letter design used by one writer in five or ten and which exists in a questioned writing does not gain in stature when it is found in the writing of a suspect. It is still a common letter. On

QUESTIONED   **EXEMPLARS**

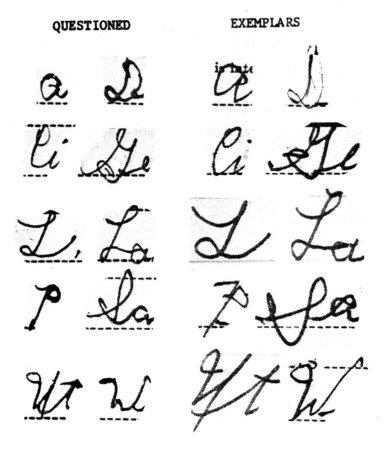

Figure 23. Identification founded on capitals, each containing personal departures by writer from system letter formations.

the other hand, a unique letter design or connection of a questioned writing has great identifying value when it is found in the writing of a suspected author. The significance of a similarity or difference flows from the singularity, the rarity, the individuality of the particular characteristic which is similar or different.

The failure of an investigator or examiner to detect the individualities of a writing does not necessarily indicate the investigator's or examiner's inadequacy. The writing may be qualitatively inadequate. Perhaps it has no tangible individuality. Or it may be so limited in quantity that the writer did not have an opportunity to inject individuality. The investigator or examiner who presumes to identify definitely every writing with which he is confronted seeks to do that which cannot be done. Relying on a tangible, concrete list of individualities as he sees them, rather than on a general impression of letter forms or "intuition," will steer the investigator of evidential writings on a truer course, irrespective of whether he intends to specialize in handwriting evaluation or purports to be expert therein.

No volume of verbiage can describe with exactitude and currency each and every personal and individual handwriting characteristic which the investigator or examiner may encounter. Although made to a common image, man was not devised in precise facsimile. The handwriting of each is different as its author is different from all other men. The various styles of the twenty-six large and twenty-six small letters of the several alphabets, the ten figures, the various punctuation markings, and the multiplicity of the interrelationships of these characters, as produced by different minds, wills, and hands provide millions of personal twists in handwriting. It is the *combination* of these individualities with their accumulative significance in a handwriting which serves to identify it.

The accompanying case illustrations exemplify combinations of individualities of established identifying value. The legends cite only the salient features of these writings and many individualties, not specifically cited, will be noted by the keen observer.

The statistician may inquire: "How many 'points of similarity' are necessary to a handwriting identification?" The mathematician may pose: "Is handwriting identification an exact science?" The jurist or administrator may question "Does handwriting identification have a scientific basis?" The defense advocate may accuse "Do not document experts make errors in handwriting identification?" Although these queries do not represent the immediate problems of the investigator of evidential writings, they are of interest to him and he should know something of their ramifications.

Two handwritings cannot be deemed to be the writing of one

Figure 24. Identification involving below average writer who attended elementary school in southern United States. Conservatism is essential in evaluating writings of this class which frequently embody many "system" similarities.

and the same person unless they agree in every fundamental element and embody no basic differences. It is not a matter of six or eight or twelve or fifty or five hundred "points of similarity." Points of similarity furnish inferences of identity between two writings as points of difference indicate their non-identity. The significance of such inferences proceeds from the relative singularity, the relative individuality in terms of all possible writers for the particular point under consideration. "Points of similarity" do not justify identifications unless they involve a combination of agreements in personal individuality which adequately isolates one and only one writer from all the other possible writers.

Would that this principle could be committed to some easy formula for the neophyte examiner of writings. However, there is no high speed parkway to measurements and interpretations of handwriting individuality. Some critiques of handwriting identification seem to suggest pique that the critic cannot be provided with a scorecard of the millions of possible handwriting individualities, with the separate probability values listed thereon, so that the critic might himself tote up the final outcome for each game of identification. Only through extensive experience in evaluating thousands of writings of all classes can one estimate accurately the relative singularity, the relative individuality of a "point of similarity" or a "difference."

In comparing two handwritings, the examiner first must determine from his knowledge of handwriting development, handwriting execution, and handwriting forms whether two writings agree in every fundamental particular. Assuming that he so finds, the examiner must then adjudge from his experience in evaluating writings of all classes the relative frequency, the relative probability of such individual agreements, and such aggregate agreement. In arriving at a judgment that two writings are the product of the same person, the examiner must have calculated that there is no likelihood of the combination of agreeing individualities occurring in the writing of any other possible writer. An ultimate conclusion which takes into consideration every individuality in the writings being examined, which is based on a knowledge of handwriting execution and on experiential research in the sing-

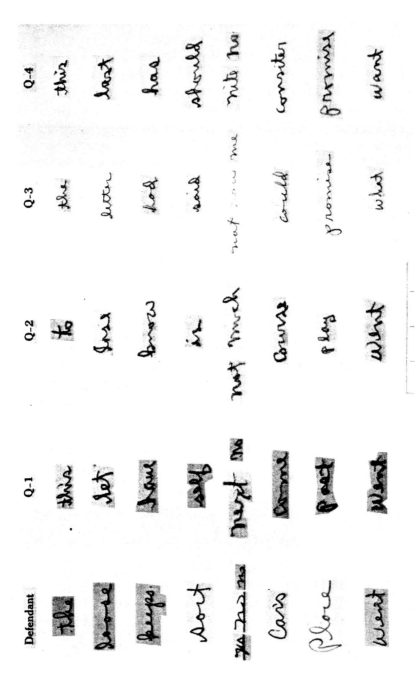

Figure 25. One of series of charts used in identifying writer of four studiously disguised extortion letters. Despite reduced writing speed and other distortion efforts, writer retained striking habits in initial letters.

ularity and recurrence of handwriting individualities obviously proceeds on scientific principles. Its mathematical lineage is evident in the calculation of the separate and aggregate probability for the individualities in the handwritings. Specific mathematical calculations on a case to case basis are the exception rather than the rule for the experienced examiner, as his carefully calculated judgment that a combination of individualities is so singular that it could exist in only one handwriting is not augmented by the physical calculation of the combination as one in three hundred billion or one in five hundred billion.

While the identification of handwriting follows scientific principles and is reducible to the laws of exact science, no responsible authority contends that it is an exact science per se. Handwriting identification is more accurately described as a technique which applies a number of arts and sciences. As to possible error, of course, document experts may err. Document experts, even as the rest of the human race of whatever station or calling, are neither infallible nor impeccable. The possibility of error exists in all calculated judgments, scientific or otherwise. The records for accuracy of competent document examiners in the United States are, however, highly impressive. They inspire confidence in those who are truly familiar with them. This author is aware of hundreds and thousands of cases wherein unerring conclusions were rendered by practicing specialists in the document field. An awareness of the possibility of error in all things human seasons the efforts of the knowing, diligent worker to greater accuracy— it never prejudices the efforts of the truly qualified, nor should it.

A handwriting identification should be accepted or rejected in the same manner as all evidence should be accepted or rejected. As succinctly stated by the late Dean Wigmore* it should be "measured by its convincingness." The identification of a handwriting must stand on its reasons, their exposition, and their illustration—the same basis on which we decide all the weighty problems of human affairs.

---

*Wigmore on Evidence, Second Edition, 1923.

HANDPRINTING AND NUMERALS

Handprinting is defined as including block capitals, sometimes referred to as lettering, and manuscript writing, occasionally described as lower-case printing. It will be understood that this definition encompasses the numerous varieties of these two classes of handprinting as well as their basic forms.

The question is heard so frequently "Can handprinting be identified in the same way as handwriting?" that it is probably advisable to preface this discussion of handprinting with an unequivocal affirmative response to this question. This affirmation of the identification possibilities of handprinting does not blanket as intrinsically identifiable each and every bit of handprinting which

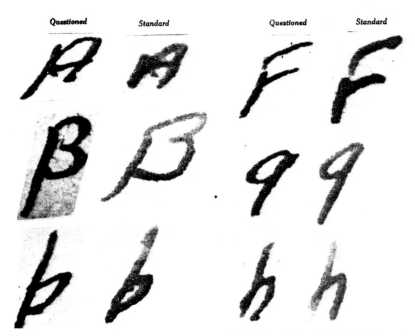

Figure 26. Handprinting agreements highlighted by individualities in initial and terminal strokes.

comes into question. Assuredly handprinting is susceptible to identification. But handprinting serves as an accurate index to its author in fundamentally the same manner as does its more utilitarian brother, cursive script. To be identifiable, a handprinting subject to inquiry must contain the individualities and characteristics of its author in adequate kind and number, and it must receive adequate evaluation in comparison with adequate exemplars of the handprinting of its author.

A number of factors has combined in recent years to augment substantially the incidence of handprinting in all types of documents. Consequently, evidential handprinting has been increasing materially and it will continue to be of even greater investigative concern. Some of these circumstances, not necessarily in the order of their relative importance, are: the trend to manuscript writing instruction in the lower elementary grades, the reversion by many writers to manuscript writing subsequent to their introduction to and early use of cursive script, the increased exposure to lettering, drafting and related forms of instruction, the progressively diminishing proficiency in cursive script by the writers of this age, the multitudinous "Print—Do Not Write" situations one now encounters almost daily, and the erroneous impression held by many criminals and others seeking anonymity that their handprinting will shield their identity much more effectively than their handwriting.

These developments need knell no alarm for the investigator of evidential documents. Quite the contrary is the fact. They presage greater success in many investigations. Frequently, a single case or even a single document will include both cursive script and handprinting and thus, two discrete, if intimately related, avenues of identification are available.

Some understanding of the distinctions between cursive script and handprinting is requisite to a thorough-going evaluation of handprinting problems. Personal individuality in handprinting springs from a slightly different beginning than it does in cursive script. The latter provides important expressions of individuality in letter connections, the effect of such connections on preceding and ensuing letters and letter designs, and significantly in its run-

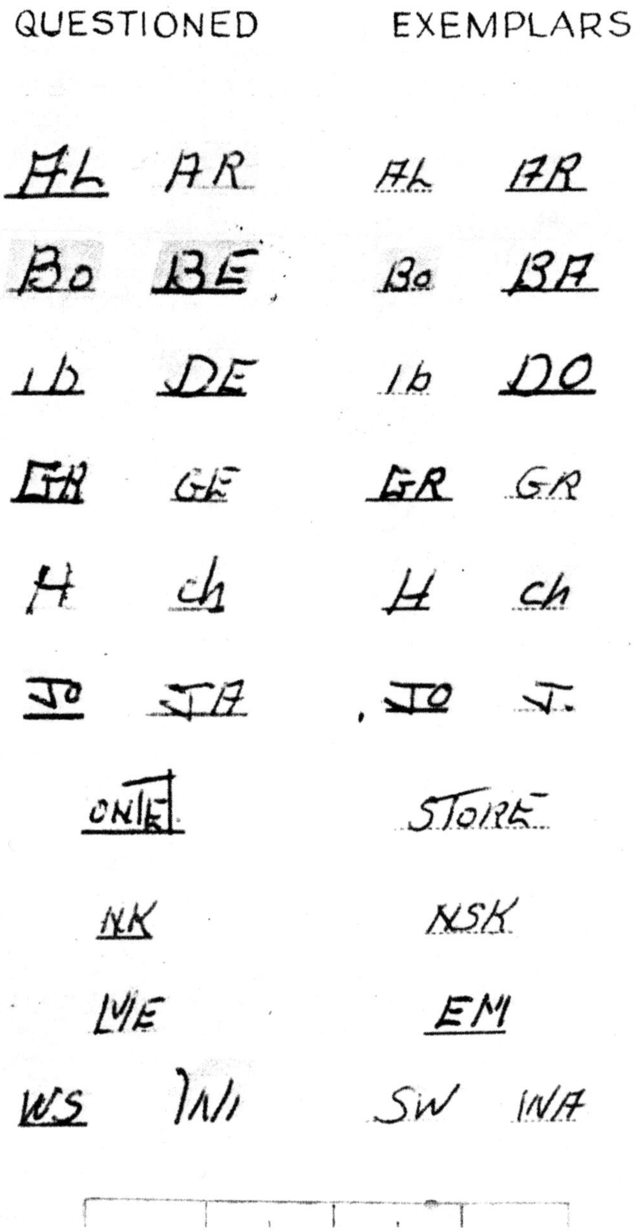

QUESTIONED   EXEMPLARS

Figure 27. Identification of occasional handprinter-observe tendency to angularity and irregular junctions.

ning execution. The majority of mature writers proceeds in cursive script by letter combinations, letter groups, words, phrases, and even sentences without a great deal of conscious effort. Cursive script does not tend to require a continual, conscious direction and redirection of the writing impulses on the part of the writer. The variety of hand and forearm movements required in executing the essentially rounded script characters tends to be fluid in the mature writer. The speed of movement alone in cursive script, not to mention its other intricacies of movement, furnishes a considerable area of individuality from writer to writer.

On the other hand, handprinting is composed substantially of disconnected letters, many of which embody disconnected components. The disjunctions between letters and within individual letters, which are inherent in the execution of printed letters, necessitate repeated direction and redirection of the writing impulses. Junctions involving sharply differing angles of movement are frequent. This tends to call for the exercise of more mental control by the average handprinter and therefore to adorn handprinting with somewhat more consciousness of execution than handwriting possesses.

A further pertinent consideration is that the average writer employs cursive script to a greater extent than he does handprinting. There is a greater variation in the handprinting of the occasional or intermittent handprinter, as executed at different sittings, than is the case in respect to the more utilitarian cursive script. This is particularly true if several handprintings by the same individual are separated by extended intervals. Individualities do not become so unconscious, and therefore so repetitive and automatic, in handprinting unless one uses handprinting systematically and extensively, in which event handprinting will become quite as automatic as cursive script.

The same general principles outlined in the preceding chapter, *The Identification of Handwriting*, likewise underlie the accurate appraisal of handprinting. Because handprinted letters are essentially disconnected and readily "detachable," as it were, for form comparisons, there is a number of prior considerations which merit especial emphasis in the investigation of handprintings. Personal individuality in handprinting is expressed principally in the selection of letter styles and designs, the conformation of individual letters, size ratios, arrangement and punctuation habits. The prime step

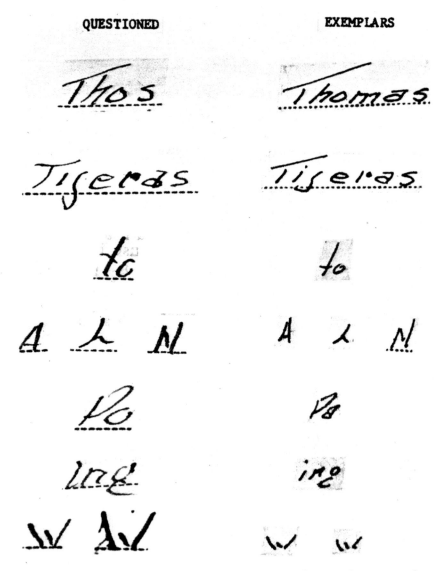

QUESTIONED **EXEMPLARS**

Figure 28. Identification based on approximately five words, noteworthy for singular *j*, *r*, *g*, and three stroke *w*.

in a handprinting inquiry should be a study of the questioned printing to establish independently its normalcy or otherwise, its exemplified skill, and its general reliability as a medium of identification. Initially, it should be pondered as a whole. Was it in total accomplished with a fluency of movement and a certainty of execution indicative of a familiarity with and a measure of skill in handprinting? Does it have that ring of automatic letter conformations and overall execution? Or was it accomplished with a conscious mental effort and non-rhythmic execution denoting either unfamiliarity with handprinting or intentional disguise? Does the handprinting have a faceless, nondescript tone or does it really impress as a reliable medium to the identity of its author?

The automatic fixed printing habits, the occasional variations, the accidentals, the rarities, and the distorted or assumed features should be catalogued meticulously. The aggregate individualities should then be weighed carefully. Do they really isolate one and only one handprinter? Does the accumulative weight of the individualities convince that it could be adduced from the subject handprinting alone and from no other? Only when the answer to these questions is a resolute "yes" has one developed the basis for identification of the author of handprinting.

The same procedural steps should be initially followed in respect to the exemplar handprinting of the suspected author. Individual letter comparisons should not be indulged without first having pondered carefully and fully the whole of the questioned printing and the whole of the exemplar printing. There is an inclination on the part of most investigators to attach unwarranted significance to pictorial similarities between individual letters at all times, and particularly is this true where handprinting is involved. Therefore, it is essential that the examiner of handprinting endeavor to acquire a firm comprehension of the mental and manual qualifications and limitations which produced the handprinting he seeks to identify through comparisons with exemplars, *but in advance of such comparisons.*

The general adequacy of exemplars for comparative purposes will be commented upon in considerable detail in the following chapter. Suffice it to say at this point that the indispensability of

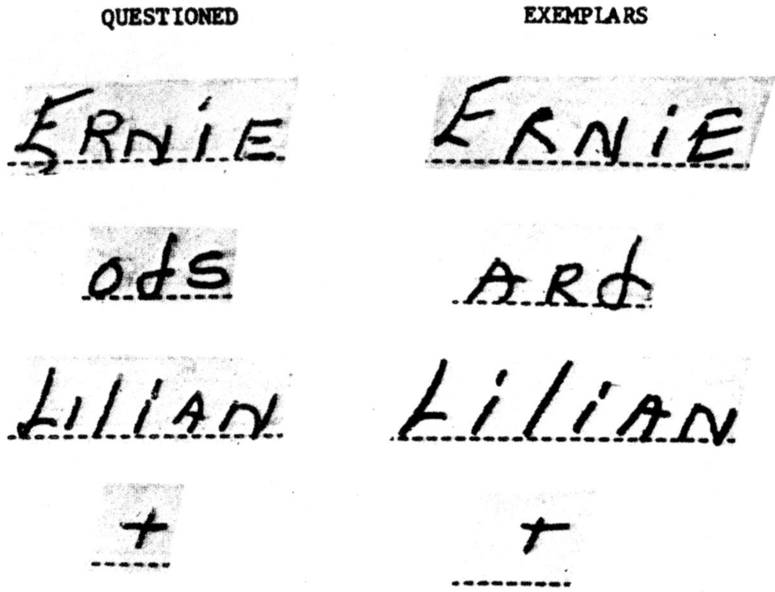

QUESTIONED   **EXEMPLARS**

Figure 29. Identification based on approximately six words—see individualities in *d*, *L*, *1*, *i*, center stroke of *n*, and ampersand.

sufficient handprinting exemplars cannot be overemphasized. Because handprinting tends to be less automatically executed than
cursive script, and because it tends to embody greater variation
than cursive script, it follows that a considerable volume of handprinting, preferably produced at separate sittings, is frequently
necessary to delineate thoroughly and accurately the personal
individualities of its author. Printing exemplars produced in the
regular course of business and witnessed exemplars produced at
the investigator's request complement each other and are equally
necessary in complex printing cases. Nervousness, self-consciousness, and undue attention to the writing process tend to be excluded from exemplars produced in the regular course of business
or events and ordinarily there is no possible motive to distort or
disguise the writer's usual habits. When such exemplars include
handprintings which antedate the questioned printing, they are
completely outside the pale of possible influence from or com-
panionship with the latter.

Request exemplars are valuable because they can be directly witnessed and more readily controlled to the verbatim subject matter which is under investigation. Specific attention can be given writing materials, writing implements, spelling, abbreviatons, arrangement, etc., to the end that conformity between the exemplars and the questioned printing is accomplished. A further and very important consideration is that a guilty subject in seeking to camouflage request handprintings will frequently revert unwittingly to abnormal characteristics, which he has previously injected into questioned handprintings. For this reason, request exemplars should be sought in all cases wherein disguise and distortion are evident in the questioned writings.

The investigator of evidential documents who does not routinely consider the necessity, availability, and applicability of request and informal exemplars places a series restriction on his own results and ultimate successes. By adopting the practice of exclusively utilizing request exemplars, the investigator permits those investigated to exert control over an important phase of his investigation, at the possible expense of successful case solutions. Similarly, he who does not obtain request exemplars to pinpoint a subject's habits in regard to misspellings, peculiar arrangements, unusual phrases, disguises, and punctuation which occur in a questioned handprinting is casting aside significant identification resources which are readily available to him. Regular-course-of-business and request exemplars together provide an insight to the handprinting individualities of their authors more readily than can either class of exemplars alone.

In comparing questioned and exemplar handprintings, the investigator should constantly bear in mind that his objective is not necessarily to effect identifications of suspected individuals or to support some other preconceived theory. The end is ever to establish the truth of the matter under inquiry. The investigator's and the examiner's search is neither for "similarities" nor for "differences" but for identifying individualities, be they in agreement or divergent.

A series of fundamental agreements in identifying individualities is requisite to the conclusion that two writings were authored

QUESTIONED   EXEMPLARS

Figure 30. Identification illustrating necessity for discrete consideration
of normal, transitional, and distorted letter forms.

by the same person, whereas *a single fundamental difference in an identifying individuality* between two writings precludes the conclusion that they were executed by the same person.

In the consideration of individual letters and letter combinations, discretion must be exercised to the end that letters from the same niche in the respective units of writing are correctly associated.

When a questioned handprinting discloses a normal, seminormal, and disguised form of a given letter, each should be evaluated with its so-classified counterpart, if any, in exemplar handprintings. The importance of following this procedure will be apparent in several of the accompanying illustrations.

Variations are within the range of each writer. Differences exist between the writings of different writers. Variations which have been produced purposefully to conceal identity, or variations which are the result of accident or outside influence, clearly do not constitute "differences." Interpretations of variation versus difference are frequently critical and require the services of the skilled document examiner. The investigator's task will be illumined by a thoughtful, orderly effort to: (1) separate normal, transitional, and distorted letters and letter combinations and (2) compare normalcy with normalcy, transition with transition, and distortion with distortion.

Despite the occasional advocate's allegation to the contrary, it is not overly difficult to distinguish between a reasoned, firm conviction and an educated or even an uneducated guess in document identification problems. The former is demonstrable. The latter are simply appeals to belief without reason. One cannot place reliance on a collection of "similarities" which are commonplace. Neither can one stand on a "difference" which reeks of deceptive or accidental execution. The test of a sound identification of two writings is a correctly affirmative response to the proposition: Is there present a combination of agreements in significant personal individualities which isolate one and only one writing personality?" When the correct answer to this proposition is "yes," there can be no true differences between the writings in issue.

NUMERALS

Many investigations of today produce myriads of evidential numerals. This is especially true of inquiries relating to embezzlements, bankruptcies, payroll falsifications, purchase and invoice manipulations, income tax evasion, bookmaking, and fraudulent checks, although numerals arise in virtually every sort of civil and criminal case situation.

Numerals, both Roman and the more common Arabic, provide valuable reservoirs of identification data. Each writer is identifiable by his numerals in the same general manner and subject to the same conditions as have been previously outlined in respect to the identification of cursive script and handprinting. Numerals are essentially disconnected units of writing. The Roman styles and the Arabic "4" and "5," as usually conformed, contain secondary strokes. Numerals, therefore, present many considerations similar to those which are pertinent to the consideration of disconnected handprinted letters. In contrast to the usual running flow of connected cursive script, the writing of numerals is usually characterized by somewhat more conscious direction and redirection of the writing impulses, as the writer accommodates his movement to the disconnected numerals and their inner disconnected components.

Each writer through the repetition inherent in his daily needs and duties develops and expresses the individuality of his own capacities and personality in numerals, as he does in the other facets of his handwriting repertory. This individuality is chiefly evident in numerals' designs, sizes and proportions, arrangement, speed and pressure of execution, comingling of numerals and other writing elements including punctuation, and connection habits, if any. The occasional or intermittent writer of numerals tends to be less automatic and to inject therein somewhat more variation than in the more used cursive script. Conversely, the accountant, the bookkeeper, the bank teller, and the billing clerk develop automatic fixed habits in numerals through the repetition which is native to their daily tasks.

As in the other areas of handwriting, many individual writers employ several classes of numerals. Ornate figures may be used

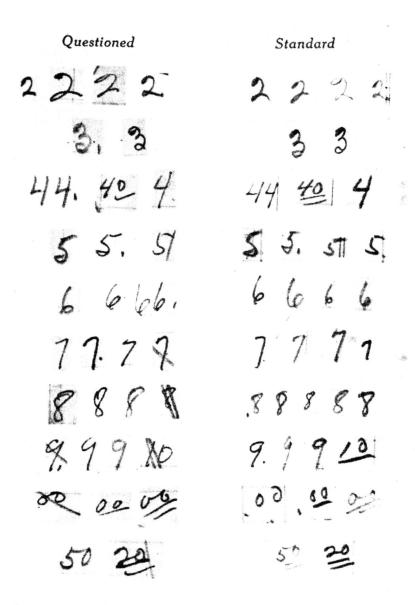

Figure 31. Identification via numerals in accounting records—note patching in *2* and *3* and variety of numeral forms.

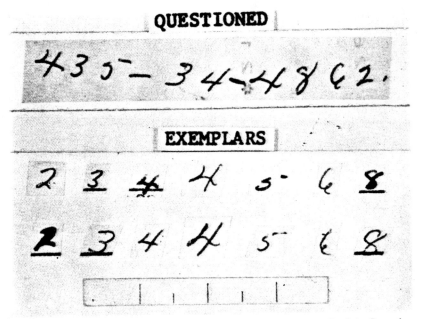

Figure 32. Identification of forger through fictitious Social Security number.

in addressing envelopes or in dating an important contract, whereas clipped "accounting" numerals may grace the family budget account and the office ledgers. Certain occupational necessities tend to develop special purpose numerals, such as, construction drawings, production charts, audit worksheets, deposit slips, or even bookmaking paraphernalia. It is important to consider first the particular class of numerals one has under inquiry in order that valid evaluations and comparisons may thereafter be conducted.

It is not difficult for many writers to develop several classes of numerals and occasionally to use them interchangeably without being fully aware of the extent of their own variations. Informal exemplars, written under a variety of conditions and from a variety of documents, are frequently essential to the solution of numeral identification problems, in order that the writer's classes of numerals and his variations may be accurately evaluated.

It is this writer's observation that the intentional distortion of numerals is somewhat less prevalent in questioned and disputed

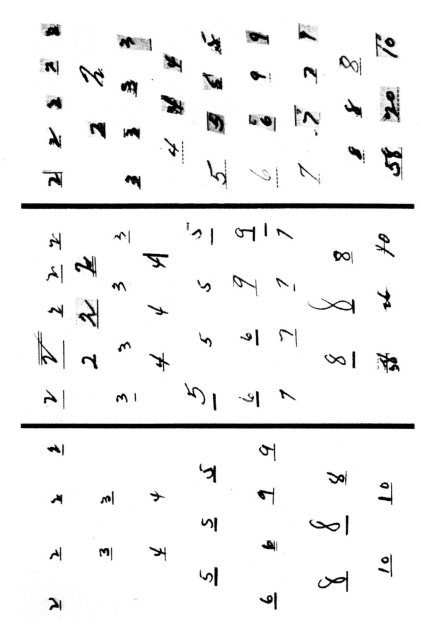

Figure 33. Left and center columns show excerpts from time cards in payroll fraud case. Right column illustrates normal writing of payroll manipulator. Relative consistency in 3, 4, 5, 6, 7, and 9 contrasts with range of variation in 2 and 8.

QUESTIONED   EXEMPLARS

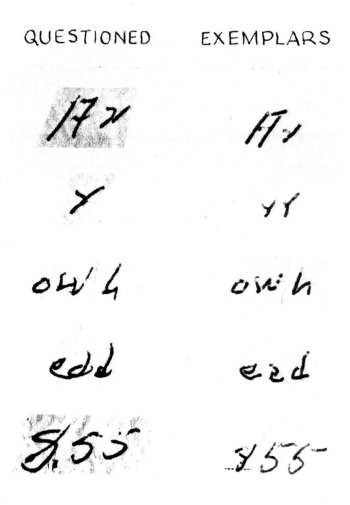

Figure 34. Identification via a two numeral and one word address.

documents than the intentional disguise of cursive script or even handprinting. Evidential documents should be carefully examined for the presence and significances of numerals as they sometimes disclose identifying habits of their author in greater degree than companion script or handprinting wherein the writer devoted a greater effort to distort his usual writing habits. It is not suggested that it is an imposing or impossible task to conceal intentionally one's identifying individualities in a few figures, perhaps a date, a telephone number, or a brief mathematical computation. Rather it is suggested that many writers omit or neglect to camouflage numerals in incriminating documents.

As to exemplar numerals, their general reliability is enhanced if they were informally prepared in the regular course of business or events, at about the same time or prior to the questioned document. To combat the possible injection of distortion into request numerals, premature and undue specificity in respect to numerals should be avoided during the investigative interview. Premature and misplaced emphasis by the investigator actually induces disguise from many interviewees. It is advisable to procure an initial portion of request numerals by interspersing them skillfully throughout a dictated narration which largely calls for cursive script. In this manner, the subject is more apt to write numerals in his usual manner than when his attention is focused on them by the specific request to write numerals alone. Thereafter, additional request numerals should be obtained which specifically correspond with the format and sequence of the questioned numerals in each case.

Thoughtfully obtained informal numerals and astutely procured request numerals complement each other and are jointly necessary to the solution of many numeral problems. Investigative thoroughness in the study of questioned and disputed numerals, followed by the intelligent acquisition of exemplars to recreate the numerals in issue in their requisite setting, are the indispensable forerunners of productive reports from the document examiner and ultimate case solutions.

HANDWRITING INVESTIGATIONS

■

THE PROCUREMENT OF EXEMPLARS

Preservation of Evidential Handwriting

The initial consideration in every handwriting inquiry is to insure that the evidential handwriting is preserved in precisely the condition in which it was originally received for investigation. This rule applies, of course, to all evidential documents whether of known or questioned origin. He who carelessly mishandles documents of any class may preclude their accurate and complete interpretation. Thoughtless underscorings, careless markings, folds, creases, and soiling which is inflicted upon or adjacent to handwriting may obscure important identifying factors therein. Such extraneous markings may lessen the weight to be given an entire handwriting at a subsequent examination or trial, and they may even vitiate its admissibility as formal evidence. The investigator should have ever before him the fact that a handwriting cannot properly be divorced from the materials, the conditions, and the circumstances which attended its birth. They are an integral part of it. Therefore, no after-the-fact markings, foreign materials, or physical changes should be injected which could becloud an evaluation of an evidential handwriting or the document on which it appears.

Specifically do not fold, staple, perforate, impress rubber or metal stamps upon, attach labels or stickers to, mark, write on, or otherwise alter an evidential handwriting. Do place small inconspicuous initials and dates in areas of the document where they do not conflict with the original writing. The reverse side of the document is an ideal location for these small identifying marks and care should be exercised that they do not strike through the paper to obstruct the writing on the obverse. Do maintain consequential documents unfolded and in transparent plastic envelopes or evidence preservers. Do not be continually handling an evidential writing—you can see it through the transparent covering, you

74

know. Do not carry handwritten documents carelessly in your wallet, notebook, or brief case on rounds of interviews. Do maintain them in their protective coverings and have photostatic copies prepared for routine interviews. With such copies you will save wear and tear on the original and several investigators can conduct simultaneously, when necessary, a number of separate inquiries relating to the same document.

Do not smear evidential handwritings with fingerprint powders or chemicals. Do consider the advisability of latent fingerprint processing in the light of the physical properties of the parent document, the lapse of time since the document in question was suspiciously handled, and the number of persons who have thereafter handled it. If your own judgment or that of your fingerprint specialist or criminalist dictates the advisability of fingerprint processing, make certain that the handwriting is photographed critically and to scale prior to the application of iodine, silver nitrate, ninhydrin, or other chemical agents.

Preliminary Considerations

Having insured the preservation of evidential handwriting in its original condition, the foundational phase of its investigation is a thorough, detailed study of the questioned document, the questioned handwriting. The scene should be envisioned which produced the document, the handwriting, the signature which is under investigation. Who were the dramatis personae? What were their physical and mental conditions? Their ages? Their interests? Their reliability? Where was the locale? What was the time? The exact occasion? What were the surrounding circumstances? The writing conditions? What were the writing implements and materials? What is the format? What is the motive, the thought content of the writing? What are the outstanding peculiarities, the individualities?

There is no alternative for this fundamental phase of the inquiry. Rushing prematurely into an investigation concerning a document, a handwriting, a signature which one has not attempted to comprehend fully is not merely unrealistic. It is a basically faulty procedure which is prone to produce poor results and to dissipate investigative manpower.

The procurement of exemplars for comparative purposes in a handwriting investigation presupposes that one or more questioned documents and handwritings have arisen or are anticipated in a given case. Of course! That is obvious, we say. But it should not be permitted to become so obvious that the questioned handwriting in any case is taken for granted. Some investigations degenerate into hit-or-miss scattershot operations. "Get some handwriting" becomes the order rather than "Study this questioned handwriting carefully and compile representative exemplars for comparison with it." Each handwriting investigation, each search for exemplars should be conducted in the light of and under the auspices and patronage of the questioned writing. Its identification is the ultimate objective. With this end result in mind, correct procedural techniques will tend to follow as a natural, logical consequence.

Handwriting exemplars should recreate the identifying elements of the questioned writing with which they are to be compared. The object of exemplars is to illustrate, fairly and completely, their author's personal habits in the creation of such handwriting as is under question or in dispute. It is not the object of exemplars to do more, and they are deficient when they accomplish less. Accurate, complete exemplars which demonstrate their authors' habits in the light of the handwriting which is in question provide the basis for reliable sound conclusions. Incomplete exemplars or those whose manner of procurement has distorted or precluded an accurate interpretation of their author's habits inherently circumvent reliable sound conclusions. Inadequate exemplars can and do result in inconclusive findings. They can even lead to erroneous conclusions.

The procurement of exemplars might be likened to a manhunt. One would not initiate a manhunt without a description of the man who was sought, his probable attire, his possible disguises, his known peculiarities, and everything else of identifying significance which could be developed concerning him. One would brief himself and his collaborators exhaustively on the identifying elements, the characteristics of the individual for whom he was searching. It would be considered inefficient and downright foolish for one to seek a suspect in the flesh without some idea of what the suspect looked like, what he acted like, and where he was apt to be found. Handwriting presents an analogous problem and one with equal if not greater tangibility.

The identifying elements of a questioned handwriting provide the core around which its investigation should revolve. These identifying elements should be before the mind of the investigator consistently in his inquiry and throughout his search for exemplars. One is not simply seeking any handwriting from suspected individuals. The object is to develop exemplars which fairly and completely illustrate a suspect's habits in the recreation of the handwriting which is under investigation. The purpose is not necessarily to obtain exemplars which seem similar to the questioned handwriting and indicate guilt on the part of a suspect. The ultimate is to acquire true and accurate exemplars of the suspect's habits and individualities so that they will reveal the truth, perhaps the innocence of the suspect.

Classes of Exemplars

There are two general classes of handwriting exemplars. The first and the better general class includes those writings which are prepared in the normal, routine course of business or personal affairs. This class will be referred to as informal or regular-course-of-business exemplars. The second and the second best general class of exemplars consists of those writings which are prepared in the presence of the investigator and at his request, for the specific purpose of comparison with a questioned document or documents. This latter class of exemplars will be referred to as request exemplars.

The relative value and the particular applicability of informal and of request exemplars represent vital information for the investigator of evidential writings. It should be understood by the law enforcement officer, the attorney, the judge, and the document examiner how each of these general classes can be utilized most effectively and weighed most accurately.

As previously discussed, handwriting is identified on the basis of the personal individualities of its author. These individualities are the result of handwriting training, experience, and usage and they are developed through constant repetition until they become quite automatic in most adult writers. These individualities are essentially unconscious expressions. As a general rule, they are produced outside the conscious concentration of the mature writer. When one writes informally, in the regular conduct of his business or personal affairs, he has no motive to disturb his usual writing habits. No reason is injected to distort or disguise the automatic routine expression of his personal writing individualities. Writing in his habitual unrepressed manner, there is no overhanging inclination to self-consciousness, mental stress, deception, nervousness, fear, or resentment. It follows that informal, regular-course-of-business exemplars are inherently more personal and more natural. Thus, they are more apt to embody the writer's true, unvarnished, unembellished individualities.

Request exemplars are prepared within or related to the law enforcement atmosphere, or at least within the circle of specific interest in a questioned handwriting. The writer by request has a point to prove. He is either interested in proving that he executed the writing in issue or in disproving his responsibilty. He is not neutral. He has a concern for what his exemplars may reveal. He has become associated in some way with the questioned or disputed writing. The writer by request usually is under some suspicion or at least thinks he is, regardless of what he is told or what he says at the time of preparation of request exemplars. Whether the writer is guilty or innocent, deceptive or just plain scared, cooperative or antagonistic, of high station or low, clever or stupid, first offender or recidivist, skilled penman or semi-illiterate, his consciousness is directed to the act of writing in some degree. Self-consciousness, deception, nervousness, intentional disguise, mental stress, fear, and other like factors must be carefully considered and reconciled in the interpretation of individualities from request exemplars. The mental attitudes and manual ability of some writers make it possible for them to distort effectively, and occasionally to exclude entirely, their normal and true individualities from request exemplars.

It is not intended to infer that request exemplars are not valuable. Nothing could be more remote from the truth. Request

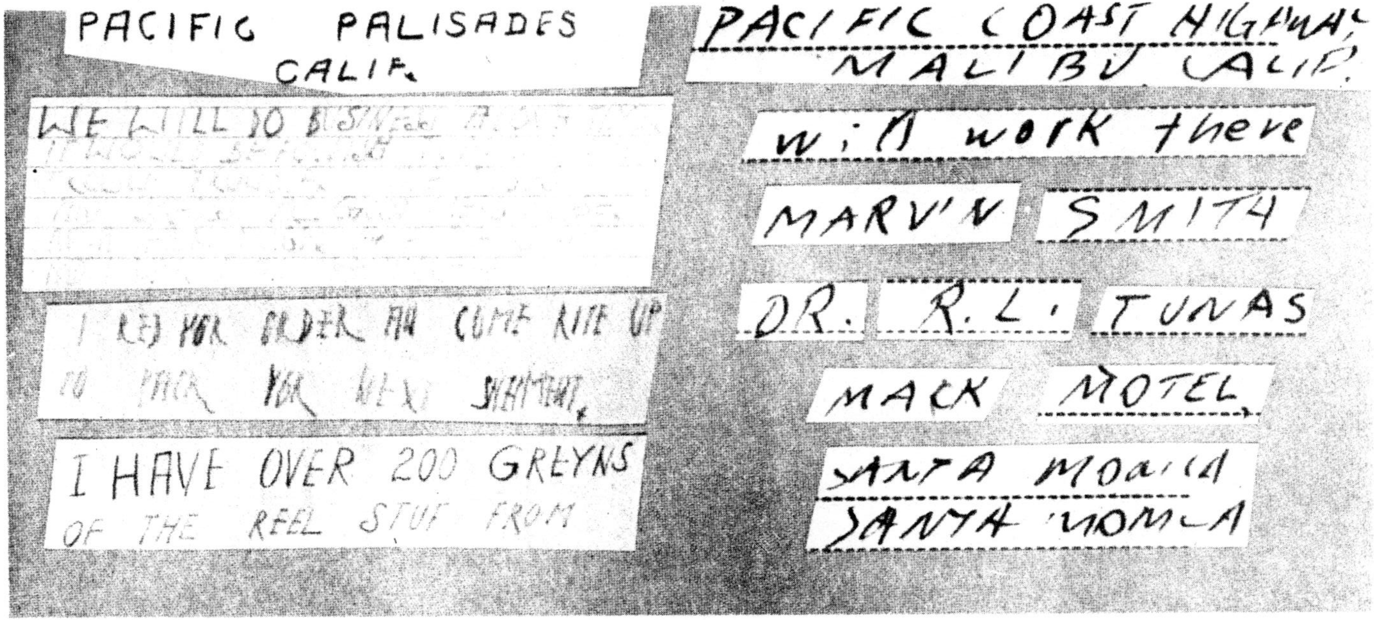

Figure 35. Left column illustrates portions of four request exemplars which subject, a university graduate, alleged to represent his normal writing. Right column contains excerpts written by subject in regular course of business.

exemplars are not only distinctly worthwhile, they are in many cases indispensable to success. Many handwriting identifications and eliminations can be and are accomplished through request exemplars alone. There is always a place and an important place for the second team. Occasionally it will outscore the varsity. It is especially adapted for particular plays. In some games it should be employed throughout. But no coach could be very successful if he consistently started his scrub team and played it throughout all his contests.

Departments having a low percentage of handwriting case solutions are urged to take a new look at their thinking and their procedures in respect to handwriting exemplars. The first team of exemplars, the informal, regular-course-of-business writings should not be virtually ignored. No department should attempt to rely exclusively on the substitutes, the self-interest, request exemplars. Some handwriting inquiries fail of solution because of the absence of informal exemplars. Still more cases necessitate tortuous and protracted laboratory studies and produce border-line conclusions because of the unavailability of informal-regular-course-of-business exemplars.

The principle which is involved may be seen by analogy in oral statements, verbal exemplars, let us say. Would anyone seriously contest that statements by an accused to sympathetic family, friends, and associates, completely removed from the law enforcement atmosphere, would be liable to elicit valuable and accurately informative data? Does not the accused react characteristically when talking to his business associates, family and friends, who know him well, and whom he could not readily deceive in any event? Would not the reliability of the accused's statements be augmented if they were made prior to his accusation? Prior to the date of the incident which brought him under suspicion and made him an accused? Handwriting exemplars present similar considerations. When written in the normal, routine flow of daily affairs, under no possible aura of deception, self-interest or unreliability, they are clearly of great value in isolating, and with facility, the true writing individualities of their authors.

A few inexperienced document examiners, unimaginative

identification laboratories and law enforcement administrators have probably contributed to the preoccupation of some investigators with request writings and a resulting exclusion of informal exemplars. In some areas of law enforcement, so much emphasis has been accorded the mechanics of procuring request exemplars during the investigative interview that the fundamental objective of exemplars has been unwittingly submerged. Concentration on request exemplars is sought to be rationalized at times as a necessary expedient to conserve investigative manpower, to insure that admissibility requirements for court presentation are satisfied, and to obtain literatim facsimiles of the questioned writing. These considerations are pertinent but partial. The principle may be embraced with both practical and scientific tenability that informal and request exemplars complement each other and are equally necessary in many difficult cases and should be available in all cases whenever possible.

Sources of Informal Exemplars

The availability of informal writings varies from writer to writer, according to the quantity and kind of writing accomplished in his daily pursuits. Familiarity with the background, occupation, business and professional relationships, social associations, and personal habits of an individual will suggest the location of exemplars which are appropriate for comparison with a particular questioned writing. The following sources are thought-promoting in this connection, particular note being taken of the existence of several exemplars on certain individual documents as, the respective signatures of the officiating clergyman or magistrate, those married, and the witnesses on a marriage record.

Personal Documents

Birth and baptismal certificates and records, family Bible, diaries, personal notebooks, telephone and correspondence listings, marriage documents, greeting cards, correspondence and postcards, hospital and medical records, prescriptions, rent receipts, memoranda about the home and office, such as a note to the milkman, memo to the charman.

Education Documents

High school and college admission applications, examination papers, written assignments, research projects, fraternity and sorority records, athletic entries.

Vocational Documents

Applications for employment, employment bureau and personnel office papers, application for professional and vocational licenses, public examinations, civil service papers, labor union documents, time cards, account books, reports and surveys, stenographic and clerical memoranda, payroll checks, clients' checks.

Financial Documents

Bank checks, notes, contracts and related correspondence, insurance documents including health and accident, loan companies' records, pension applications and checks, lease agreements, deeds, title companies' documents, expense accounts, credit applications, for example, to a department store.

Social, Recreational, Fraternal Documents

Documents relating to clubs, lodges, civic organizations, PTA associations, political groups, religious organizations, and non-profit groups.

Corporate Documents

Applications for gas, electricity, water, telephone, refuse disposal service, incorporation documents as, for example, documents filed with state agencies, original telegram messages, applications and reports to intra and inter-state traffic and commerce agencies, filings in connection with real estate developments, corporate minutes, books of account, invoices.

Motor Vehicle Documents

Applications for registration, installment contracts on vehicle purchases, operators' and chauffeurs' licenses and applications therefor, insurance papers, reports of accidents, reports of loss or theft, orders for service, court documents relating to accidents, credit card applications and invoices based thereon. The latter frequently lead to hotel and motel registrations based on routes of travel, as gleaned from credit purchases.

Military Documents

Selective service records, National Guard, Army, Air Force, Navy, and Coast Guard papers, tax exemption filings and loan, real estate, pension, medical, and educational documents related to military service.

Governmental and Public Records

Official archives, Veterans Administration records, tax documents relating to property, personal, use, corporate, income and payroll revenues at local, county, state and federal levels, immigration and naturalization records, patent office applications, civil suit documents, briefs, pleadings, bail bonds, affidavits, waivers, powers of attorney, social security records, bankruptcies, death certificates, voting registrations, library applications, probate records and supporting papers, postal and customs documents.

Criminal Documents

Arrest records, parole and probation reports, jail and penitentiary records, writings obtained by other agencies in prior investigations, writings obtained by your own agency in prior investigations, complaints and reports to police departments, sheriffs, district attorneys, etc., exemplars obtained incident to booking procedures.

Miscellaneous Documents

Documents obtainable from friends, associates, family and neighbors, delivery receipts, decoy and otherwise, return receipts for registered mail, decoy and otherwise, express records and receipts, motel and hotel registrations, building plans, airplane logs, passports, shipping papers, purchase orders. Do not forget the janitor and the maid. Many cases have been solved by writings recovered from the trash can or waste basket, a laundry list, or a complaint to the window cleaner.

Proof of Exemplars

Proof of authorship, of course, must be considered carefully in connection with informal exemplars. This is properly the responsibility of the investigator who obtains such exemplars. The simple and most satisfactory method of proving authorship is

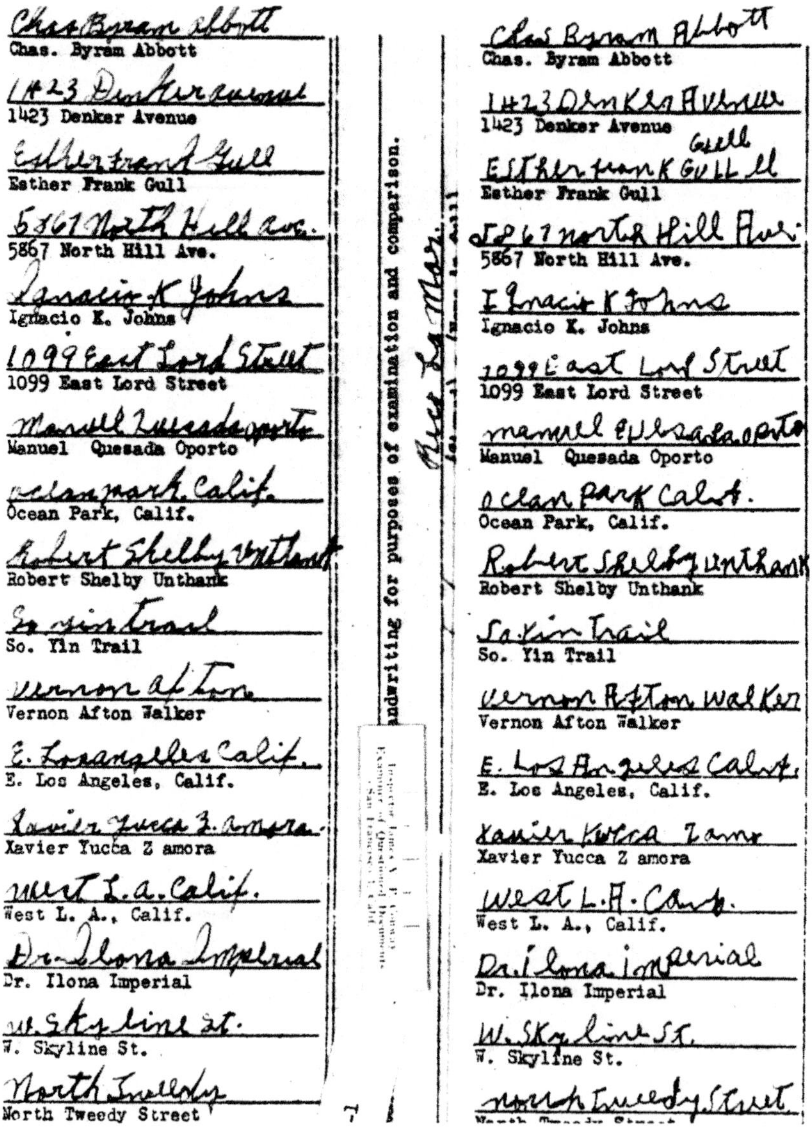

Figure 36. Variations in exemplars of unskilled writer prepared, respectively, in 1953 (normal) and in 1955 (disguised). Writer was 31 in 1953.

usually by interrogation of the writer in question. Strangely enough, many investigators who evince not the slightest hesitation in requesting a suspect to prepare exemplars during the investigative interview are reluctant to interrogate the same suspect concerning informal exemplars. The suspect who will voluntarily prepare request exemplars will also ordinarily identify exemplars which he authored informally, in the regular course of business. The majority of suspects in criminal cases and subjects in civil matters furnish request exemplars willingly and without any compulsion. Many babble about how anxious they are to cooperate. Even the recalcitrant who refuses, as is his right, to furnish request exemplars will frequently have no aversion to a conversation which will identify many of his informal writings which will prove eminently suitable for comparative purposes.

A rather astounding misapprehension has been noted at virtually all levels of law enforcement respecting the questioning of suspects concerning exemplars written outside the presence of the investigator. Cases have been observed wherein investigative and trial expenses running into thousands of dollars have been incurred because an investigator did not timely inquire of the accused, "This is your handwriting, is it not?" Absurd situations are created wherein a defendant's Uncle John must be subpoenaed from Tallahassee to Seattle to identify correspondence being introduced as exemplars, which the defendant himself would have freely discussed and identified as his handwriting, had he been properly questioned in the preliminary stages of the investigation. Situations have occurred wherein the omission of timely questioning negatived the evidential admissibility of such exemplars, because Uncle John was not available to identify the correspondence from his far away nephew in the law's toils.

Too frequently also, it is assumed that a writing provides a reliable criterion of the characteristics of a given individual, because it bears his name or what purports to be his signature. Again it may unreasonably be presumed that a writing will somehow wend its way into evidence because "everybody 'knows' it is the defendant's handwriting." In the assemblage of exemplars, the objective is to compile writings which reliably and thoroughly reveal the subject's individual writing habits in the light of the particular questioned writing, *and which at the same time are admitted by the subject to be his writing or can be proved so to be.*

Exemplars can be proved by the testimony of a witness who observed the act of writing. Exemplars can also be proved by circumstantial evidence which associates the subject unerringly with their execution. But the question must always be preconsidered carefully, "What witness can and will identify this exemplar as the defendant's writing?" And an excellent ready answer is "I showed this writing to the defendant and he told me that he wrote it and he also described the time, the place, and the circumstances of writing it."

When an interview involves a written document, and more particularly when it includes a request for the witnessed preparation of exemplars, it focuses attention on handwriting, as such. There is scarcely any investigative disadvantage thereafter to a full exploration of the subject. An investigator who adopts a mysterious, ivory-tower attitude concerning exemplars, prospective exemplars, and their intended uses usually succeeds in tieing only his own hands. If the interviewee has actually written an incriminating signature or other writing, he is aware of the implications of exemplars, whether he admits or denies authorship. If he proposes to lie or to evade concerning the identification of informal exemplars, better to extend him plenty of "rope" than to restrict his areas of falsehoods.

The simple questions by the investigator during his initial interviews with subjects, "You remember writing this application for employment?" "You recognize your handwriting on these rent checks which you issued for your apartment rent?" "This is the registration you wrote when you checked into the Biltmore?" or, "Suppose we go down to your bank, office, and home and you can turn over to me handwriting exemplars which you feel fairly and accurately illustrate your handwriting?" in many cases will spell the difference between success and failure in identifications via handwriting exemplars. When these types of questions are posed timely and skillfully and under the aegis of a completely fair but withal searching investigation, they will produce a surprisingly high percentage of affirmative responses.

Variations in Exemplars

As heretofore cited, the questioned writing provides the base on which exemplars are superimposed to build an identification. The investigator should be aware that many writers tend to vary somewhat in style, size, letter conformations, and design selectivity according to the particular kind of writing they are accomplishing. The investigator's thinking and efforts should be directed, therefore, to the procurement of exemplars of the same kind, or subclassification of writing, which is represented in the questioned writing being investigated.

A writer may inject variations in his intimate and family correspondence which do not regularly appear in the memoranda and directives which he sends to his office staff. One may have a particular signature which he reserves for his firm's checks and correspondence. Certainly, he will have a cursory scrawl for the

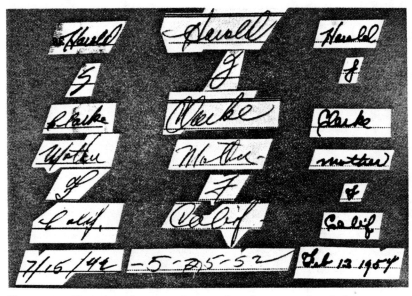

Figure 37. Variations in normal exemplars by somewhat below average writer executed, left to right, in 1942, 1952, and 1954. Writer was 21 in 1942.

delivery boy, the message center, lecture and research notes, and the prescriptions to the pharmacy. He may adopt a formal flourished signature for an important contract, deed, statute, and his last will and testament. When one addresses envelopes and post cards, he may assume peculiarities which do not appear very often elsewhere in his writings. His writings on blueprints, maps, and production charts may bring innovations.

Lower case printing, block lettering, numerals, and accounting entries pose additional writing situations which do not have much in common with, say the cursive initials on the time card or the endorsement on the payroll check. If one is a big enough "shot" to be bothered by autograph seekers, surely he will have learned to concoct a special signature for that purpose. One may have various special purpose writings and he may deliberately change certain writings from time to time.

The point is that writing is a practical, fairly readily understood expression when looked at squarely and reasonably. There are relationships among the various kinds of writing each of us performs. Obviously, the greatest relationship exists between two of our writings of the same kind. The investigator then will find his efforts most productive and rewarding when he can procure exemplars of the kind corresponding to the kind of writing which is in issue in a given case.

There will be case situations wherein informal writings: (a) are not sought, for valid reason or otherwise, (b) cannot be located, (c) are not clearly provable, or (d) are qualitatively or quantitatively inadequate. In these situations, the investigator must resort to request exemplars. Recognizing that request exemplars are self-interest writings, susceptible to involuntary distortion and voluntary camouflage, the investigator should direct especial attention to the neutralization of those factors which could abnormalize the recreation of a questioned writing by a subject who is writing under request conditions. One should take cognizance that the mishandling of interviews designed to produce request exemplars can accentuate those factors—self-consciousness, deception, nervousness, mental stress, fear, abnormal writing positions, deliberate disguise, etc.,—which distort writing habits, just as surely as the circumspect handling of such interviews can neutralize these factors.

The Forgery Claimant

Consider the typical sort of handwriting inquiry proceeding from the claim by John Smith that a check has been forged against his bank account, or that the endorsement on his payroll check has been forged. Although John may be an upstanding citizen with a reputation for complete veracity, it should not be assumed automatically that the protested check has been forged. Neither can it be assumed that the forgery, if such occurred, is a simple, simulated, or traced forgery. Never let it be said that you "investigated" an alleged forgery without first endeavoring to determine from the document in issue that it was in fact a forgery, and a particular kind of forgery. One should be certain that a check is truly "dead" before seeking its "murderer" and he should consider carefully how the check met its demise. One will run across occasional "suicides."

Neither the authorship nor the irrelevancy of any notations, markings, or data on an alleged forgery should be presumed. Memoranda should be prepared progressively by the investigator as he establishes responsibility for initials, addresses, telephone numbers, identification notations, erasures, and the materiality of possible individualities such as choice of pen or pencil, color of ink, position of signature, type of identification used, etc.

The complete document should be examined critically, obverse and reverse. Does it contain any carbon traces or indentations? Does the writing appear to have been unnaturally drawn rather than written in a free unrestrained manner? What stands out about the alleged forgery? With the results of these preliminary observations in mind, handwriting exemplars should be obtained from the forgery claimant. Remember that the investigator is not necessarily casting aspersions on John Smith's claim of forgery by seeking exemplars of his signature and writing. Rather the fact and the method of forgery are to be studied via exemplars so that the forgery may be intelligently and thoroughly investigated.

The best exemplars to prove or disprove the genuineness of the disputed signature of John Smith are signatures written by John in the regular course of business, on the same class of documents, prior to and about the same date as the disputed signature. The best exemplars for comparison with a May 1948 check which John Smith asserts is a forgery are checks which John admittedly and provably drew against his bank account from about March to July 1948. The best exemplars for comparison with a disputed endorsement of November 1952 are endorsements which John admittedly and provably wrote on payroll or other checks in the regular course of business from about September 1952 to February 1953.

Such exemplars recreate the setting, the character, the time of the disputed documents. By including checks written prior to the alleged forgery, such exemplars eliminate the danger of being misled by self-serving planted signatures, written after the alleged forgery was disclaimed. By consisting of documents of the same class and kind, such exemplars preclude obstructions in the form of variations resulting from one of John Smith's several styles of writing. By including a variety of checks written over a number of months, such exemplars provide an adequate cross-section of John Smith's habits under normal, day to day writing conditions.

In most forgery investigations, interview of the claimant is called for in the earliest investigation stages. Frequently, this is prior to an opportunity to obtain informal exemplars of the forgery claimant. Regardless of the stage of the investigation when the forgery claimant is first interviewed, it is proper and advisable to request him to prepare a number of exemplars of his endorsement, or the manner in which he prepares and signs checks, or signs his name on whatever class of document is in question.

Do not exhibit the questioned document to the claimant immediately prior to the procurement of such request exemplars. But be realistic. He has probably seen it before your interview. He is usually the prime mover in the forgery investigation. Ask the claimant about his prior examination of the averred forgery. What caused him to conclude that it was a forgery? Make note of his

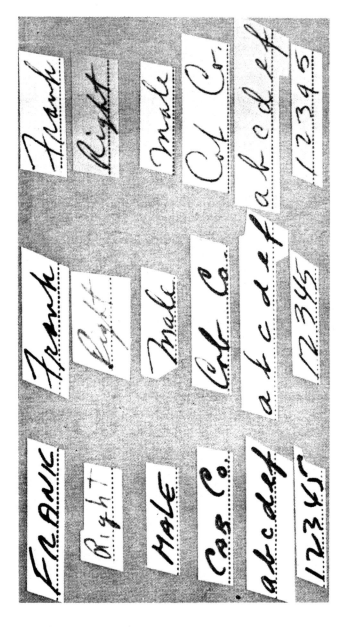

Figure 38. Variations in normal exemplars by average writer prepared, left to right, in 1950, 1951, and 1954. Writer was 31 in 1950.

answers. They may change later. Tell him why you prefer to wait until after he has prepared exemplars in your presence to permit him to examine or to re-examine the alleged forgery with you. You are simply endeavoring to preclude the writing and format of the questioned document from influencing his exemplars, consciously or unconsciously. When it is impracticable to obtain exemplars prior to the claimant's immediate examination of an alleged forgery, note of such circumstance should be incorporated in the case memoranda for future consideration.

In obtaining request exemplars, the claimant-writer should be seated in a natural writing position. Supply him with fountain pen, steel pen and holder, ball pen, pencil, or whatever instrument was used to prepare the questioned writing. When a forged endorsement is claimed, have the claimant write endorsements on blanks checks of comparable size and writing space. If blank checks are not available, blank slips of paper of corresponding size may be used. When the questioned endorsement is written on printed lines, blank checks or slips of paper with similar ruled spaces should be used.

As the claimant prepares each exemplar, remove it from his immediate vision, while he prepares the next one. This procedure is much preferable to having him write a series of signatures on the same piece of paper. The investigator should be casual about the entire proceedings so as to induce naturalness in the exemplars, and in the light of the questioned document. If the latter was probably written in a standing position at a bank counter or under some unusual writing conditions, the claimant should be asked to prepare several exemplars in like manner. The investigator should indicate on such exemplars the manner of their preparation. Similarly, he should show by a small unobtrusive number the order in which the various exemplars were written.

When questioned writings include a street address, city and state, telephone number, military designation, identification number, etc., the subject should be specifically requested to include such particulars in his exemplars. Additionally, he should be questioned for the precise significance of these data.

If the issuance of an entire check is alleged, the disputant should be supplied with comparable blank checks, or slips of paper of corresponding size and with appropriate spacings and rulings. He should be asked to fill in all the particulars on the exemplar checks in his usual manner of preparing checks. From dictation, he should be given the date, amount, payee's name, and the other particulars of issuance. Specific directions as to the subject's method of writing or expression should be avoided. When they are unavoidable, memorandum should be made of the directions given, for future consideration. It is important for the investigator to remember at all stages that his object is neither to establish nor to disprove the claimant's position, but to determine the truth of the matter through adequate exemplars.

There is considerable advantage to causing exemplars to be written at several different times during a single interview, rather than having them prepared in one continuous writing operation. A desirable plan is to intersperse routine questions for ten or fifteen minutes at several points in the interview to interrupt the preparation of exemplars and divert the subject's attention temporarily from writing, as such. The interviewer should maintain control of the situation with the end objective of fully developing the claimant's writing habits in the recreation of the questioned document.

All exemplars should be unostentatiously initialed and dated. A further suggested procedure is to have the subject state in his own handwriting that "These handwriting exemplars are being supplied to Inspector John Doe of my own free will for purposes of examination and comparison."

Incident to discussion of his allegation of forgery, the claimant should be asked to examine and identify any informal exemplars theretofore obtained. If none has been developed, a series of questions should be propounded to elicit from the claimant his business and other associations through which authentic regular-course-of-business exemplars may be examined, if and when necessary. For example, the availability of canceled checks should be clarified for possible comparison with a questioned check, and the location of payroll or clients' checks should be established for possible comparison with disputed endorsements. The claimant

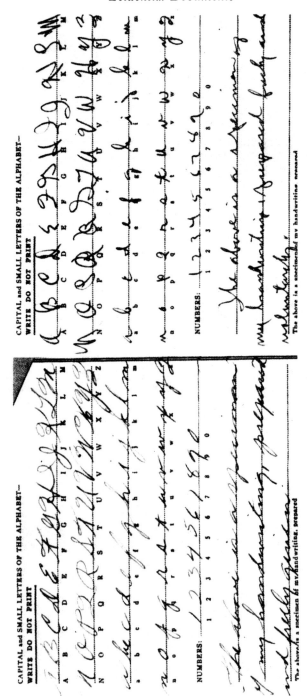

Figure 39. Variations in exemplars by skilled writer, 35 years of age, as shown by excerpts written at separate sittings on same day.

should be asked himself to produce several signatures written in the routine course of his daily affairs. Frequently, in fact, usually, the subject will have excellent exemplars on his person, such as, signatures on his motor vehicle operator's permit, fraternal society membership cards, receipts, labor and professional organization cards, military and selective service documents, and the other multitudinous identification cards one seems required to possess in ever increasing numbers.

When a forgery claimant is reliable and truthful, as most of them are, request and informal exemplars together usually will promptly and clearly support his credibility, even to the unpractised eye. Should deception be involved, these two classes of exemplars together will establish the fact much more readily than will a complete reliance on request exemplars alone.

Examine the exemplars which the claimant prepared at your request. Determine whether they agree with each other, and with those exemplars which he executed in the regular course of his daily pursuits. If an agreement among these writings is apparent, it is a considerable indication of the claimant's reliability. At least, one knows that he has acquired reliable exemplars from which to uncover the truth. If the exemplars produced by request disagree with those executed in the normal course of events, the investigator is placed on notice that the claimant may be unreliable. In any event, the disagreement must be resolved. Point out the discrepancy to the claimant. Get his explanation now. It may save much time later. Are his explanation and attitude reasonable, or do they give further indication of his unreliability? Particularly the investigator should determine whether it seems evident that the claimant intentionally distorted his request exemplars. If so, he should be specifically questioned about this circumstance. The investigator has everything to gain and nothing to lose by a full discussion.

A very logical question, frequently heard, concerns the quantity of exemplar signatures necessary for purposes of comparison with an alleged forgery. As the regular-course-of-business signatures are qualitatively superior to request signatures, the availability of one or the other or both of these classes of exemplars controls somewhat the number which is requisite to determine forgery or authenticity. Signatures, like their authors, vary greatly in their complexities and accordingly there is no binding rule of number which will suffice or even be necessary in every case. A single informal exemplar could conceivably be adequate to establish a clumsy forgery. In the general run of cases encountered in law enforcement, three to five exemplar signatures of the forgery claimant might be adequate in some cases, five to ten would probably be adequate in most cases, and fifteen to twenty undoubtedly would be adequate in the vast majority of cases.

Considerations Relevant to Class of Forgery

Having considered the questioned signature or writing itself, and having obtained suitable exemplars of the individual who alleges forgery, the investigator's next step is to compare the questioned writing with the aggregate exemplars. Everyone cannot be expected to be a specialist in comparing writings. But every law enforcement officer, attorney, and just plain citizen should in each and every case of this sort seek to determine whether he is confronted with an obvious forgery, and if so, whether it is an imitation or a simple forgery. The investigator of evidential writings must proceed on broad principles, it being understood that in many cases he will necessarily consult his document examiner for advice in the earliest as well as the later stages of forgery investigations.

From the investigator's standpoint, an alleged forgery which closely resembles the pictorial form of exemplar writings must be considered either genuine, or a forgery by imitation, that is, a tracing or a simulation. If such alleged forgery contains the trademarks of forgery by tracing or simulation, as outlined in a preceding chapter, the investigator should proceed on that basis, particularly if the claimant's reliability has been otherwise well established. When the investigator is uncertain from his preliminary comparisons whether an alleged forgery is genuine writing or an imitation thereof, he should forthwith solicit the counsel of his document examiner. He should not become disillusioned if occasionally the document examiner's report shows that such a questioned writing is a simple forgery in a writing of the same class and system as is employed by the individual whose writing was forged.

An alleged forgery which is grossly dissimilar to exemplars of the purported writer may be considered by the investigator, preliminarily at least, to be a simple forgery. In occasional cases, subsequent developments in the field or the laboratory will disclose such writings to be distorted genuine writings. If the investigator's preliminary consideration offers any suggestion that distorted genuine writings may be involved, here again he should enlist the services of the document examiner for guidance. In brief, the investigator must endeavor to reach a conviction, personally or in collaboration with the document examiner, as to the sort of forgery or alleged forgery with which he is confronted before he can properly attack its solution.

An important fact to remember in preliminary comparisons of claimed forgeries is that a questioned writing cannot embody better handwriting—more fluent, with greater skill demonstrated in letter formations and connections—than a suspected author possesses. One cannot exceed his writing capacity in signing his own name or forging the signature of another. Conversely, a writer may deliberately execute a signature or other writing, which he plans to disavow later, at sub-normal speed and erratic movement. Regular-course-of-business exemplars, it is reiterated, facilitate determinations of true writing capabilities.

The investigation of traced or simulated forgeries embodies some elements which are quite divergent from those which encompass the simple forgery. The investigator should not waste time and effort comparing tracings, *which are not writings*, with the *writing* of suspected forgers. Similarly, it must be conceded that it is pointless to compare simulations which closely copy the form of authentic writings, *and are also not writings*, with the *writing* of suspected forgers. Finally, it should be borne in mind that in those instances wherein inaccurate simulations are encountered, the influences of the model authentic writing must be subtracted completely from the forgery, and only those remaining particulars wherein the forger injected his own *writing habits* should be compared with the *writing* of suspected forgers.

As a practical matter, this simply means that the investigator of traced and simulated forgeries will accomplish little, if anything, from comparisons of these two classes of forgeries with the writings of suspected forgers. Accordingly, investigative effort should be directed along other lines. It may be noted, nevertheless, that it is usually advisable to procure exemplars from suspected forgers in these classes of forgery investigations incident to interrogation. Even though the investigator knows that such exemplars will not be fruitful, rarely does a suspect and especially a guilty suspect embrace the security of this intelligence.

Perhaps the most pertinent consideration in traced and simulated forgery inquiries, is the model authentic signature or writing which was used by the forger. Where, when, and how did he obtain the model or models? Does he still have them or have they probably been destroyed? What authentic documents have been missed or are still missing? A bank statement with canceled checks? Indentification cards? Driver's license? Military documents? If none appears to have been stolen or "borrowed," are there indications the forgery was accomplished by a family member or business associate? Did the forger use the correct class of writing for his model, or did he betray himself by using a cursory signature on personal correspondence as the model from which to simulate a formal check or contract signature? Did the forger use an older signature for his model on a document of current vintage? Or did he use a current signature as his model in simulating Aunt Minnie's signature on her alleged will of twenty-five years ago? Is the forgery so faulty in form that it is evident the forger relied on his memory and did not have a visible model from which to simulate?

Frequently forged writings involve a traced or imitated signature plus other writings, perhaps a date, an amount, or an address, which represent non-imitative writings, simple forgeries. A typical example is the forged endorsement wherein the forger imitated the true payee's signature but was forced to inject his own *writing* habits when he was called upon to write an address as part of the endorsement. In these types of situations, the address or other non-imitative writing in which the forger was reduced to his own writing resources should be the focal point for comparative efforts with the writing of suspected forgers.

Fortunately from the standpoint of identification, the majority of handwritten forgeries met in law enforcement are simple, non-imitative forgeries. Simple forgeries as a class embody individualities of their forger authors which are adducible for their identification.

The Forgery Suspect

The procurement of exemplars of the writing of suspected forgers necessitates several considerations additional to those which are essential in obtaining exemplars from the forgery claimant. First, more exemplars are necessary from the forgery suspect. In writing the name of another, the average forger is performing an act less automatic, less practiced, and less familiar than the signing of his own name. The result tends to restrict his writing individuality. A forgery by a given writer is ordinarily less individualized than that writer's own signature. Additionally, disguise in forgeries is an ever present element. Therefore, a large quantity of exemplars is essential to demonstrate thoroughly the habits of the forgery suspect in writing the letters, letter combinations, words, figures, and punctuation marks which appear in forgeries of which he is suspected.

Again the value of regular-course-of-business exemplars must be recognized in respect to the forgery suspect to an even greater extent than in the case of the forgery claimant. There is no inference, as previously pointed out, that request exemplars are not likewise essential. When the forgery suspect is interviewed, the procurement of request exemplars is an integral part of that interview. Equally salient should be a discussion with the suspect looking to the location and identification of writings which he prepared in the regular course of business and which are available for comparative purposes. The latter will not be necessary in every case, but the investigator should know where they can readily be found when he does need them.

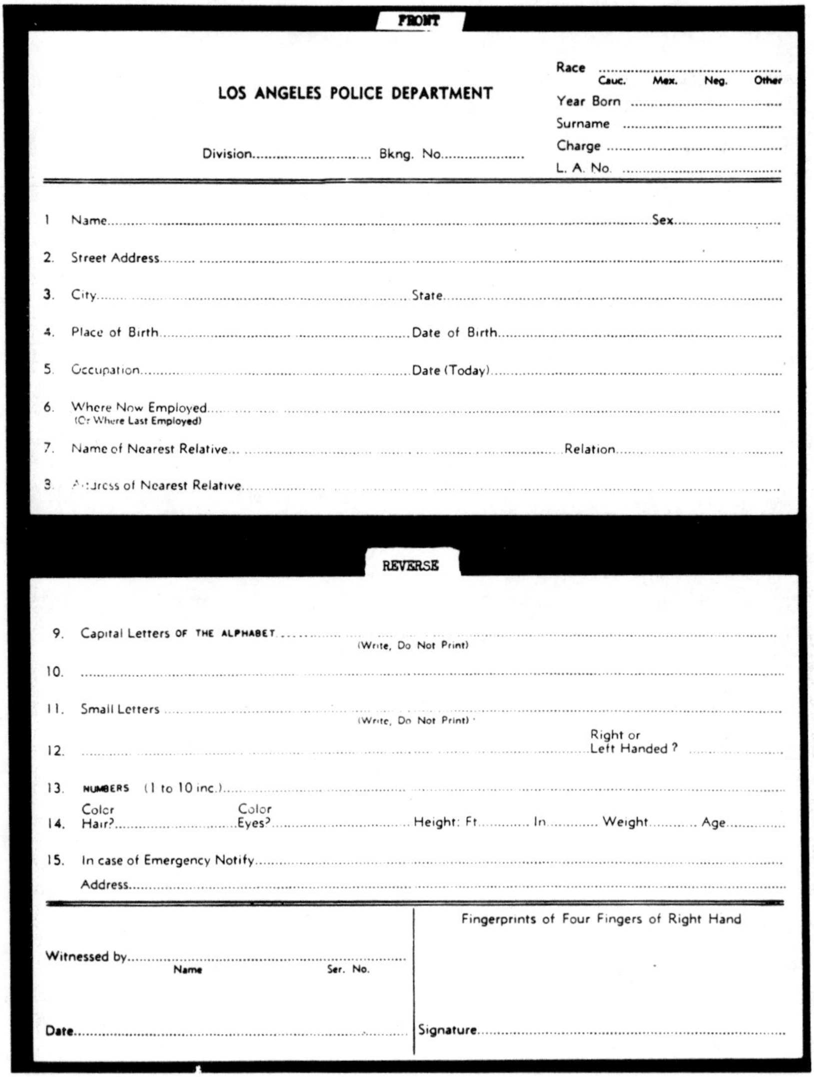

FRONT

LOS ANGELES POLICE DEPARTMENT

Division.............................. Bkng. No....................

Race ....
Cauc. Mex. Neg. Other

Year Born ....

Surname ....

Charge ....

L. A. No. ....

1 Name...Sex..........................

2. Street Address...

3. City...State...

4. Place of Birth...Date of Birth...

5. Occupation..Date (Today)..

6. Where Now Employed..
(Or Where Last Employed)

7. Name of Nearest Relative...Relation..........................

8. Address of Nearest Relative...

REVERSE

9. Capital Letters OF THE ALPHABET...
(Write, Do Not Print)

10. ....

11. Small Letters..
(Write, Do Not Print)

12. ....Right or Left Handed ? ....

13. NUMBERS (1 to 10 inc.)...

14. Color Hair?...............................Color Eyes?.......................Height: Ft............ In............ Weight........... Age..............

15. In case of Emergency Notify..
Address...

Witnessed by..
Name Ser. No.

Date...

Fingerprints of Four Fingers of Right Hand

Signature...

Figure 40. Exemplar form, 8″ by 5″, used to excellent advantage by Los Angeles and other police departments to obtain writing from persons arrested.

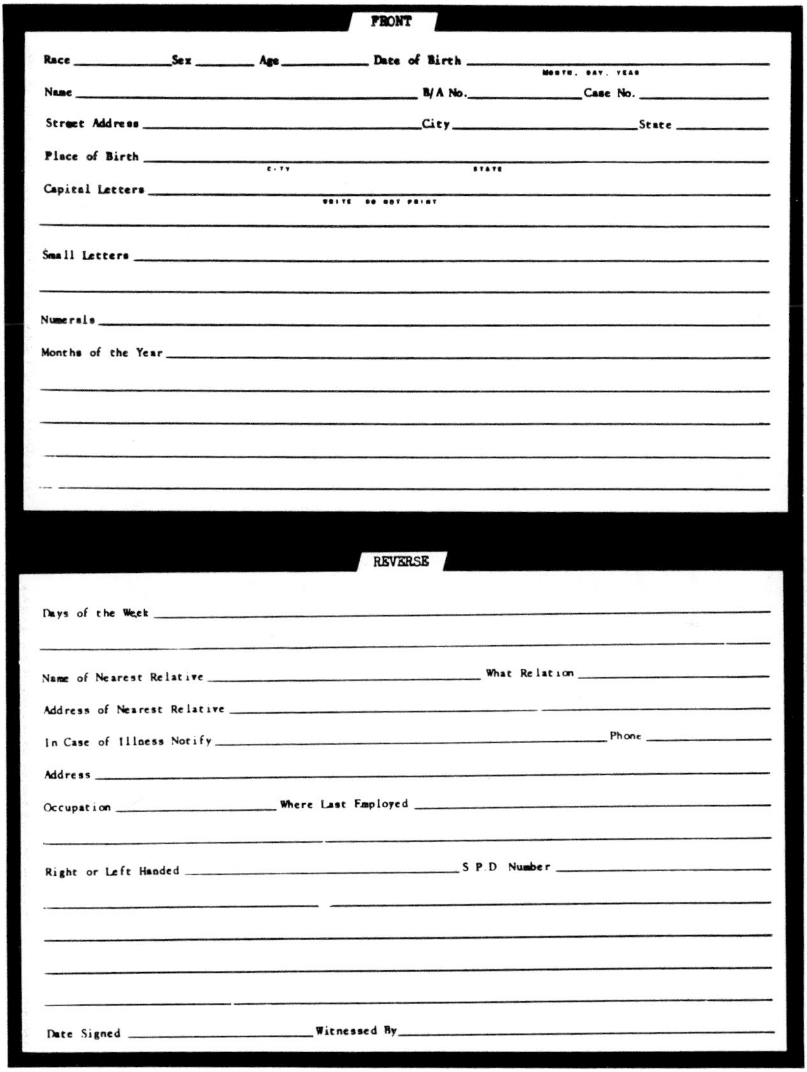

FRONT

Race ______ Sex ______ Age ______ Date of Birth ______ (MONTH, DAY, YEAR)

Name ______ B/A No. ______ Case No. ______

Street Address ______ City ______ State ______

Place of Birth ______ (CITY) ______ (STATE)

Capital Letters ______ (WRITE DO NOT PRINT)

Small Letters ______

Numerals ______

Months of the Year ______

REVERSE

Days of the Week ______

Name of Nearest Relative ______ What Relation ______

Address of Nearest Relative ______

In Case of Illness Notify ______ Phone ______

Address ______

Occupation ______ Where Last Employed ______

Right or Left Handed ______ S P D Number ______

Date Signed ______ Witnessed By ______

Figure 41. Efficient exemplar form, 8″ by 5″, used by Seattle and other police departments.

The procedural suggestions already cited in respect to the forgery claimant's preparation of request exemplars are equally applicable to the forgery suspect. He should be provided the opportunity to display his true habits in the light of the writing position, writing materials, arrangement, words, figures, and phrases of the questioned writing. It is distinctly inadvisable to barge bluntly into a request that the suspect write, for example, the name on the questioned check about the time he comes through your office door. The practice of barely seating a suspect and having him write only the name on a questioned check or in a questioned document two or three times should not be confused with the intelligent procurement of reliable, adequate exemplars. There may be a poorer method of acquiring exemplars than this absurd practice but it does not come readily to mind.

A good method of "breaking the ice" as it were, is initially to ask the subject to write his name, address, names of next of kin, place of employment, and other personal history data. As the interviewer progresses to the recreation of the questioned writing, he should pass through similar writing combinations. For example, if the questioned writing consists of the check endorsement "William McGillicuddy," ask the suspect to endorse "Michael Woddy," "Walter Gilbert," "Wilhelm McWilliam," "Gill Cody," and "Bertram McPhail" on a number of specimen checks, before he is requested to write the literatim endorsement which is in issue. The suspect's attitude as you proceed into the latter may tell you as much as does his writing.

Some departments have adopted excellent printed forms which are used in this *preliminary* phase of the acquisition of request exemplars from forgery suspects. A number of such forms is illustrated. They are distinctly valuable in bridging the gap from the informal exemplars to the self-interest, the request exemplars. They tend to be accepted by many suspects as a part of routine questioning procedures. When the matter is adroitly handled by the interviewer, suspects are not so apt either to refuse to complete these forms or to disguise their writing or to direct undue attention to the writing process.

Additionally, printed specimen forms of this type are especially helpful in identifying recidivist forgers. It is neither expensive nor time consuming to compile handwriting exemplar forms from persons questioned and arrested in connection with forgery and related offenses. Separate forms completed at several questionings and arrests are of inestimable assistance in associating forgery and other complaints with old offenders. This is particularly true of professional forgers who are adept at distorting their handwriting. A further and important consideration is that when exemplar forms are on file for a given individual, some examination of his writing can be made before he is directly approached for questioning in current investigations.

We have approached the point in law enforcement when the procurement of handwriting exemplars for potentional identification with the millions of evidential documents in circulation should be just as routine a part of questioning and booking procedures as fingerprinting.

It should not be accepted in any sense, however, that causing a forgery suspect to complete a "handwriting card" will provide all the exemplars which are needed in all cases. There should be no confused thinking in this regard. Exemplar forms such as those illustrated are excellent cross-section exemplars for general handwriting evaluation. They provide ease of examination for repeat offenders because any searcher can immediately familiarize himself with the location of all the letters of the alphabet, numerals, and character combinations which are in the same location on each exemplar form. Each department can inject names and street names which are most likely to be found in questioned writings of the locality where the forms are used. But no form of this type was intended to or could provide the handwriting answer in all cases. The procurement of exemplars in each investigation is geared inexorably to the questioned writings which are the subject of that investigation. The use of printed exemplar forms, which this author highly recommends as a part of exemplar acquisition, should not be permitted to obscure the former basic consideration.

It should be unnecessary to state, but this author's experience has shown the necessity nonetheless, that exemplar card forms of the type illustrated were intended to provide handwriting leads

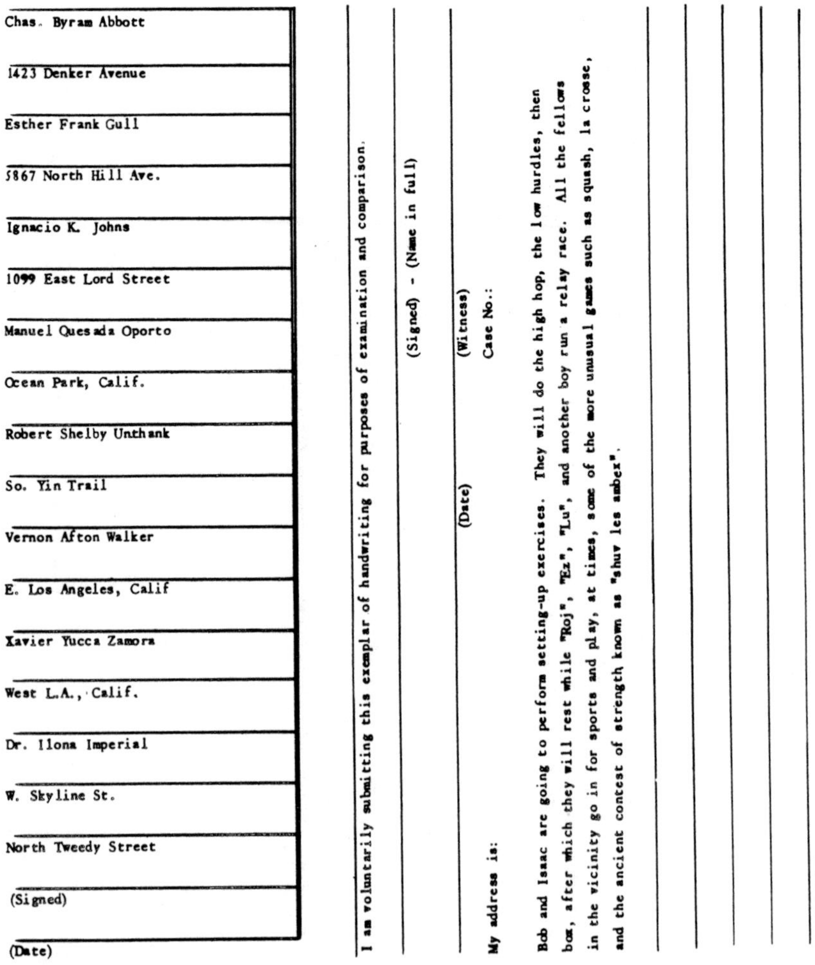

Chas. Byram Abbott

1423 Denker Avenue

Esther Frank Gull

5867 North Hill Ave.

Ignacio K. Johns

1099 East Lord Street

Manuel Quesada Oporto

Ocean Park, Calif.

Robert Shelby Unthank

So. Yin Trail

Vernon Afton Walker

E. Los Angeles, Calif

Xavier Yucca Zamora

West L.A., Calif.

Dr. Ilona Imperial

W. Skyline St.

North Tweedy Street

(Signed)

(Date)

I am voluntarily submitting this exemplar of handwriting for purposes of examination and comparison.

(Signed) - (Name in full)

(Witness)
Case No.:

(Date)

My address is:

Bob and Isaac are going to perform setting-up exercises. They will do the high hop, the low hurdles, then box, after which they will rest while "Roj", "Ex", "Lu", and another boy run a relay race. All the fellows in the vicinity go in for sports and play, at times, some of the more unusual games such as squash, la crosse, and the ancient contest of strength known as "shuv les amber".

Figure 42. All purpose exemplar form, 8″ by 9″, which can be adapted to contain names and addresses common to locality in which used.

and handwriting identifications primarily in forgery cases. They were not designed to provide the complete solution in cases involving extended writings, such as anonymous letters, although they will frequently provide important leads in such investigations. It should be fairly evident that the letter combinations in names and addresses are usually considerably different than the letters

POST OFFICE DEPARTMENT   CASE No: ....   SURNAME: ....
INSPECTION SERVICE   YEAR BORN: ....
LOS ANGELES, CALIFORNIA   DATE: ....   RACE: ....

NAME: ....

STREET ADDRESS: ....   Arthur Bob Charles

CITY: .... STATE: ....

PLACE OF BIRTH: ....   Don Edward Funk

DATE OF BIRTH: .... AGE: ....

HEIGHT: .... Ft. .... In. WEIGHT: .... BUILD: ....   George Henry Imig

COLOR OF HAIR: .... COLOR OF EYES: ....

RIGHT OR LEFT HANDED? ....   Joe Kenneth Lamb

OCCUPATION OR TRADE: ....   Mary Nan Olson

Where now employed
or last employed? ....

NAME, ADDRESS and   }   Paul Quentin Ray

RELATIONSHIP of your   }

NEAREST RELATIVE   }   Samuel Tom Unthank

CAPITAL and SMALL LETTERS OF THE ALPHABET—   Vernon Will Xavier
WRITE DO NOT PRINT

A   B   C   D   E   F   G   H   I   J   K   L   M   Yolanda Zamora

N   O   P   Q   R   S   T   U   V   W   X   Y   Z   1234 N. East Ave.

a   b   c   d   e   f   g   h   i   j   k   l   m   5678 S. West Blvd.

n   o   p   q   r   s   t   u   v   w   x   y   z   9012 E. North Pl.

NUMBERS: 3456 W. South St.
      1   2   3   4   5   6   7   8   9   0

The above is a **specimen of my handwriting, prepared**

freely and voluntarily.   SIGNATURE

     WITNESS: ....   DATE: ....

                                                                  GPO 965500

Figure 43. Exemplar form 8½″ by 10½″, used by postal inspectors and others, which effectively covers capitals, small letters, numerals, and given names frequently encountered in forgeries.

and letter combinations found in lengthy communications. The investigator of an anonymous letter who obtains a "handwriting card" only as an exemplar shows beyond any doubt that he has not studied the anonymous letter which he is supposed to be investigating, and that he does not understand the fundamental principle that exemplars should recreate the identifying elements of the questioned writing with which they are to be compared.

Specific precautions should be taken when request exemplars are in preparation, so that the suspect's writing is not influenced by any other writing. It should be insured that no other writing is within the subject's vision and no "leading" pronunciations or misspellings should be dictated in a manner which would or could inject non-volitional peculiarities into the subject's exemplars. It should be understood also that a subject should not be caused to copy or imitate the form of a signature or other writing incident to the preparation of exemplars. However, forgery suspects should invariably be questioned as to whether they are familiar with or have ever seen the genuine writing of the individual whose writing has been forged. A suspect should be caused to take a definite position in this regard at the outset of the investigation, so that he cannot later fashion a defensible position to suit his own purposes, which may not be consistent with the facts as they develop.

The genuine writing of the individual whose writing has been forged should always be considered by the investigator and it should always be submitted to the document examiner who is called upon to examine the writing of any forgery suspect. Any influence the former may have had on a forgery can best be evaluated through concurrent examination of each. Such influence, or the lack of it, is a material consideration in the evaluation of the writing of any suspect. The perpetrator of a forgery either wields or avoids the influence of the writing of the individual whose writing he is forging. When exemplars of a suspected forger are submitted to the document examiner, *invariably* he should also be provided with exemplars of the individual whose writing was forged, so that the document examiner may readily assess the volitional versus suggestive qualities of the forgery, as a preliminary to consideration of the writing of the forgery suspect.

Extended Writings

When extended writings such as a complete letter or series of communications are in issue, the same fundamental thinking and procedures as have been heretofore cited in respect to the forgery claimant and the forgery suspect should obtain. Lengthy writings virtually exclude tracing and they tend to preclude simulation. They usually represent the natural or the disguised writing of their authors, without the influence of a second writer. Accordingly, from a qualitative standpoint, extended writings provide auspicious grounds for expressions of individuality.

The most revealing exemplars are informal exemplars of appropriate writing class. The best exemplars for comparison with an anonymous letter would be letters written by the suspected author in the normal course of events, perhaps to friends or relatives, contemporaneously and containing comparable words, phrases, and letter combinations. Letters' sizes, arrangement of writing on the page, margins, methods of expressing dates and addresses, contractions, misspellings, mixtures of cursive script and handprinting, unusual and unique phrases, foreign and colloquial expressions afford important bases for identifying individualities. These and other identifying elements of extended writings should be carefully catalogued by the investigator prior to interviewing suspected writers, so that full advantage may be taken of their identifying value incident to the procurement of request exemplars.

When a subject is to be interviewed concerning a single letter, after preliminary handwriting such as that in personal history data has been obtained, it is usually advisable to have the subject prepare, from dictation, the complete wording of the letter several times. Should the letter be quite lengthy, or when a series of letters is under inquiry, it is preferable to select represensative material from the various texts, and then to have the subject prepare, from dictation, several exemplars of this representative material. The writer's range of variation can be plotted more readily when he is caused to repeat the same wording several times. In addition, *it is decidedly more difficult to disguise the same text two or three times, than it is to camouflage a collection of unrepeated material.*

There are investigative situations when it is inappropriate to dictate to a suspect the identical text which appears in a questioned writing. In such eventualities, the investigator should prepare in advance a narrative statement which embodies the key words, letter combinations, phrases, numerals, etc., appearing in the questioned writing, for subsequent dictation and redictation to the subject.

Post Litem Motam Exemplars

Writings produced by an accused after evidential writings have come into dispute and solely for the purpose of establishing his own contentions should always be exposed to careful scrutiny and received with extreme caution. In many courts, such writings are held inadmissible in behalf of their manufacturers for the very obvious reason that their reliability is suspect. Investigators and attorneys should be alert to the end that objections are timely raised against such exemplars, should they be introduced during a trial, without an adequate showing of their competency and reliability. Ludicrous spectacles have occurred when a defendant, after studying the testimony of a document examiner concerning his handwriting individualities, is permitted to manufacture spurious, self-interest exemplars for the specific purpose of defeating the truth.

Exemplars volunteered by a witness during his direct examination are similarly objectionable, although on cross-examination it is proper and sometimes essential that a witness who has denied evidential writings be asked to prepare exemplars for comparative purposes.

In every case, handwriting exemplars will not be less than adequate and justice-serving, if their procurement is characterized by strict, yet reasonable, adherence to the principle that exemplars should recreate the questioned writing with which they are to be compared.

TYPEWRITING

From the eighteenth century, efforts were directed by numerous inventors to develop a mechanical method of producing rapid legible writing. The manual script of that era with its artistry and heavy shading was laborious and time consuming. The recording of any considerable volume of verbiage was a major undertaking indeed. In addition, the varying proficiency of individual handwritings made it highly desirable for government, the church, education, and commerce that a simple mechanical means of producing universally legible writing should be perfected.

The first recorded attempt to invent a typewriter is found in the records of the British Patent Office. On the seventh of January, 1714, almost two and one-half centuries ago, a patent was granted by Her Majesty, Queen Anne, to Henry Mill, an English engineer. The opening sentence of this first typewriter patent wherein Henry Mill wrote his brainchild into history is of interest:

> "Anne, by the grace of God, to all to whom these presents shall come, greeting. Whereas our trusty and well beloved subject, Henry Mill, hath, by his humble peticion, represented unto us, that he has, by his great study, paines, and expence lately invented and brought to perfection 'An artificial machine or method for the impressing or transcribing of letters singly or progressively one after another, as in writing, whereby all writings whatsoever may be engrossed in paper or parchment so neat and exact as not to be distinguished from print.' "*

A century later, in 1829, the first United States patent for a mechanical writing machine was issued to William A. Burt of Detroit, Michigan. Neither the initial effort of Henry Mill nor the later patent of Burt led to production or commercial success.

In 1867, Christopher Latham Sholes conceived the idea of a type-writer which mechanically impressed the upper case letters

---

*From booklet of June 1941 by the Underwood Elliot Fisher Company.

of the alphabet onto a piece of paper. From Sholes' ingenuity developed the Sholes, Glidden and Soule Type-Writer. This type-writing machine was patented on June 23, 1868. It is indeed a strange looking contraption by today's standards. It may be viewed at the Smithsonian Institute, Washington, D. C. After five years of the struggles which seem to beset most pioneers, on March 1, 1873, Sholes entered into an historic contract with the then Remington Arms Works, Ilion, New York, to produce the Sholes-Glidden Type-Writer. Early in 1874, Model Number One of the Remington Typewriter became available to the public. Remington Model Number Two, which first wrote both upper and lower case letters, was introduced in 1878.

From these beginnings have developed the millions of type-writers, mechanical and electrical, of the variety of brands which are in daily use by millions of people, producing millions of documents of all classes. Most of the latter, like most of their authors, are above reproach and will run a routine unquestioned course. But out of this welter of typewritten documents, there emerges a significant percentage which comes to constitute evidential type-writing, which must be examined, interpreted, and evaluated by investigator, document examiner, attorney, judge, and jury.

As early as the turn of this century, typewriting evidence had begun to appear in the courts of this country.* Fifty years later, the typewritten documents in United States v. Alger Hiss, decided January 21, 1950, in the Federal Court for the Southern District of New York were to rock the nation and the world. One has but to look around him at the progressive shift from hand-writing to typewriting on numerous documents of daily appearance to appreciate the tremendous impact and significance wielded by the typewriter today and to recognize the continuing and inevitable increase in evidential typewriting.

Evidential typewriting provides a fertile field for the investigator. The two principal typewriting questions are(1) whether an evidential typewriting was accomplished on a suspected typewriter, and (2) whether an evidential typewriting, prepared on

---

*Levy v. Rust, 49 Atl. 1017 (N. J.), 1893.

a known typewriter, was actually typewritten on its purported date. Collateral to the first of these questions is the determination of the make or brand of typewriter on which a questioned typewriting was prepared. Tertiary problems include whether all of a typewritten document was prepared continuously in a single typewriting operation, and whether an evidential typewriting was prepared by a suspected typist.

Frequently, the enforcement officer must endeavor to locate the typewriter on which an evidential typewriting was prepared from among many, perhaps hundreds, of possible typewriters which may have been so used. There is a number of basic considerations which need to be understood by the investigator if he is himself to solve these and related typewriting problems or to participate effectively in their solution by others.

One of the primary considerations is that the product of each make or brand of typewriter is individual from that of typewriters manufactured by other companies, and usually individual from the typewritten work of typewriters marketed under different brand names. The typeface designs of each manufacturer differ from the typeface designs ordinarily employed by other typewriter companies. Accordingly, it is usually possible to differentiate, for example, a communication written on a Royal typewriter from a letter prepared on an L. C. Smith typewriter, or a message typewritten on an Underwood from a narration composed on a Remington.

A note of conservatism should be recorded in respect to the differentiation of typeface styles and designs according to the different brands of typewriters. Several factors obtain which have a bearing on the classification of a particular brand of typewriter through analysis of its typeface styles and designs and their impression qualities. Included among these factors which complicate somewhat this general area of typewriting examinations are: (1) Instances have occurred when one or more typewriter companies have copied or matched the typeface designs of a second company. This means that the basic typeface designs used by Company A on its typewriter product may also appear on typewriters manufactured by Company B under its own brand name. Usually slight changes are injected in one or several characters incident to such copying or matching. These variations are ordinarily minute and the particulars in which they have been adopted may not be represented in a brief questioned typewriting. (2) There are instances when two or more complete typewriters, marketed under different brand names, have been produced in the same factories from identical parts and common typeface designs. (3) Numerous European typewriters of a variety of brand names employ common typeface designs. European brand typewriters have filtered into the United States in increasing numbers since 1946. In addition, at least three domestic manufacturers are marketing typewriters in this country under their own domestic brand names, which are either completely manufactured in Europe or are equipped with type manufactured in Europe.

One of the major United States manufacturers has adopted a special identifying mark on a common letter, known to document examiners, in order to identify its typeface designs which are copies or matches of the designs of another manufacturer. Distinct assistance in these problems would be accorded if all typewriter companies would similarly tag their typeface formations which are derived from the styles and designs of other manufacturers.

The typewriters coming within the purview of "1," "2," and "3" above do not currently represent a material percentage of the typewriters which are relevant to criminal and civil investigations. A few are being encountered now and the number is increasing. These circumstances dictate that the investigator and document examiner should recognize that in classifying the *typeface* styles, designs, and qualities of impression in an evidential typewriting, one is usually, but not invariably, also identifying the manufacturer's brand name of the *typewriter* used to prepare such evidential typewriting.

It is emphasized that these factors which sometimes impede the precise classification of typewriting material as to brand name of the parent typewriter do not obstruct the much more important and the more frequently encountered problem of identifying an evidential typewriting with a particular suspected typewriting machine. The identification of the individual typewriter will be elaborated hereinafter in this chapter.

It is ordinarily possible to determine the approximate date of manufacture of the typewriter which prepared a given typewritten document. Each make of typewriter undergoes changes in its typeface designs from time to time. Through knowledge and recognition of these progressive changes, it is possible to establish, for example, that an extortion letter was typewritten on a Corona typewriter, equipped with elite type, manufactured after 1938, or that a disputed invoice was prepared on a Remington typewriter, equipped with pica type, manufactured prior to 1940.

The classification of typewriting material as to brand of typewriter and the approximate date of manufacture is accomplished by comparison with reference files which are maintained by practicing document examiners and major identification laboratories. These files are necessarily quite extensive as they are designed to contain exemplars of all styles of typefaces, with the progressive changes therein, of all the brands of typewriters whose work is apt to be encountered in this country. Exemplars of matched and copied typeface designs, foreign typefaces, data concerning the usual and exceptional manufacturing processes and practices are coordinated with the exemplar material.

Obviously it is not practicable for the average investigator to attempt to acquire and to maintain the dated history of all the typeface styles and designs which have been, are being, and may be used on evidential documents. It should not be erroneously assumed that typewriter mechanics, repairmen, or sales representatives have or are familiar with these data. Reference files for classifying and dating typewriting are maintained by the laboratories of the Federal Bureau of Investigation, Postal Inspection Service, Treasury Department, Veterans Administration, many state bureaus of identification, a few local departments of enforcement, and leading document examiners in private practice. The important thing for the investigator to know is the location of such reference files, which are available to him and his department, when it becomes necessary to establish the brand and approximate date of manufacture of the typewriter which prepared a questioned typewriting.

PRELIMINARY EXAMINATION OF TYPEWRITING

A typewritten document can ordinarily be definitely identified with the individual typewriter on which it was prepared. Such identification—holdup instructions, espionage documents, threatening letters, a deed of title, a will, fraudulent checks, etc.—is frequently indispensable to the solution of major civil and criminal cases. Through an understanding of how such identifications are effected, the investigator will be enabled to direct his own efforts efficiently in their accomplishment.

The identification of a specific typewriter is effected chiefly through the following factors, in combination: design and size of the typefaces; horizontal alignment of the typefaces; vertical alignment of the typefaces; perpendicularity or otherwise of the typeface impressions; striking qualities of the typeface impressions, including uneven strike-ups, light, heavy, rebounding and inconstant strike-ups; and scars, breaks, damages and other defects in the typeface surfaces.

The first of these factors—design and size of the typefaces—concerns typeface characteristics which are the result of the manufacturing designs for a group of typewriters. The other factors relate largely to individualities which are the result of operation and usage of the individual typewriter. Every investigator of evidential typewriting cannot be expected to become expert in every phase of typewriting identification. Anyone who has reasonably good vision, a modicum of objectivity, and who will follow a few simple rules can eliminate many suspected typewriters which are non-identical to a questioned typewriting because of differences in basic typeface designs and spacings. The imperfections from usage, the defects resulting from operation of the individual typewriter, will remain to a considerable extent the responsibility of the document examiner. Even in the latter area, the alert investigator may become proficient in isolating typewriting individualities and in effecting many at least tentative typewriting identifications.

The vast majority of typewritten documents which the investigator encounters will have pica typefaces or elite typefaces. The former are ordinarily spaced ten characters to the horizontal inch and the latter are usually spaced twelve characters to the horizontal inch. At the outset, it is advisable to measure the horizontal spacings of the letters and other characters appearing in a type-written document to determine the number per horizontal inch. Should there be ten to the inch, only those typewriters with such spacing should be considered in further investigation. Should there be twelve characters to the inch, only typewriters with such spacing merit further attention, and so on.

This sentence is typewritten on a Smith-Corona Standard Typewriter, Serial No. 88E4003350-11, having elite typefaces spaced twelve letters to the inch, the usual horizontal spacing for this type style.

This sentence is typewritten on an Underwood Standard Typewriter, Serial No. 11-7083352, having elite typefaces spaced twelve letters to the inch, the usual horizontal spacing for this type style.

This sentence is typewritten on a Royal Standard Typewriter, Serial No. HHP-4845941, having pica typefaces spaced ten letters to the inch, the usual horizontal spacing for this type style.

This sentence is typewritten on an IBM Executive Model Typewriter, Serial Number 41-116202, equipped with Modern typefaces and proportional spacing.

This sentence is typewritten on a Remington Statesman Model Typewriter, Serial Number ES 2259153, equipped with Monticello typefaces and proportional spacing.

Figure 44. The usual horizontal letter spacings. Note points of similarity between typefaces of IBM Executive and Remington Statesman (introduced in 1957).

Some fifteen years ago International Business Machines Corporation departed from previous typeface spacing practices in its Proportional Spacing Machine, the predecessor of the currently marketed Executive Model. This typewriter introduced a new concept of typewriter letter spacing, similar however, to the type spacing of conventional printed type. The basic principle is simply that all letters are allotted horizontal space in conformity with their relative widths.

On IBM's Executive Model, each character is horizontally spaced according to a system of units, $1/32''$, $1/36''$, or $1/45''$, depending on the particular typeface style. Executive Modern and Executive Secretarial are founded on 1/32" units, for example, while Executive Heritage is based on 1/36" units, and Executive Charter stems from 1/45" units. The smallest lower case letters, "f," "l," "i," "t," and "j" occupy two horizontal units in most styles. The largest lower case letters "w" and "m" are accorded four and five horizontal units, respectively, in most of the available typeface styles. The capital letters occupy four units except the wider "W" and "M" and the narrower "I," "J," and "S" in most typeface styles.

Typewriting which employs proportional rather than static horizontal letter spacing is readily cognizable by a comparison of the horizontal space accorded the small letters "i," "l," "f," "t," and "j" with that allotted the wide letters "m" and "w." When one has recognized that a questioned typewriting was prepared on a proportional spacing typewriter, his further investigative efforts should be restricted to such typewriters.

It is characteristic of most foreign typewriters that their horizontal letter spacing varies from that used by manufacturers in this country. Pica typefaces on many foreign typewriters are pitched at 2.5 mm. and 2.6 mm. rather than the 2.54 mm. pitch (ten to the inch) used in this country. Elite typefaces on many foreign typewriters are pitched at 2 mm., 2.1 mm., and 2.3 mm. rather than the 2.12 mm. pitch (twelve to the inch) employed on our domestically produced typewriters.

The point is that the horizontal letter spacing should be carefully measured as a preliminary phase of typewriting examination to the end that investigative efforts are thereafter restricted to only those suspected typewriters which have the horizontal spacing in issue.

The number of lines per vertical inch should also be measured in every questioned typewriting. Usually, there are six lines to the inch on the conventionl American typewriters. Should there be wider or narrower vertical line spacing, the investigator is placed on notice that he is dealing with a special purpose typewriter, a foreign typewriter, or a proportional spacing machine. The vertical line spacing of the International Business Machines Corporation's

Executive Models is commonly from 5.25 to 5.28 lines per inch for most typeface styles. Other vertical line spacing is available on the IBM Executive Models and on the standard models of the various other manufacturers, according to customer preference. Within the past few years also, selectivity of vertical line spacing has been provided on some typewriter models.

The important consideration for the investigator is that the vertical line spacing of an evidential typewriting should be determined by accurate measurements and only those suspected typewriters which have vertical line spacing corresponding to that which is in issue should merit further investigation.

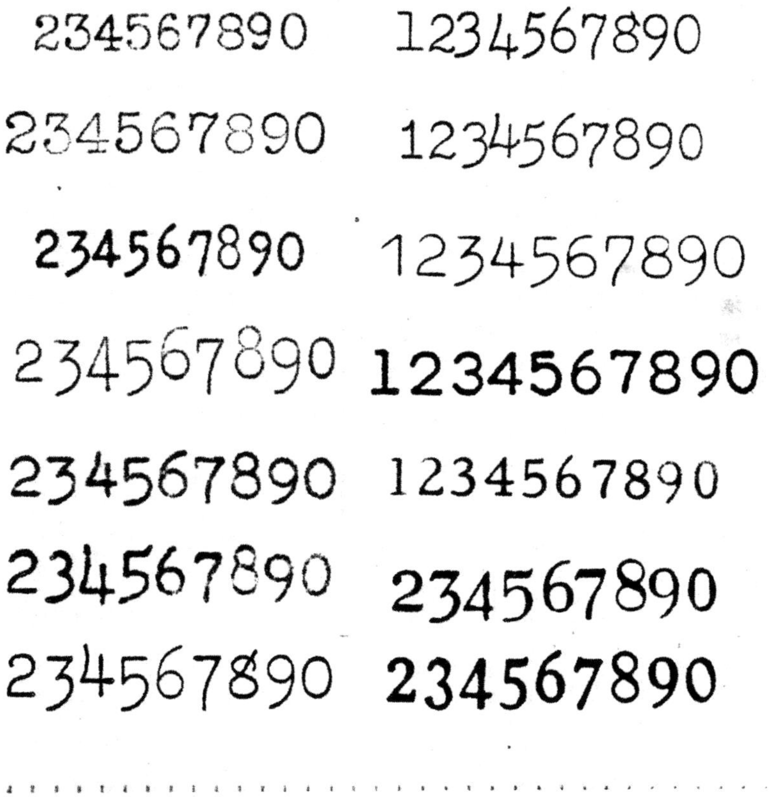

234567890   1234567890

234567890   1234567890

234567890   1234567890

234567890   1234567890

234567890   1234567890

234567890   234567890

234567890   234567890

Figure 45. Standard, billing, uncial, gothic, and shaded numeral typefaces. Style of numerals should be established at outset of a typewriting inquiry.

A further important step which is advisable in the preliminary examination of any typewritten document concerns the numerals. The numerals may be standard, uncial, billing or modified billing, gothic, or shaded typefaces. The general class and style of numerals should be established at the outset of inquiries concerning typewritten documents which bear numerals so that investigative attention can be concentrated on typewriters equipped with the proper style and will not be misdirected to typewriters equipped with a different style.

DISTINCTIVE LETTER DESIGNS

Careful consideration of letter sizes, horizontal letter spacing, vertical line spacing, and numeral designs alone will cull from further attention many typewriters which otherwise could be considered suspect in respect to the preparation of an evidential typewriting. Thereafter, there is a number of letters in which even the novice should be able to detect design agreements and differences.

Consider the letters "W" and "M." Do the center sections of these letters extend as far as the right and left sides of these letters, or are they shorter? If the "W" has a long center, does the center have a serif at its tip or is it formed without a serif thereat?

Examine the letters "w" and "m." Does the former have a long or a short center section? Do the former, if it embodies a

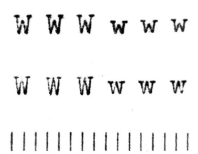

Figure 46. The old and the new. Short centers were adopted in the *W* and w approximately as follows for most typeface styles: Corona–1938, IBM –1930, Smith–1938, Remington–1946, Royal–1950, Underwood–1945, Woodstock (Allen)–1951.

longer center, and the latter have a serif at the tip of the center section or are they without such a serif?

Appraise the letter "t." Is its crossbar longer on the right side, longer on the left side, or is it equidistant on each side of the staff of "t"? Does the curved lower extension of the "t" turn upward at a point to the left of, to the right of, or about even with the right terminus of the crossbar of the "t"?

Evaluate the comma. Does its tail extend very significantly to the left of the dot, or only very slightly to the left of the dot?

Torpedo Portable Serial Number 878920

abcdefghijklmnopqrstuvwxyz
1234567890!"#$%_&'()*+¼:@,.?,./¢;½=-
ABCDEFGHIJKLMNOPQRSTUVWXYZ

GOSSEN TIPPA PORTABLE Serial Number 105741

abcdefghijklmnopqrstuvwxyz

234567890- -¾½;¢,./ "#$%_&'()*!¼:@,.?

ABCDEFGHIJKLMNOPQRSTUVWXYZ

ADLER STANDARD serial number 2089965
abcdefghijklmnopqrstuvwxyz
'#$%_&'()*+¼°:@÷,.?234567890-=½!;¢ea,./
ABCDERGHIFJKLMNOPQRWTUVWXYZS

SIEMAG"De Luxe" 131876

1 2 3 4 5 6 7 8 9 & ° + * é " ' (- è _ ç à) =
A Z E R T Y U I O P ¨ £ a z e r t y u i o p ^ $
Q S D F G H J K L M % frs q s d f g h j k l m ù 1/
W X C V B N ? . / § w x c v b n , ; : !

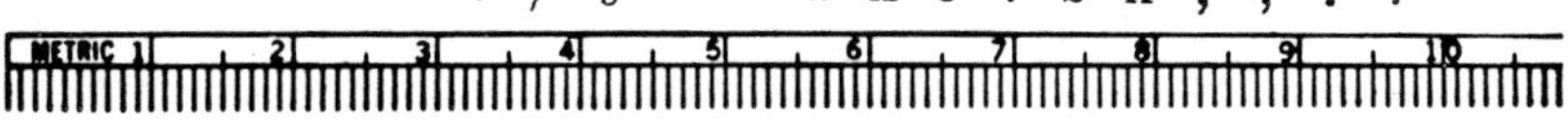

Figure 47. Exemplars of similar foreign elite typefaces appearing on typewriters of four different brand names.

GOSSEN TIPPA PORTABLE Serial Number 94179

abcdfeghijklmnopqrstuvwxyz

234567890-$\frac{3}{4}\frac{1}{2}$;¢ "#$%_&'()*!$\frac{1}{4}$:@,.?

ABCDEFGHIJKLMNOPQRSTUVWXYZ

ADLER Standard UNIVERSAL No. 96 89 95

```
Q  W  E  R  T  Z  U  I  O  P  A  S  D  F  G  H  J  K  L
q  w  e  r  t  z  u  i  o  p  a  s  d  f  g  h  j  k  l
;  "  =  %  &  (  )  _  §  /  Y  X  C  V  B  N  M  ?  !
1  2  3  4  5  6  7  8  9  0  y  x  c  v  b  n  m  ,  .
```

TORPEDO PORTABLE   Serial Number 874866

abcdefghijklmnopqrstuvwxyz
1234567890 !"#$%_&'()*+$\frac{1}{4}$:@,.?,./¢;$\frac{1}{2}$=–
ABCDEFGHIJKLMNOPQRSTUVWXYZ

MONTANA LUSCE PORTABLE Serial Number 22676

abcdefghijklmnopqrstuvwxyz

"#$%_&'()*$\frac{1}{4}$:@?.$\frac{3}{4}$ 234567890-$\frac{1}{2}$;¢,./

ABCDEFGHIJKLMNOPQRSTUVWXYZ

VOSS

```
Q  W  E  R  T  Z  U  I  O  P  U  Y  X  C  V  B  N  M  ?  !  '
q  w  e  r  t  z  u  i  o  p  ü  y  x  c  v  b  n  m  ,  .  -

A  S  D  F  G  H  J  K  L  Ö  Ä  ;  "  /  %  &  (  )  _  §  +  :
a  s  d  f  g  h  j  k  l  ö  ä  1  2  3  4  5  6  7  8  9  =  ß
```

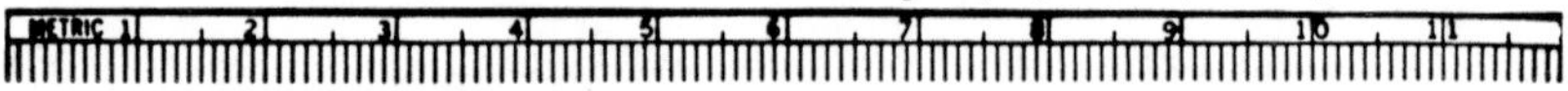

Figure 48. Exemplars of similar foreign pica typefaces appearing on typewriters of five different brand names.

Consider the letter "g." Is the upper circle much smaller and
a different shape than the lower circle or oval, or is it about the
same size and shape? Is the upper circle of the "g" very closely
positioned in respect to the lower circle or oval, or is there a
considerable space between these two sections of the "g"?

It should be borne in mind that different ribbon conditions may tend to make writing on the same typewriter seem different. A line of typewriting or a complete document written through a heavily inked ribbon superficially looks considerably different than the work of the same typewriter through a dry ribbon, which has about outlived its usefulness. Similarly, a line of typewriting or a complete document prepared with a very heavy touch will on perfunctory glance appear different than the work of the same typewriter via a light touch. Due cognizance must be taken of both ribbon condition and the touch of the operator throughout all stages of every typewriter investigation.

MALALIGNMENTS

Horizontal malalignments occur as typewriter individualities when a character defectively strikes to the right or left of its normal, allotted striking position. The inexperienced examiner should apply discretion to his consideration of apparent horizontal malalignments. The mechanical escapement of the ordinary typewriter is constructed so as to invoke right-to-left movement of the carriage, and therefore the paper, in units of one-tenth or one-twelfth of an inch. It is well known that non-rhythmic typists occasionally "jam" the typewriter action so that typefaces are impressed on the paper prior to the completion of the carriage movement. Typefaces which appear to strike "to the right" are deserving of prior attention. In any event, it should be established that a horizontal malalignment persists through a number of strike-ups, to the same extent, and is not the product of the typist's irregularity, before it is concluded that such malalignment is truly individual to the particular typewriter.

A further sort of malalignment, more readily recognizable, occurs as a typewriter individuality when a character defectively strikes above or below the line of writing. As previously cited, single spaced typewriting is ordinarily spaced six lines to the vertical inch. With this line spacing, each line occupies one-sixth of an inch, and all characters are footed to the base of their allotted one-sixth inch. Before concluding that a given character strikes "high" or strikes "low," it should be preconsidered that a true

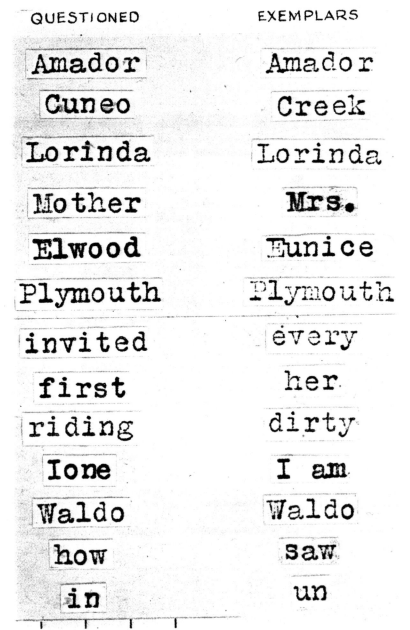

QUESTIONED   EXEMPLARS

QUESTIONED	EXEMPLARS
Amador	Amador
Cuneo	Creek
Lorinda	Lorinda
Mother	Mrs.
Elwood	Eunice
Plymouth	Plymouth
invited	every
first	her
riding	dirty
Ione	I am
Waldo	Waldo
how	saw
in	un

Figure 49. Typeface individualities of Remington typewriter identified in scurrilous postal card case: *Aa*—low, *C*—worn on left side, *L*—left tilt, *M*—left tilt, *E*—light at lower left, *P*—heavy on bottom, *v*—left tilt, *i*—right tilt, *I*—left tilt, *W*—heavy on right and left tilt, *w*—left tilt, *n*—broken lower right serif.

strike-up occurs only when the typewriter carriage is at rest, either in the upper or in the lower case. Shifting of the carriage sometimes produces illusions which are misinterpreted. The examiner should establish that a character which appears to strike above or below the line of writing persistently so misaligns, completely independent of the up and down movements of the carriage, before concluding that such malalignment is truly individual to the particular typewriter.

The interpretation of possible malalignments on typewriting of the IBM Executive Models and any similar proportional spacing typewriters cannot, of course, be accomplished by the conventional methods of measurement which are applicable to typeface spacings which are constant for all the characters. Suffice it to say in this general treatment of the subject that the investigator may readily recognize the work of proportional spacing typewriters and restrict his investigative efforts to such typewriters. The development of identifying malalignments within the tolerances of the unit spacing horizontal system and the variable vertical line spacing system is a proper task for the document examiner, who is equipped with test plates designed to the particular horizontal unit spacing and vertical line spacing which is found in a given document.

PERPENDICULARITY

Deviations from perpendicularity are typewriter individualities which provide promising avenues of investigation. The wear and tear received by the type bars frequently will result in the leaning or tilting of a character to the right or left of vertical. A material deviation from ninety degrees is usually rather apparent to the naked eye. Especially is this true of letters which contain one or more sections which, when correctly aligned, stand in ninety degree relationship to or parallel exactly the line of writing. Vertical deviations seem more apt to develop in those characters which approach the platen from the outer areas of the typebar segment, such as the "p," "l," "w," "a," and "q," although they may and do develop in any character.

The less perceptible deviations from perpendicular of one or two degrees are as individual as an obvious tilt of four or five

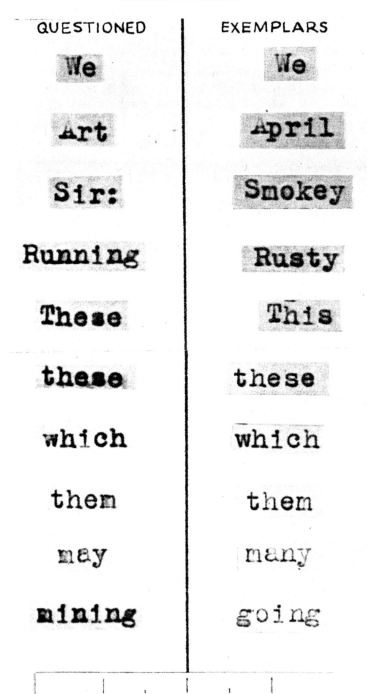

Figure 50. Typeface individualities identifying two documents prepared five years apart in mail fraud case: *W*—heavy on right, *A*—heavy on bottom, *S*—heavy on lower half, *R*—damaged at right extremity, *T*—damaged at left end of lower serif, *h*—right serif bent, *w*—missing right serif, *m*—damaged center section, *a*—tilts to left, *g*—tilts to right.

degrees. The smaller but highly significant vertical malalignments usually must remain in the province of the document examiner who is equipped with special typewriting protractors for accurate measurement, but material lack of perpendicularity in characters such as the "i" and the "l" should attract even the casual investigator.

STRIKING QUALITIES

It is generally understood or at least tacitly accepted that each typeface—and it might be well to recall that there are at least eighty-four separate faces on the ordinary typewriter—is constructed so that its letter design strikes the platen evenly, with uniform pressure on the entire letter design surface. Through the wear and tear of the typewriter's operation, individual typefaces develop a lack of uniformity, an unevenness, in the pressure exerted against the platen. This may cause a particular letter to strike heavy on the top, the bottom, right side, left side, or on one of its corners. A character which so strikes unevenly usually is referred to as "off its feet."

Additional striking individualities occur when a letter persistently strikes heavy or light over its entire surface. This category of individualities requires a very critical evaluation in the manually driven typewriter, in order to discount the influence of the typist's touch. Letters which strike heavy or light within the touch control system of the electric typewriter provide a more promising area of individuality.

Rebounding letters are frequently individual to a given typewriter. Here again, caution must be exercised to the end that typist or class individuality is not misinterpreted as typewriter individuality. Some lightweight portable typewriters, when in use by the non-rhythmic typist who emphasizes a heavy touch, develop carriage vibration which will intermittently produce rebounds or double strike-ups, especially following the last letter in a word or sentence. This latter class of rebound is a group characteristic rather than the individual typewriter characteristic and should be so construed.

Uneven or otherwise defective strike-ups which are the result of imperfect typebars and typeblocks usually will be reflected both

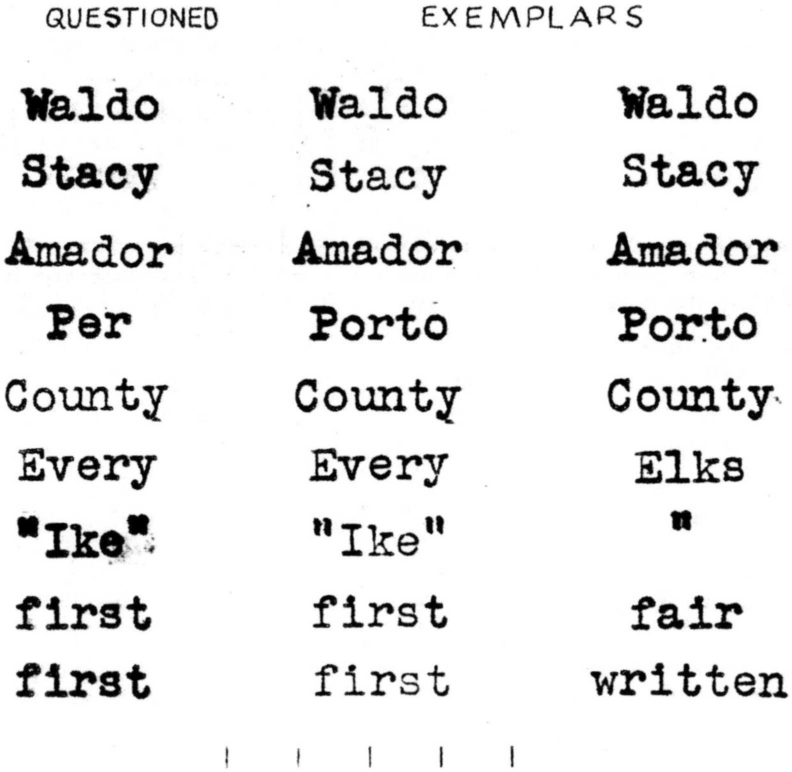

QUESTIONED   EXEMPLARS

Waldo	Waldo	Waldo
Stacy	Stacy	Stacy
Amador	Amador	Amador
Per	Porto	Porto
County	County	County
Every	Every	Elks
"Ike"	"Ike"	"
first	first	fair
first	first	written

Figure 51. Less perceptible individualities identifying typefaces of rarely used Smith-Corona typewriter in anonymous letter case: *W*—rebounds, *S*—rebounds and has scar on left side of upper curve, *A*—rebounds and strikes heavy on bottom, *P*—rebounds and has scar at right side of upper curve and damage at lower right extremity, *C*—strikes heavy at terminus, *E*—strikes light at upper left, "—rebounds, *r*—floats to right of perpendicular.

in the upper and lower case strike-ups for the particular character. Thus, an upper case "A" or an upper case "O" which is heavy on the left side will be reflected in the lower case "a" and "o" which are similarly "off foot."

TYPEFACE DEFECTS

The real clinchers of most typewriting identifications are broken serifs, scarifications, flattened and damaged portions of typefaces. These individualities are the tattoo marks, the crossed eyes, the jagged scars, the short arms, the amputations of type-writing identification. Every document examiner has experienced the firm conviction of identity which comes from the development of a relatively few typeface breaks and scars which concurrently exist in a questioned and in a known typewriting. Taking into consideration the eighty-four plus typefaces of the common type-writer, style and design agreement, spacing agreement, alignment agreement, perpendicularity agreement, striking agreement, and agreement in even three or four scars or damaged typefaces present an irresistible basis for the conclusion that two documents are the work of one and the same typewriter.

DATING PROBLEMS

An evidential typewriting which is challenged as to the date of its preparation should first be considered in the light of whether the typeface designs were in existence, without deviation, on its alleged date. Many criminal violations and false claims necessitate "turning back the typewriter." The forger of a backdated will, deed, promissory note, or check and the fabricator of a fraudulent employment record or property assignment rarely have the capacity and facilities to make certain that they are using a typewriter of the proper vintage. Employment by the forger of a typewriter having typeface designs which are clearly incompatible with the alleged date of his forgery provides unmistakable evidence to unmask and rebut the forgery.

The dates of first usage and the periodic changes of the various typeface styles are of record in the typewriting reference files previously referred to in this chapter. These data frequently are decisive when the date of preparation of a typewritten document is subject to question and challenged. In these situations, the investigator should consult a document examiner or laboratory which maintains the appropriate reference files at the outset of his investigation. By way of illustration, a typewritten will was produced several years ago bearing the date "September 19th, 1919." This two page instrument seemed to enjoy an aura of respectability in that it conveyed a considerable estate to a renowned institution of higher education. The will had come to light

under somewhat peculiar circumstances and counsel for the lega-
tees, while convinced in good faith of the authenticity of the will,
very wisely decided that in the interests of both caution and thoroughness, it would be circumspect to have the will scientifically
examined by a document examiner.

Laboratory examination revealed that this will could have
been typewritten, at the very earliest, in late 1939, or not until
twenty years after its alleged date of preparation. The basic typeface style was first introduced in 1927. Subsequent design changes
in this style which were evident in the typewriting of the will
occurred progressively from 1928 through 1934. The numeral
designs appearing in the will were first introduced in 1936 and an
alteration in the design of one of the numerals was made in late
1939. In addition, the typefaces of the will indicated considerable
wear from usage, demonstrating that the typewriter had enjoyed
a great deal of use between its manufacture and the actual preparation of the "will." It is difficult to conceive any more definite
and convincing proof of forgery. Needless to add, the signatures
to the will likewise were replete with evidences of forgery.

As the manufacturer's changes date the parent typeface designs, the defects and conditions arising from its operation date
the work of the individual typewriter. This is an important phase
of typewriting examinations which all too frequently is neglected.

Each typewriter develops its malalignments, damaged typefaces, and other deviations from standard progressively throughout of its usage. Exemplars of the work of a typewriter throughout
its usage establish when its various defects first occurred. The dated
history of a typewriter which is in daily or almost daily use, such
as in a business, governmental, or professional office, ordinarily can
readily be established. Such can be accomplished by recovering
from the files and correspondents of the particular office, letters,
statements, invoices, and so forth, prepared in the regular course
of business, during the period in which the subject typewriter was
in use.

In many disputed probate matters, questioned property assignments, contested contracts, patent disputes, compensation and
medical claims, and income tax frauds it becomes vital to establish

Figure 52. Three typewriters having vertical script typefaces differentiated by initial point of *h*, alignment of *a*, and beginning curve of *e*.

the true date on which important documents were prepared on a known typewriter. If a typewriter placed in use in September of 1946, developed a broken southeast serif in the letter "A" in March 1948, and a scarification at the northwest serif of the letter "i" in July 1949, the dates these defects developed bear witness pro or contra the alleged dates on which documents were typewritten on this typewriter. A will correctly dated January 4, 1948, must disclose neither the damaged "A" nor the scarified "i." A notification of contract dissolution properly dated May 16, 1948, must disclose the broken "A" but not the damaged "i." And a list of expense items legitimately dated August 13, 1950, should reveal both the imperfect "A" and the defective "i," and so on through the typewriter's complete history.

Even the secondary condition of the typefaces of a known typewriter and its ribbon condition may afford additional bases for very closely approximating the date of preparation of a document on such typewriter, or for establishing definitely that a disputed document was not prepared on its purported date. A typewritten medical record was questioned because it was alleged that such record was prepared after the filing of a civil suit, rather than on its alleged date, which corresponded with the time of alleged initial treatment and diagnosis. Various typewritten records were available as exemplars of the work of the subject typewriter throughout the periods in issue. These records illustrated that the typefaces of this typewriter were quite dirty, with filled-in letters "a," "e," "o," "d," "b," and "p," for some time prior and about *three weeks subsequent* to the date of the disputed record. These exemplar records further established that the ribbon was worn and frayed during this same period. The questioned record, in sharp contrast, revealed that when it was typewritten the typewriter had been equipped with a new ribbon, that its typefaces had been cleaned, and that there were no filled-in letters. The "tailored" record clearly was not typewritten until at least three weeks after its purported date.

SUBSTITUTIONS

A further problem which arises in respect to evidential typewriting concerns whether a typewritten document was prepared in a single typing operation or whether it contains secondary additions, perhaps appended fraudulently after the document was signed. As previously pointed out, each typewriting line is ordinarily allotted one-sixth of an inch, all lines are parallel one to the other, and the individual typewritten characters are commonly alloted one-tenth or one-twelfth of an inch horizontally. Any disturbance in these basic relationships indicates that the document's position in the typewriter did not remain constant throughout its preparation. The extent of such basic inconsistencies indicates whether the typist inconsequentially moved the document, perhaps incident to an erasure or other correction, or whether the document was completely removed from the typewriter and later reinserted.

When everything in an evidential typewriting except, let us say, three or four disputed words is in correct basic alignment, and the three or four disputed words misalign as a unit, the conclusion is self-evident that the latter were "added" after the initial typewriting. Occasionally, forgers are not even thoughtful enough to use the same typewriter for fraudulent additions. Some years ago, a rather prominent individual piously offered in evidence an administrator's deed dated 1915, covering large Florida land holdings. The deed originally was typewritten on a Remington of proper vintage. Several key words and money amounts on the bottom of the second page of this deed were typewritten on a Woodstock, manufactured after 1928. The "additions" misaligned as a unit and they barely covered erasures of the original wording. More positive proof of fraud is difficult to envision.

The investigator will intermittently be confronted with typewritten documents which bear obviously genuine signatures but which the apparent signers deny with vehemence and apparent sincerity. Corporate minutes, admissions of indebtedness, financial records, and perhaps a letter proposing marriage or an acknowledgment of paternity are among the sorts of documents in this class. Careful consideration of these matters at times reveals that the signer actually signed a similar document which was thereafter "revised" with additions prejudicial to the signer. In a document of this class, the position of the signature in relation to the pertinent typewriting should be examined to ascertain whether one or the other appears "crammed" or whether they provide a symmetrical relationship one to the other and to the document as a whole. It is sometimes patent that a typewriting, and particularly the final part of it, had to be restricted to too small a space, or extended to too large a space, in order to simulate a reasonable relationship to a prior signature.

When documents of this class embody several pages, the beginning and ending words and phrases of each page should be scrutinized to detect any cropping or circumlocution which may have been necessitated by a fraudulent insertion or substitution of an entire page. In the latter connection, suspected pages should be carefully inspected by ultra violet rays and varieties of low angle illumination sources to detect chemical and mechanical erasures of prior handwritings. Forgeries are occasionally "composed" by removing a handwritten message and thereafter typewriting a fraudulent message or statement above a genuine signature.

Mentally embracing the intentions and probable attack of the forger may be a complex task for the investigator. But reckoning the points at which the forger may have attacked an evidential typewriting is less imposing if: (1) all interested parties are analytically questioned and all aspects of the disputed documents are imaginatively considered in the light of all pertinent representations, and (2) a qualified document examiner is consulted on all doubtful issues.

EXEMPLARS

As heretofore noted, it will ordinarily be the responsibility of the document examiner to advise, when necessary, the make and approximate age of the typewriter on which an evidential typewriting was prepared, to effect, when necessary, the ultimate identification of an evidential typewriting with a suspected typewriter, and to determine, when necessary, the approximate date an evidential typewriting was written on a known typewriter. In the latter two situations, the field investigator is the medium through which typewriting exemplars are acquired on which the document examiner may base sound conclusions.

The investigator who develops skill in the acquisition and evaluation of exemplars will accomplish many case solutions without the necessity of specialized assistance of any sort. A valid confession resulting from a thorough revealing investigation transcends the conclusions of the document examiner. The important thing for the investigator to keep before him is that thoroughness on his part, prior to, incident to, and subsequent to the procurement of typewriting exemplars, as with handwriting exemplars, will provide the basis for sound, reliable case solutions, whether accomplished in the field, in the laboratory, or via the cooperative efforts of both field and laboratory.

The procurement of typewriting exemplars may be divided into five steps: (1) Study of the questioned typewriting by the investigator, (2) Procurement of regular-course-of-business exemplars typewritten on or near the date of the questioned typewriting, (3) Preparation of exemplar typewriting by the accused writer, if any, on his typewriter, (4) Preparation of exemplar typewriting by the investigator on suspected typewriter, and (5) Procurement of the suspected typewriter itself by the investigator.

There is no substitute for a thorough examination of the questioned typewriting prior to the actual acquisition of typewriting exemplars. The very least which should be accomplished in this examination is the determination of horizontal and vertical spacing and the basic numerals designs. A more skilled observer might also delineate spacing malalignments, deviations from perpendicularity, characters striking "off foot," broken serifs and other typeface damage, if such there be.

The investigator who submits to the document laboratory ten-to-the-inch pica typewriting for comparison with twelve-to-the-inch elite typewriting discloses his own failure to perform two elementary measurements. Similarly, the investigator who submits typewritings which embody standard design numerals for comparison with typewritings which have uncial or accounting design numerals, testifies to his own inability to conduct a rudimentary observation.

If the investigator can himself isolate but *one* single individuality involving a typeface of a questioned typewriting—perhaps a broken serif—this plus the general measurements and styles of the typewriting will immeasurably speed his further investigative efforts. The skilled investigator does not search for just any typewriter. Rather he searches for a typewriter equipped with elite type, twelve characters to the horizontal inch, six lines to the vertical inch, uncial numerals, short center "w," and a broken southeast serif on the letter "n," or a typewriter equipped with pica type, ten letters to the horizontal inch, five and one-half lines to the vertical inch, standard numerals, long center "W," "w" and "M," and a flattened "u." As with handwriting, typewriting exemplars should be procured strictly in the light of the questioned typewriting with which they are sought to be identified.

Typewriting exemplars written in the regular-course-of-business, contemporaneously with the questioned typewriting are especially valuable. They duplicate the typeface and operation conditions of the suspected typewriter on the date which is in issue. Such exemplars are particularly necessary when any considerable period has elapsed between the date of a questioned typewriting and the date of locating a suspected typewriter. The latter may have undergone changes in the interim. Perhaps it was serviced and realigned by the repairman. A damaged typeface may have been replaced. Inquiry should be made in this regard but "before" and "after" exemplars are more reliable than unsupported statements by an interested individual as to whether his typewriter was repaired, reconditioned, or injured. Perhaps the suspected typewriter was dropped to the floor. Conceivably in a serious matter and possibly in any case, one or more of the typefaces could have been deliberately altered by filing or mechanical mauling.

Desperate suspects are sometimes very ingenius. In any event, questioning of the owner of a suspected typewriter and others as appropriate, should be conducted to elicit the location of exemplars which are timely to the questioned typewriting and typewritten on similar paper. If the questioned document is a letter on calendared stationery, the effort should be to acquire similar typewritten letters on comparable paper stock. If the questioned typewriting involves postal cards or shipping tags, the endeavor should be to obtain contemporaneous typewriting on similar stock, and so on.

When a suspected typist and suspected typewriter are located simultaneously, it is advisable to request the suspect himself to prepare typewriting exemplars. It is preferable that these exemplars be prepared with the typewriter in the condition in which it is first found, assuming that it is operable. That is, do not at the outset change the ribbon, clean the typefaces, or otherwise change the typewriter's initial condition. Such action may thereafter be necessary or advisable in individual cases but it should be deferred until after preliminary exemplars have been prepared.

Exemplars prepared by the suspected typist should be accomplished in such manner that all avenues of identification are brought to bear on the suspect. The questioned typewriting should be dictated so that the suspect will utilize his personal habits of arrangement, capitalization, spacing, abbreviations, and especially phrasing and spelling. All parts of the questioned typewriting should be dictated, incident to the procurement of request typewriting exemplars, unless it is very lengthy, in which event representative sections should be carefully selected for typing at least twice by the suspect. Special attention should be given numbers and dates, unusual phrases, and errors. It should be remembered that if one omits individualities such as misspellings, he is handicapping his own investigation, and perhaps helping to exonerate the guilty or to deprive the innocent a full opportunity of establishing his innocence.

It is rarely possible to develop sufficient individuality in the work of the practised touch-system typist to identify his typewriting through its typing peculiarities alone. The self-taught unpractised typist frequently embodies adequate individuality in his typewriting alone to identify it from proper exemplars. In either case, all facets of the questioned typewriting should be thoroughly exploited by exemplars which illustrate the suspect's habits in each and every significant particular of the questioned typewriting. And as with handwriting, regular-course-of-business and request exemplars together will reveal more about one's typing habits than will either class of exemplars alone.

The investigator should himself typewrite the complete text of the questioned typewriting two or three times on the suspected machine. If the questioned typewriting is extremely lengthy,

Exemplars of the typeface impressions of Underwood Standard
Typewriter No. 11 - 7 183 352, located in Suite 313 of the
Rincon Annex Building, San Francisco, prepared at 8.45 p.m.
on January 6, 1957, by Inspector Richard Roe, Case 12345-E.

qwertyuiop asdfghjkl zxcvbnm

q w e r t y u i o p a s d f g h j k l z x c v b n m

QWERTYUIOP ASDFGHJKL ZXCVBNM

Q W E R T Y U I O P A S D F G H J K L Z X C V B N M

234567890-½¢;/.,

2 3 4 5 6 7 8 9 0 - ½ ¢ ; / . ,

"#$%_&'()*¼@:?.,

" # $ % _ & ' ( ) * ¼ @ : ? . ,

ahbhchdhehfhghhhihjhkhlhmhnhohphqhrhshthuhvhwhxhyhzh

AHBHCHDHEHFHGHHHIHJHKHLHMHNHOHPHQHRHSHTHUHVHWHXHYHZH

Touch Variation:

aaa bbb ccc ddd eee fff ggg hhh iii jjj kkk lll mmm

nnn ooo ppp qqq rrr sss ttt uuu vvv www xxx yyy zzz

AAA BBB CCC DDD EEE FFF GGG HHH III JJJ KKK LLL MMM

NNN OOO PPP QQQ RRR SSS TTT UUU VVV WWW XXX YYY ZZZ

Carbon Impressions

q w e r t y u i o p a s d f g h j k l z x c v b n m

Q W E R T Y U I O P A S D F G H J K L Z X C V B N M

2 3 4 5 6 7 8 9 0 - ½ ¢ ; / . ,

" # $ % _ & ' ( ) * ¼ @ : ? . ,

Now is the time for all good men to come to the aid of their party
NOW IS THE TIME FOR ALL GOOD MEN TO COME TO THE AID OF THEIR PARTY

Figure 53. Recommended method of obtaining complete strike-up of
typefaces, supplemental to typing questioned material verbatim in each case.

representative sections should be selected for typewriting at least twice by the investigator. He should also prepare exemplars of all the characters on the typewriter according to the accompanying illustration. In preparing these exemplars, a firm, even, and not excessively heavy touch should be employed, except in that portion of the exemplars reserved to "touch variations." In this portion of the exemplars, the first strike-up of each letter should be heavy, the second should be medium, and the third should be a light touch. The section of the exemplars captioned "Carbon" may be prepared using a commercial carbon ribbon, if one is available. Lacking such a ribbon, the "carbon" exemplars may be prepared by shifting the typewriter to "stencil" position, and typing on a piece of clear carbon paper superimposed on a blank sheet of paper. It is preferable that the typefaces are cleaned and brushed prior to the preparation of the "carbon" exemplars as the purpose of these exemplars is to obtain a critical imprint of the typefaces without the intervention of the cloth ribbon.

As a practical matter, it is frequently impracticable for the investigator to take possession of a suspected typewriter and to submit the typewriter to the document examiner for laboratory study. Such action must depend on the realities and the practicalities of the case situation. The investigator should not overlook the opportunity of obtaining possession of suspected typewriters, particularly in cases of major importance and more especially if such typewriters are relatively new. Identification of the new typewriter is a difficult task because it is usage which develops typewriter individualities. Definite identifications are routinely accomplished by the document examiner solely on the basis of exemplars and without ever seeing the suspected typewriter itself. But in difficult cases involving relatively new typewriters, the opportunity to examine and operate the suspected typewriter may reveal to the examiner minute individualities, which are not readily perceptible from exemplars alone, or about which he has some element of irresolution from exemplars alone.

In all cases involving possible tampering or altering of typefaces, the typewriter should be submitted to the document examiner for study, if it is available.

A superficial consideration of this brief treatment concerning the procurement of typewriting exemplars might cause the unthinking to conclude that the time required to investigate, let us say, five hundred suspected typewriters would be prohibitive. Nothing could be farther from the truth. The purpose of analysis and thoroughness is to reach sound conclusions at a saving of investigative manpower. It should be clearly understood that the investigator should terminate his consideration of any suspected typewriter, immediately when he determines that it could not have been used to prepare the questioned typewriting which is the subject of his inquiry. The thoughtful, discerning acquisition of exemplars *in the light of the questioned typewriting* will eliminate non-identical typewriters rapidly.

Let us assume that responsibility must be established for a typewritten extortion note, suspected to have been typewritten in one of three large municipal departments, each having several hundred typewriters. The investigator in charge should first examine the extortion note, or preferably have it examined by a document examiner, for the purpose of determining the general characteristics and outstanding individualities, for example: Royal typeface formations, standard or portable, pica, ten characters to the inch, six lines to the inch, standard numerals, short center "W" and "w," northwest serif of "y" broken, "p" leans three degrees to left of vertical, "o" is flattened on right side. Each participating investigator should be briefed on these general and specific characteristics. Following the suggested exemplar format which is illustrated herein, hundreds of typewriters will be eliminated in the first line of the exemplar, on the basis of spacing, numerals, or both. Most of those not so eliminated will be separated from further consideration when the investigator strikes the "W," "w," "y," "p," or "o." Only those typewriters which are not definitely eliminated after appraisal of the points derived from the questioned typewriting, should be subjected to the complete procurement of exemplars. Properly directed, a team of three men can process as many as a thousand suspected typewriters in less than a day, if they are massed at two or three locations.

ANONYMOUS LETTERS

Anonymous letters present a challenge at one time or another to every level of law enforcement. Their proper investigation requires some consideration of the kinds of people who are most apt to engage in anonymous letter writing, why they do so, and how descriptive identifying data concerning them may best be developed.

Anonymous letter inquiries should proceed from a thoughtful study of the objectives and thought content of the anonymous letter writer, as revealed from within the letters themselves. Based on conversance with thousands of anonymous letters of all types, it is this author's firm conviction that responsibility can be established in virtually every multiple anonymous letter case, provided that studious, enlightened, and thorough procedures are adopted timely and consistently pursued.

Many anonymous letter inquiries are unnecessarily prolonged or completely fail of solution because they are characterized by misdirected dabbling in the theories of the victims. Another common defect of unproductive, tortuous investigations is a premature, misplaced emphasis on the mechanics and media of the letters. Trotting about from one victim to another and inquiring "who would have it in for you?" with an ever ready pad for handwriting exemplars is scarcely a discerning approach. Occasionally, irreparable harm is visited on innocent individuals, who are falsely suspected for lengthy periods, chiefly because it was not recognized that the motives and needs of the innocent are divergent from the anonymous driving forces which spew havoc wielding letters. In other instances, the rights of victims are seriously invaded for extended periods, because the thought content of the letters has been neglected, and the culprit reaps the added satisfaction from investigative ineffectiveness.

We are not here primarily concerned with the isolated anonymous letter, written on the spur of momentary rage or passion,

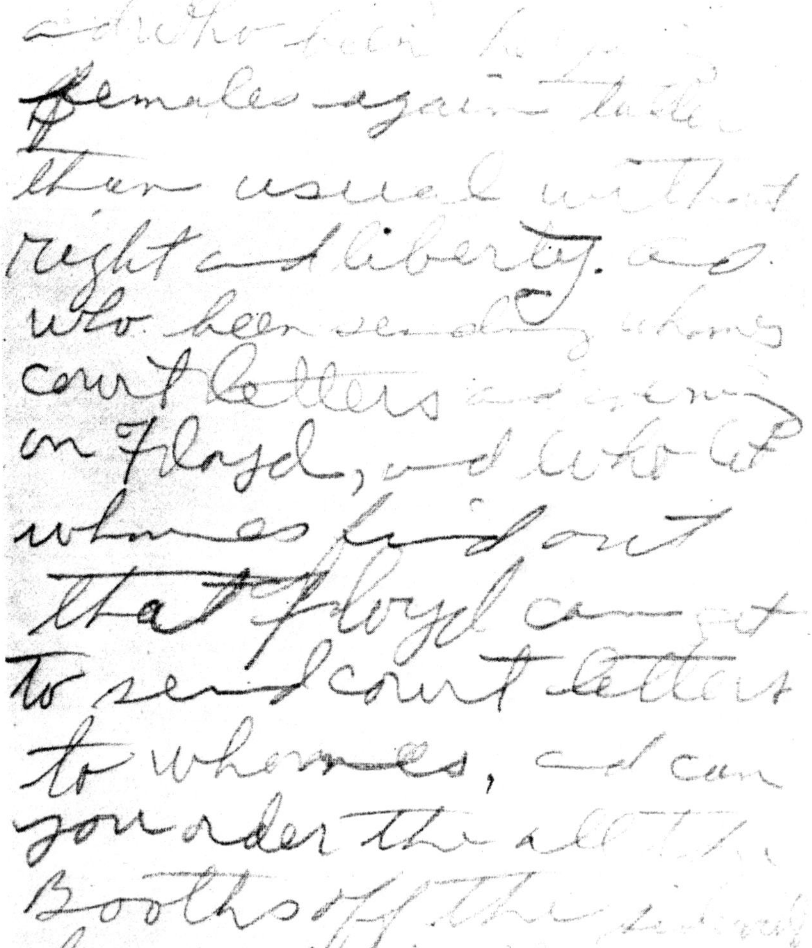

Figure 54. Writing of psychotic disclosing size variations, corrections, corrupt letter forms and general lack of mental-manual coordination.

or during an alcoholic binge. This sort of letter usually trademarks its origin by its contents. Ordinarily, it is not recurrent and does not present an imposing law enforcement problem.

As a general rule, anonymous letters written by the true psychotic are readily cognizable, even by the non-specialist in the field of psychiatry. At least there are some distinctive marks in the work of the psychotic which can alert the investigator and the document examiner to seek the specialized appraisal of the trained psychiatrist in doubtful matters. Letters by the psychotic usually lack coherence, continuity, intelligence, and consistent purpose. The secretaries of prominent public figures rather expect a batch of such rambling missives with each provocative public occurrence involving their employers. They may emphasize acts which are unreasonable and ridiculous on their face. The psychotic usually does not carefully and consistently cover his anonymity because for him there is not the understanding so to do which characterizes the non-psychotic.*

The detection of the psychotic anonymous letter writer will at times require considerable ingenuity because of his unpredictability, but the pressure of actual harm to the victim addressees of the psychotic letter writer is not commonly present. When it is, security measures are indicated which are outside the scope of this discussion. The following comments respecting the psychoneurotic "poison pen" and the obscene mail circulator are also pertinent to detection of the psychotic writer who poses the threat of harm to the recipients of his unbalanced attentions.

It is the purposeful, usually psychoneurotic, letter writer who succumbs to one, then ten, then is driven to hundreds of vicious, intensely harmful epistles who plagues society and law enforcement. This sort of letter writer merits the earnest study of every investigator of evidential documents because the course of human history indicates that his anonymous handiwork will always be in evidence. The consequences of the activities of these usually compulsive letter writers are frequently grave and far reaching. Serious physical illness and mental stress are visited on their victims. Changes of residence and employment may be enforced, prop-

*The author speaks as a layman in respect to the field of psychiatry.

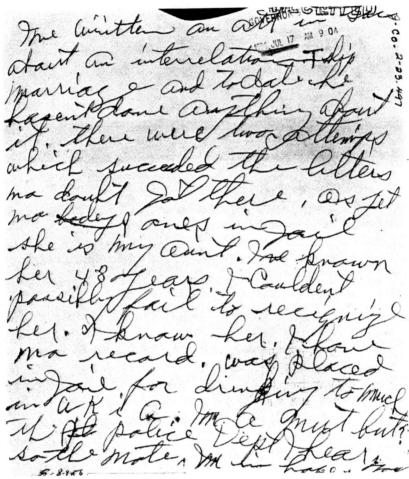

Figure 55. Writing of psychotic replete with corrections, lack of pen control, and deficient coordination.

erty depreciation may be caused, family relationships are disturbed beyond readjustment, personal reputations are besmirched, societies, even governments have been affected. Anxiety and tension from series of anonymous letters have led to suicides, physical violence, and the involvement of entire communities in suspicion, hatred, and unrest.

Occasionally, the view is expressed that to ignore anonymous letters is the best way of stopping them. Experience has demonstrated that to ignore compulsive letter writers is to spur them to more extensive, more damaging invasions of the rights of their victims. Complete exposure of the "poison pen" and the obscene mail circulator spells the only effective termination of their activities. The prompt solution of these cases of multiple anonymous letters should be stressed to prevent the secondary evils which stem from their continued circulation, as well as the primary nuisances invoked on their initial targets. It is characteristic of most series of anonymous letters that they begin in mildly offensive vein and are aimed at one or a few individuals. When not terminated promptly by investigative action, the objectionable nature of their contents, and the number of victims usually increase progressively until the guilty writer is ultimately identified and apprehended.

Most "poison pen" artists are women, so the liberty will be taken of using the feminine gender in the ensuing references. This is not to imply that men do not engage in anonymous letters, but to indicate that men are outnumbered by their feminine contemporaries in this form of expression. It may be noted additionally that men with feminine traits and women with masculine leanings deserve mention in a consideration of those who may give vent to this distorted form of expression.

The anonymous letter writer is usually also a "victim" either by way of herself receiving one or more letters or being referred to derogatorily in letters directed to others. Becoming a "victim" satisfies at least two fundamentals for the "poison pen." She is enabled gracefully to invade the inner circle of victims, to keep pace with their comments, to experience first-hand their reactions, to grovel in the general mischief, and to maintain a rein on their suspicions. Planting, directing, routing, and skillfully fending off suspicions may even supersede the letters themselves in the prime satisfactions of the "poison pen." Secondly, as a "victim" herself, she can point out, should she come under direct suspicion or be accused, how "illogical" it would be for anyone to direct objectionable statements to herself, to those near and dear to her, or to vilify herself and her loved ones.

Common motivations for anonymous letters are jealousy, envy, revenge, sex frustration, feelings of personal inadequacy, guilt complexes, the urge to wield power and influence—to be a "big shot," to push others around. Other causations lie in business, professional, and social rivalries, neighborhood and civic disagreements, perverted efforts to right some real or imagined wrong or injury, racial and religious prejudices, feelings of "not belonging"—being a "have not." As anonymous letter writers become more and more involved in these activities, frequently they are virtually possessed by the feelings of superiority derived from their deception of friends, associates, police, investigators, and victims. This is especially. true if as a "victim" the culprit has, foxlike, joined the hounds to chase herself and is gleefully supplying distorted data and misinformation to confound the investigation.

Quite evidently a disturbed personality is prerequisite to inclusion in this dubious group which seeks mischief from anonymous written expression. The depths of such a dreamworld do not consume the well adjusted person, busily engaged in fruitful thoughts and labor. It is equally apparent, in this author's view, that the keys to the identification of these disturbed personalities reside first in their personal and personality characteristics as expressed within their abnormal missives.

In effect, the successful investigator of anonymous letters must identify the plot, the time, the characters. All the letters in a given series should be assembled for concurrent study. Arrangements should be made so that additional letters in the series are turned over to the investigator promptly following their receipt by the victim-addressees. This should not be a hit-or-miss operation. A few or even one missing letter may provide key information or may confirm an investigative theory, tentatively inferred from other letters. All persons addressed and mentioned in the letters should be identified with particularity. Their relationships and associations should be developed by frank interviews so that the true significance of the connection of their names with the anonymous letters may be accurately postulated.

The "poison pen" may be a bank president, a church organist, an engineer, a carpenter, a ribbon clerk, an artist, or a housewife. But he or she is not a normal bank president, church organist, engineer, carpenter, ribbon clerk, artist, or housewife. The thoughtful scrutiny of all the principal and minor characters in an anonymous letter drama, in the light of the personal and personality characteristics of the anonymous letters' script, will serve to illumine the abnormal leading player, the "poison pen."

A chart should be carefully compiled showing when the letters first appeared, when and where they have been mailed or otherwise dispatched, and when and where they have been received. This chart should encompass an analysis of the times of day and the days of the week which can be adduced from the letters. What occurred to "set off" the letter writer in the first instance? Why are most of the letters received on Monday, for example? Does the weekend provide the only opportunity for the culprit to write extensively without observation? Or is the volume and timing of writings such that it follows the "poison pen" must live substantially alone in order to be able to avoid observation while in the acts of preparing and dispatching the letters? Do lapses in the appearance of the letters coincide with vacations or illnesses of possible suspects? What incidents involving the various principals have temporal or geographical relevance to either accelerated or diminished activity on the part of the letter writer? Do the points and times of mailing indicate the use or non-use of an automobile for mailing or otherwise dispatching the letters on their evil way?

The contents of the letters should be studied chronologically and in the light of conditions and events surrounding the principals and possible suspects. While the targets of the letters may seem to vary, and the subject matter may seem to change superficially, there is but a single disturbed personality producing them. What is the writer "getting off her mind"? What is the underlying theme or themes? Is the melody always the same or has it variations and, if so, what is their significance?

Read the letters aloud. Use the inflection which is indicated by the choice of words and style of expression. This will assist in focusing attention on the real intentions of the writer. The preparation of typewritten copies of handwritten letters for independent study by several investigators is helpful. Your stenographer may

even unravel some of the mystery as typewritten copies are prepared by her.

It must be kept in mind that the acts of authoring and sending
anonymous letters are themselves illogical and abnormal. One cannot blindly apply principles governing normal, logical conduct
in evaluating the disturbed writer who is obsessed with this abnormal method of loosing her feelings. Your objective is to isolate
from the letters themselves, and the external data you develop from
selective interviews of the principals and their associates, the abnormal preoccupations, impulses, and *needs* which are driving
the anonymous writer to this form of expression. In viewing
suspects developed in these cases, one may well ponder: "Which
needs to give vent to this perverted mode of expression?"

Anonymous letters carry a message of the disturbed impulses
producing them which can probably be best deduced, as each
letter is progressively analyzed, by applying these considerations:
What was the writer thinking when this letter was written, when
these words were said? What was urging the writer at that time?
Why did the writer say what was said to the particular individual
to whom it was said? Why did the writer *feel the need* of the statements, as made? What did the writer hope to accomplish?

Statements such as "why don't you quit your job" may
really be expressing the writer's envy of the greater capabilities
of a fellow employee. Remarks such as "keep your filthy glances
away from Jane Doe" may really be expressing the author's erotic
interest in the recipient and jealousy for Jane. Insulting references
to reputation, attire, family, friends, and home may really denote
resentment of the superior station of the addressees and the inse-
curity and incapacity of the author of such references.

The "poison pen" herself may be and frequently is in rather
vague understanding of her own prevailing emotional and neurotic
problems. What she says and does cannot fail to reveal them to
others who conduct competent scientific observations. If the
investigator is unable to paint a picture of the disturbed personality
which is expressing itself via anonymous letters, he should consider
enlisting the assistance of a competent psychiatrist. The latter by
studying such series of letters can frequently provide invaluable

help in describing the preoccupations of the letter writer, in outlining the personality pattern which the investigator must identify.

The importance of adequate preliminary studies of anonymous letters themselves is perhaps best indicated by the truism that the background and purposes of the letters coincide precisely only with the guilty from among the possible suspects. There is scarcely another type of case wherein the investigator has the opportunity to learn so much about his quarry from the corpus delecti, as he does in an efficiently planned and understandingly conducted anonymous letter investigation.

Any considerable volume of anonymous letters may be replete with evidential data concerning the probable sex, age, education, intelligence, possible occupation, and perhaps national or sectional origin of the writer. Unusual interests and pursuits occasionally are indicated. The educated writer who feigns illiteracy will be unable to camouflage successfully her true capabilities throughout a considerable series of letters. Compare the last letter with the first. Are they consistent or do they reveal intentional deception? Even the prim writer usually discloses her prudishness despite the injection of vulgarities or obscenities which would curl the hair of a "wharf-rat."

A detailed study should be made of all errors and individualities in spelling, grammar, capitalization, punctuation, and expression. Margins, paragraphing, arrangement, dates, and numerals merit analysis. Selection of paper, carbon paper, typewriter, pen, pencil, ink, stamps, method of sealing, style of address, manner of folding, neatness or lack of it, lipstick traces—all should receive careful evaluation.

As the anonymous letter inquiry involves a series of recurrent offenses, it requires and should receive a different approach throughout than an exclusively after-the-fact investigation. At least a tentative identification of the guilty writer should be accomplished through study of the letters and the various principals, victims, associates, and other persons mentioned. Thereafter, efforts should be concentrated on associating such individual with the handwriting, typewriting, ink, paper, and other physical properties of past letters, and utilizing chemical tagging, other marking

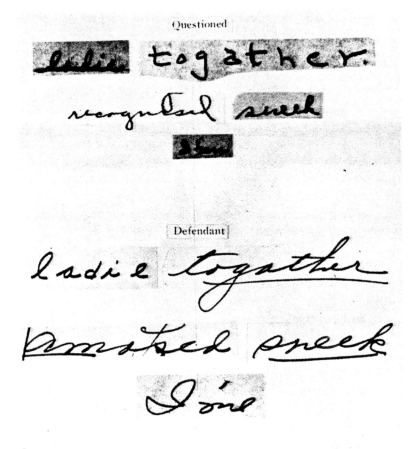

Figure 56. Spelling errors having identifying significance in scurrilous letter case despite high order of disguise injected into questioned writing.

devices, and personal surveillance to detect prospective future letters.

The ultimate objective should be apprehending the responsible individual in the act of preparing, possessing, mailing or otherwise dispatching letters identifiable with the series. It should be recognized that the "poison pen" or obscene mail circulator who adopts a masquerade of diabolical anonymity is not likely to expose readily her or his alter ego in the absence of a showing of direct proof of such guilt.

The opportunity to supply pre-marked stationery, stamps, and ink to the suspect should be explored. The feasibility of tagging the hands of the suspect with invisible chemicals should receive painstaking attention. Fluorescent powder and paste are frequently very useful in this connection, applied to the clothing, pocketbook, automobile, writing media, typewriter, door handles, or telephone. Subsequent letters can readily be inspected by ultraviolet illumination for telltale evidences.

Scatter-shot accusations should be scrupulously avoided. They serve only to indicate the accuser's ineptitude. The use of the so-called lie detector is distinctly questionable in active anonymous letter investigations. Its use, especially on a large scale, tends to promote the same brand of tension and unrest which is the object of the anonymous letters themselves. In this recurring class of offense, its use may precipitate an untimely confrontation of the suspect, which is out of step with the development of physical and other evidence. At best, the most favorable indications of deception recorded by a "lie detector" will simply confirm what should be evident from a carefully coordinated study of the letters and logical suspects themselves.

As the guilty author is usually also one of the victim-complainants, and barring that circumstance at the very least a highly interested party, the investigator has a facile opportunity to maintain communication with the logical suspect and himself select the most propitious time for confrontation. During preliminary conversations, receptivity rather than garrulity will best serve the investigator. A pose of naivete may assist him greatly. It requires considerable skill for the guilty writer of anonymous letters to avoid undue interest in the investigator's progress, and undue satisfaction that she has not been exposed. *But it is well nigh impossible for such a subject to avoid projecting, with studied indirection, to the receptive, skilled listener a variety of invalid alibis.* Given the right setting and opportunity and without any accusation whatsoever, the guilty anonymous letter writer will invariably protest too much. Only the guilty, it might well be remembered, manufactures a false alibi. Only the guilty needs an alibi.

The investigator by maintaining rapport with suspected

writers and acquiring familiarity with their mental processes and surroundings is in sound position to anticipate future letters, and to apprehend the culprit in the act of preparing, possessing, dispatching, or delivering incriminating letters. Additionally, an understanding of the causes for the letters and the thought processes which produced them is of inestimable assistance in obtaining an ultimate confession. A vague understanding of the "reasons" for anonymous letters and misconceptions concerning their authors are serious stumbling blocks in interviews designed to elicit the truth from the guilty.

In summary, the advised investigation of anonymous letters consists of a coordinated, analytical survey leading to: (1) the personality of their author as revealed from within the letters and in the light of the external circumstances surrounding the principals, (2) the personal individualities of handwriting, typewriting, composition, and other media of preparation as revealed in the letters, (3) the characteristics of dispatch and delivery as revealed by the letters and through interviews of the recipients, (4) the personalities and individualities of possible suspects as revealed through selective interviews of the principals, and studies of the actions, verbal statements, and writings of suspects, (5) identification of the guilty through comparison of personal and personality characteristics, handwriting, typewriting, chemical tagging, and consideration of alibis and false alibis, (6) surveillance of the identified writer, and (7) apprehension, confrontation, and confession.

It may conservatively be averred that the last development is probably more important to the guilty anonymous letter writer than it is to those charged with the detection and apprehension of such persons. Experience has shown that baring the soul is a necessary primary ingredient in the treatment and rehabilitation of the "poison pen" and obscene mail circulator.

GRAPHOLOGY

Graphology is commonly defined as the art of determining character, disposition, and aptitudes from the study of handwriting. This art, pseudo-science, science, or quackery, depending on the commentator, is much misapprehended, being rather absurdly endorsed as a firmly established science by some and unilaterally decried as errant humbug by others. Some of this diversity arises from a disparity of terms and their application both by enthusiastic graphologists and their eschewing critics.

To the man in the street "character" means that aggregation of distinctive mental and moral qualities which differentiates each man from his contemporaries, or at least isolates him in a well defined grouping, for example, honest, reliable, punctual, poised, truthful, industrious, well adjusted, sober, intelligent. Similarly, the unqualified position that one can adduce character "from handwriting" directly implies that such discernment of character proceeds from handwriting alone, no more and no less.

Too many American document examiners have unreservedly disavowed the psychological manifestations of handwriting and its thought content, while too many European graphologists and American opportunists have ascribed exaggerated, if not completely false, scientific basis to graphological theories which have not been established through experimental research. Some of the latter theories are so unreasonable and vague that no thinking student of the subject would waste time on them.

The one extreme is typified by the unimaginative subjective comparator, steeped in measurements and statistics, who poses as a document expert, but who essentially is an unknowing measurer and counter of letter conformations. This sort of examiner is virtually helpless when he is asked to compare non-literatim writings. He highly urges request exemplars because they are readily amenable to his unimaginative letter-for-letter comparisons. He shuns data collateral to writings. Indeed, they

151

might influence him, he piously opines. He vaguely rates graphic forms as similar or dissimilar with token or no cognizance of such basic psychological considerations as: Does this writing reliably reflect its author's normal writing habits? Does this writing reflect a mature writer whose capabilities were volitionally or non-volitionally obstructed, or does it reflect an immature writer? Does this writing reflect a mature writer whose capabilities were non-volitionally impeded by writing instrument and writing surface, or does it reflect deliberate distortion? Does this writing contain indications of nervousness, lack of mental or manual control, incoherence, unpredictability, exhibitionism, disinterest, timidity, or carelessness?

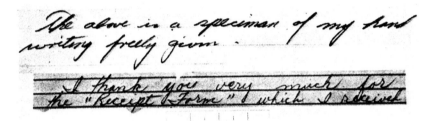

Figure 57. Prima facie appraisals of writing may be misleading. Upper sentence was written by college president. Lower phrase was written by Micronesian indigene of small Pacific island with little scholastic training.

The opposite extreme is denoted by the fuzzy thinking pretender who mysteriously asserts that doublelooped "a's" and "o's" reflect deceit, short blunt "t" crossings are indicative of cruelty, vertical writing denotes poise and self-possession, anon ad absurdum. This all-seeing seer may even purport to be able to determine authenticity in writings sans comparisons with proved exemplars. He disdains analytical comparisons as beneath his omniscience.

The truth, within the bounds of present knowledge, lies in the intermediate zones between these two extremes. Certainly it is true that one's handwriting tends to reflect its owner's personality, attitudes, and proclivites to some degree as do his walk, his talk, his dress, his gestures, and his mannerisms. Frequently, one's handwriting affirmatively reflects deceit, impatience, irritability, haste, carelessness, affectation, vanity, exhibitionism, inebriation, physical disability, or mental illness. Such characteristics are demonstrated at times by a combination of thought content and purpose, graphic forms, and especially by the manner of their execution. These factors usually must be interpreted from a considerable chronology of the subject's handwriting and in the light of the external representations urged for the writing and its parent documents.

It is one thing to acknowledge that one's handwriting, including all its direct and indirect subjective and objective ramifications tends to reflect the characteristics of its author, and may on occasion clearly isolate personality traits and attitudes timely to a particular questioned handwriting. It is quite a different matter to aver, as some graphologists have done, that one's "character" may be accurately delineated from the graphic forms alone of a single signature, a single line of writing, the address on an envelope, a brief note, or even one fairly lengthy communication.

The scientific document examiner will rely on broad tested principles and he will specifically not rely on skimpy writings and uncharted, nebulous theories. To every writing he first applies a knowledge of how writing is taught and how writing training, experience, usage and materials are reflected in every writing. He knows that deviations in the writing of the immature, unskilled penman present quite different considerations than discrepancies from normal in the writing of the mature, skilled writer. He knows that unfamiliar or faulty pens, paper, and pencils require translation into and from all written work. He has learned to recognize the volitional and non-volitional factors of body, will, and intellect which affect handwriting from observing these manifestations in hundreds of writings by hundreds of writers.

He has learned that the tremor of fraud, the tremor of age, and the tremor of illness require exceptionally critical interpretations as they have much in common at times. He marks well that a single signature or a few lines of writing are relatively barren ground for psychological manifestations whereas a series of anonymous letters or a lengthy personnel folder may provide fertile fields for expressions of individual characteristics of the writer's personality.

He recognizes the faulty execution which is associated with the cardiac and the incoherent execution which is characteristic of many psychotics, but he does not presume to invade boldly the arena of differential diagnosis via handwriting interpretations. He concedes that many evidential handwritings are not susceptible to even guarded estimations of their authors' characteristics and attitudes, within the limits of current scientific experience. Especially, the qualified document examiner has learned that there is no simple toteboard to provide the speculator with the prevailing odds on honesty, health, love, credit risk, crime, and non-malignant warts from a scrap or two of handwriting.

The man on the town who pays a dollar or two to the night-club graphologist for a character reading may receive his dollar's worth if he gets a chuckle from that worthy's "analysis." The well intentioned who invest any time or money in a course in "graphology" or "grapho-analysis" would be well advised to save even a four-cent stamp on their initial inquiry. There just is not any jiffy do-it-yourself kit to provide the uninitiated or anyone else with the "simple rules to character analysis" via handwriting.

Some time ago a "certified grapho-analyst" was retained by a firm of attorneys who represented the proponents of a holographic will disposing of approximately four hundred thousand dollars. This so-called analyst submitted a rather lengthy report, stating among other things:

> "A thorough mathematical comparison of the will of the above named deceased has been completed, and indicates the factual proof of its authenticity. To a positive degree of comparison it stands tested as authentically the original. It definitely is not a forgery. It was written by XXX himself. The writing of XXX displays certain individual personality characteristics scarcely visible to the naked eye. Unusual indications slip into unexpected spaces, parts of strokes, on dots, and even the dashes. This writing was definitely his own. Even his emotional nature is genuinely expressed. The natural shading designates the greater degree of the authenticity of the fact. He was a man who had

achieved the art of self-control when he needed it, very definite in making decisions, and rather non-committal; a man who would not make instantaneous decisions, for he required and took the time to form his conclusions. He was inclined to be touchy when one interfered with his plans. He was a person to allow little things to annoy him and was quickly irritated. He was positive to the point of stubbornness. These are a few of his outstanding qualities which held a rigid influence until the last, even though he had not the physical effort nor endurance to express his feeling. All in all he was a fine fellow. He was staunch and very fair minded."

The will in question proved to be a clumsy simulated forgery. The forger abjectly so confessed in formal testimony. The quoted statements bespeak their own presumptiveness and nescience. They fail to explain, however, why a law firm in these enlightened United States would engage such "assistance" in a weighty matter involving hundreds of thousands of dollars.

Everyone concerned with evidential documents should be aware that extravagant graphological claims have no scientific basis. No thinking inquirer should be a party to pronouncements by a graphologist who is not qualified by training and experience to detect authenticity or spuriousness. Particularly, no responsible investigator should demean his efforts by consulting a graphological seer who purports to ascertain the past or to foretell the future of an individual from his handwriting.

In cases involving an extended series of writings such as an anonymous letter investigation, the investigator should not hesitate to consult the well grounded document examiner for assistance in describing the kind of a writer who is responsible and where he is apt to be found. Through searching evaluation of the thought content, graphic forms, indications of writing training, experience and usage, arrangement and modes of expression, grammatical ability, word usage, etc., the document examiner is frequently able to catalogue highly descriptive personal and personality characteristics of the writer.

These studies should not be confused with graphology. They are essentially a summary of the physical and psychological manifestations of the handwriting and its thought content, plus all the direct and indirect facets of the documents on which it appears. The reliability of interpretations of this sort, as in respect to all conclusions from evidential documents, lies in the reasonableness, convincingness, and demonstrability of the inferences which are urged.

WRITING MATERIALS

Writing media which are particularly related to day-to-day evidential document problems will be considered in this chapter. Comment has been intentionally restricted to those aspects of writing materials which seem most frequently to concern the field investigator. Areas will be discussed wherein investigative effort and laboratory analysis can be highly productive. Some of the limitations which exist in the analysis of writing materials will also be enumerated.

BALL POINT PENS

The ball pen, or the ball point pen as it is commonly referred to, is encountered today everywhere documents are found. Its use has become so common that some knowledge of its origin, usage, and effects should be within the grasp of all who are concerned with evidential documents.

Relevant United States and foreign patents date back over sixty years. Only four years after Lewis Edson Waterman patented his capillarity ink fed "fountain pen" in 1864, John Loud made what seems to have been the first application for a United States patent covering a pen which employed a rotatable ball instead of nibs as the writing edge. Production does not appear to have resulted from Loud's efforts. In 1895, Askew patented what was essentially a marking paste, U. S. Patent No. 533492 dated April 30, 1895. Askew's mixture consisted of lampblack based in castor oil. Several years later, Werner patented a rotatable ball unit, U. S. Patent No. 600299 of March 8, 1898. Apparently a very limited quantity of ball point writing instruments was manufactured around the turn of the century, based on the Askew-Werner patents. This early device was crude and it had no material impact on the manufacture of writing instruments or their general use in this country or elsewhere.

Substantial efforts to produce a commercially feasible ball pen seem to have lapsed until about 1935. In the latter year, a ball pen called the "Rolpen" was manufactured in Czechoslovakia by Klines and Eisner, French Patent No. 807679 dated October 19, 1936. Sales of the Rolpen were confined to the Continent and they were not extensive. When World War II halted production in 1939, only about twenty-five thousand Rolpens had been distributed.

In 1939, the Hungarian, Ladislao J. Biro, who had been attempting to perfect a workable ball pen unit for a number of years, obtained French Patent No. 839929, dated January 7, 1939. Biro was unable to initiate production in Europe and he went to Argentina in 1940. By about 1943 he had manufactured his first production model. This ball pen was considerably less than an efficient or even satisfactory writing instrument but it aroused considerable interest in South America, as a departure from the fountain pen. In 1944, some of the early models produced in Argentina came to the attention of the military procurement agencies in this country as the result of Air Force interest. The latter proceeded from the claims of Biro's backers that the writing fluid of his ball pen would not leak at flying altitudes and that it was not affected adversely by radical changes of temperature and humidity. The military indicated large scale procurement, provided a satisfactory ball pen was offered, and as a result leading United States manufacturers of writing instruments sped engineering and production studies.

On October 29, 1945, after limited research, the Reynolds ball pen was introduced into the United States retail market via a large New York department store. A fanfare of nationwide publicity attended the unveiling of the Reynolds ball pen. Eversharp began distribution in April 1946, followed by Eberhard Faber and Shaeffer in November 1946, and thereafter by a long list of other manufacturers, large and small. It is estimated that eight million ball pens were sold in this country in 1946 and annual sales soared to triple or quadruple that number by 1948.

The experiences of most users of the ball pen in the four years following its introduction in this country were highly unsatisfactory. When the ball pens of the 1945-49 period wrote at all, the ink faded, migrated through the paper, transferred to hands and clothing, and in general reduced the optimistic purchaser to a state of low pessimism about the future of the ball pen as a writing instrument.

The ink formula of the Hungarian, Fran Seech, provided a step forward for the ball pen industry in 1949. Seech's ink was adopted by Frawley in his Paper Mate and improved writing experiences followed by the users of the Paper Mate and the contemporaneous models of the leading manufacturers. Belated research has ameliorated the early errors in ball pen writing inks, design, mechanical components, and assembly. The ball pen of 1958 is exerting a tremendous impact on the writing habits of millions of Americans. This writer would estimate that four out of five pen users in this country today are employing the ball pen, at least for routine writing duties.

TYPICAL FOUNTAIN PEN DESIGN   **BALL-POINT PEN DESIGN**

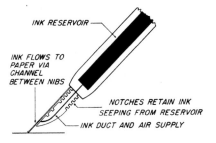
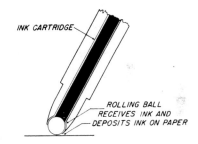

Figure 58.

By referring to the accompanying illustrations, it will be seen that the ball pen is essentially a rolling printing device in which the ball impresses a line of writing onto the paper. The steel or sapphire ball rotates in its socket and receives its oleaginous ink supply at one point of its rotation and transfers this ink to the paper at a further point of its rotation. In direct contrast, the two nibs of the fountain pen release a flow of fluid ink between them as they strike and move across the paper. Because of these different modes of ink transport and impression, the writing line of the ball pen is readily distinguishable from the writing line of its fountain pen counterpart.

Tell-tale unevenness of inking within the ball pen writing line is evident under the microscope. Usually this irregularity in inking is discernible to the naked eye. Excess globules of ink frequently appear after a sharply curved stroke or at the point of an abrupt change of writing direction. Such globules result from changes in the axes of rotation of the ball. "Unused" ink, scraped from the surface of the ball on its rollback for a new supply, accumulates at the lip of the ball socket, until mutation in the axes of rotation transports this accumulation to the writing line.

The most common diameter of the ball is approximately .04 inches. The diameters of fine and large balls range from about .03 inches to .05 inches. The ball is held in its socket by a slight crimping of the outer rim of the socket.

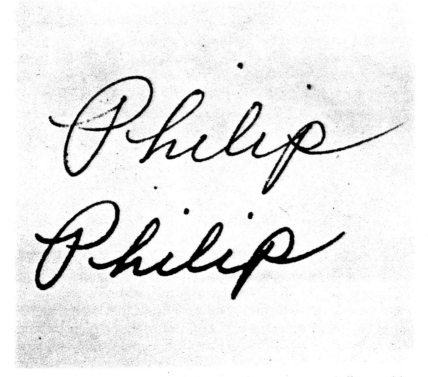

Figure 59. Gooping at points of direction changes in upper ballpen writing distinguishes from even surge of fluid ink in lower writing.

The early ball pen disclosed a pronounced tendency to clog at the outer socket area preventing the smooth rotating of the ball and transport of the ink supply. Skipping due to stalled rotation of the ball was common. Defects in ball design and assembly have been largely eliminated. Skipping may still be encountered when one attempts to write with a ball pen on a glazed or highly calendered writing surface, which does not afford sufficient center friction to rotate the ball. Also, those whose needs require writing with the ball pen in an "upside-down" position usually find that the ball will fail to rotate sufficiently to deliver an adequate and constant ink supply to the writing line. In general, however, the operability of the current ball pens being distributed by the leading manufacturers is satisfactory for the majority of writing situations.

Ball pen ink might be likened to an oily, semi-fluid paste. Common early ingredients were an oleic acid plus a mineral or vegetable oil vehicle and dye coloring agents. As previously noted, the early inks tended to diffuse, strike through the paper, smear, leak via the outer socket area, and fade, sometimes practically to illegibility. In addition, lint pick-up from the paper caused clogging. Decidedly noticeable ink "gooping" at points of change of writing direction was a characteristic of the early ball pen. Current ball pen inks disclose an improved, usually resinous, vehicle and the inks in the ball pens marketed by the reputable manufacturers today, from the standpoints of writing execution, legibility, and permanence, produce a substantially satisfactory writing line for most writing situations.

Aside from utility and operability, there is a material difference in the personal reaction of the writer who uses the ball pen, in comparison with his work with the fountain pen. Personal individuality is not reflected in ball pen writing to the extent that it is in the line of the conventional fountain pen. Handwriting individuality is significantly reduced in writing accomplished with the ball pen. Identifications via handwriting are accordingly more difficult and more dependent on letter conformations when ball pen writing is concerned.

The ball tip tends to produce a writing line of relatively static width and intensity. Intricacies of pressure are not readily isolatable. Pen position and delicate pen emphasis can rarely be determined with certainty. Writing speed is difficult to establish critically. Stops and starts within a word or even within a letter must be viewed with experience, extreme thoroughness and conservatism. Repetition of what appear to be unusual breaks in the continuity or hiati in movement weigh to a conclusion of writing habit but single instances merit guarded acceptance as personal writing individuality. They may reflect the individuality of the ball pen rather than the personal individuality of the writer.

The ball pen actually provides shelter for the forger. A poorly functioning ball pen produces an irregular inked writing line, replete with imperfections. In considering questions of suspected forgery by simulation, it is not always possible to differentiate definitely an authentic signature accomplished with a faulty ball pen, from a simulated forgery accomplished with the faulty movement of the forger. The forger's tremor, hesitation, uncertainty, and studied consciousness of the writing operation are readily translatable from the path of the fountain pen's nibs with constant ink release. But the roll of the ball at best does not disclose the defective movement of the writer so obviously. At worst, it may preclude a clear cut solution of intricate signature problems.

It should be apparent that exemplars written with a ball pen, especially when limited in quantity, should be supplemented in most cases by exemplars written with a fountain pen, so that the examiner can readily establish the writer's individualities of movement. It should also be patent that documents of gravity should not be executed with a ball pen.

This writer knows of no reliable method by which the precise age of ball pen writing on a document can be determined from the ink line itself. In time, estimates of relative age may be adducible. Formulas for ball pen inks have changed radically and continually in the ball pen's brief history. A variety of brands has filtered into the market and pens representing the various stages of development of the ball pen continue in existence. Any could prospectively be employed in an attempt to "date" a document. Conclusive evidence of forgery would be certain if a ball pen signature purported to have been written prior to the availability of ball pens in 1945, or if analysis disclosed a post-1950 vehicle in a ball pen signature with an ante-1949 date. But there is to this point no body of information respecting the behavior of ball pen ink, subsequent to its impression in a line of writing, which assists materially in solving the question of age.

A number of studies has been conducted looking to the "identification" of the ball pen inks supplied in the pens of the various manufacturers. The use of the word "identification" frequently misleads the non-technical observer. Probably "classification" is more descriptive from the practical standpoint. In any event, it should be understood that the ink from no ball pen is identifiable with the pen itself. The ink may be classifiable as belonging to the same group of ball pen inks which are supplied in the kind of a pen which is in question. Obviously, such a classification or grouping has little probative value if fifty million pens with the same ink classification have been distributed. Its value is not enhanced by the further circumstance that individual ink manufacturers supply more than one manufacturer of ball pens.

Differences in the composition and action of ball pen inks may prove vital when questions arise as to whether two units of writing were produced with the same pen. It may be alleged that a testator signed a will and then handed his pen to the witnesses who signed the document with the identical pen. Or the bank teller may testify that he handed his ball pen to the accused forger who thereupon wrote what developed to be a forged endorsement. The circumstance that the inks belonged to the same group would not positively confirm use of the same ball pen, although it would be of corroborative significance. However, differences in the inks would clearly establish that the same ball pens were not used.

Differences are commonly disclosed by microscopic study of the writing line, color evaluation, ultra-violet light, infrared and color filter photography. Further methods, which necessitate some slight disturbance of the writing line incident to analysis, involve the use of chemical agents, paper chromatography, and paper electrophoresis.

Differences, however disclosed, in two ball pen inks should not be pyramided automatically into the additional conclusion that ball pens of different manufacturers are necessarily involved. Ink changes have been rapid among manufacturers and within the products of individual manufacturers. Different inks have been used in pens of the same brand. Pending complete stability in the manufacture of ball pen inks, it will be possible to differentiate individual ball pens more readily than individual brands of ball pens. As a practical matter, the former question is of greater interest and applicability to those concerned with evidential documents.

The determination of the sequence of intersecting lines of writing is not always possible where ball pen writings are involved. The sequence of a heavy ball pen stroke which was overwritten heavily by a sharp pencil or a fountain pen may be as obvious as scratches in fresh paint. Conditions of paper surface, paper backing, time between the writings involved in the intersecting lines, and individual writing habit intervene to render many questions of sequence indeterminate. One who becomes certain that he can invariably "see" under the microscope which of two intersecting ball pen, ball pen and pencil, ball pen and rubber stamp, ball pen and typewriter, or ball pen and fountain pen lines is uppermost might profitably have an associate test his perspicaciousness. Better to establish one's limitations in private study and experiment than to have them exposed on cross-examination, when corresponding tests may properly be presented to the witness.

The transferability of ball pen writing, for example, a signature, has been mentioned as an objectionable feature of the ball pen, especially during its early history. The heel of the hand, and even a hard boiled egg or the peeled surface of a raw potato have been cited as feasible of use to transfer a genuine signature on one document to a second spurious document. The transfer would be accomplished by impressing the transferring agent, say the hand, on the genuine signature, receiving the impression, and then stamping it on the second document. The practical dangers of such transfers appear to have been exaggerated, although it was no great feat to transfer the *form* of a signature written with many of the early ball pen inks. The rapid drying resinous inks which predominate today are not readily susceptible to such transference. More important, it is not possible to transfer the indentation of the ball point and its rolling path. The furrow of the rolling ball and the quality of its ink line under the microscope distinguish ball pen writing from the flat, lifeless form of a "transferred" writing.

THE LIQUID LEAD PENCIL

The liquid lead pencil was experimentally introduced by Scripto in early 1954. No sales, as such, were made in that year but about fifteen hundred experimental models were distributed to various companies for evaluation tests. At the same time, Parker was engaged in experimentation and testing of its projected "World's First Liquid Lead Pencil." Scripto began commercial manufacture in January 1955 and concentrated distribution of

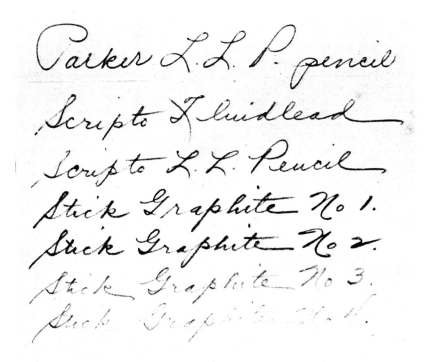

Figure 60. Telltale globules of liquid lead contrast sharply with line quality of common lead pencil.

its product commenced throughout the United States on or about January 23, 1955. While Parker had pre-announced its liquid lead pencil, commercial distribution of the latter did not take place until late April 1955. Country wide distribution by Parker was completed about June 1955. Clearly, therefore, no authentic document written with a liquid lead pencil could be dated prior to 1954 and probably could not have been written before January 1955.

The operation of the so-called liquid or fluid lead pencil is substantially similar to the operation of the ball pen. The "lead" or "graphite" is actually a suspension of carbon black in a carrier which effectively prevents diffusion of the writing line.

The writing line of the liquid lead pencil contains the same tell-tale evidences of its ball transport as does the ball pen. Sharp changes of writing direction are characterized by fringe deposits and gooping of the liquid carbon in the outer ranges of the writing line. Additional distinguishing features of the liquid carbon writing line, as compared with the writing line of the common stick graphite pencil, are: The liquid carbon line is a colder black or gray-black in tone. The liquid carbon line, because of its oleaginous base and finely ground carbon in suspension, does not embody the distinctive powdery layering of the stick graphite line. The liquid carbon line does not smudge as does stick graphite, particularly the softer varieties of the latter. The ball point of the liquid lead pencil does not vary from sharpness to dullness as its cylindrical stick graphite predecessor has been doing in its wood encasements since the eighteenth century. The constancy for width and intensity of the liquid lead pencil writing line contrasts with the variability of the stick graphite pencil line, which ranges from sharp-thin to dull-thick. This distinction is especially evident in handwriting of some length, such as a two or three page letter.

The liquid lead pencil writing line, like the stick graphite line, is not eradicable by the usual ink solvents or bleaches. It is removable by abrasion which usually disturbs the paper fibers sufficiently to render the alteration quite evident. No method is known or anticipated to learn the age of a liquid lead pencil writing line, through analysis of the writing line itself. Recordable changes do not occur in the carbonaceous line after it is impressed on the paper which would lend themselves to estimations of age.

The same precautions previously cited in respect to ball pen writing lines should attend the consideration of the sequence of intersecting lines involving the liquid lead pencil.

WRITING INKS

The principal fluid writing inks in common use today are (a) the iron gallotannates, such as the blue-blacks popularly advertised as "permanent" and which may broadly be referred to as iron or iron base inks, (b) the synthetic dye inks, such as the frequently observed aniline blues, usually marketed as "non-permanent," and (c) the carbon blacks, including India and drawing or lettering inks.

The practical questions which arise most commonly involving ink are: (1) Were two documents written with the same ink? (2) Were all portions of a given document, for example, the date, text, signature and witnesses' signatures written with the same ink? (3) What is the age of an ink writing? (4) Are two ink writings the same age? (5) Is all the ink in what purports to be a single unit of writing the same age?

Not all of these practical questions are solvable by technical methods alone within the present field of knowledge. Research continues and the day may come when all or almost all ink problems will be susceptible to definite determination. But that day is not yet.

Perhaps more misunderstanding is prevalent concerning what can be accomplished in relation to ink problems than in respect to any other single area of document analysis. When a competent document examiner reports his inability to determine from the ink alone whether a signature was written on, let us say, July 16, 1917, he may be greeted with a few raised eyebrows. The self-styled expert who infers that in some mysterious manner he is able to discern from the ink alone that the signature was actually written on July 16, 1918, or perhaps September 23, 1922, may be met with open arms by the partisan litigant, without a hard look at the crystal ball of this "genius" from which he must derive such wondrous conclusions. It is important for the investigator to know something of what cannot be accomplished as well as what can be accomplished through ink analysis.

It is known that leading manufacturers of ink utilize similar formulas. A single manufacturer may use the same formula for years without changing the ingredients. Ink manufactured to the same formula will analyze and react to tests the same, whether ten bottles or ten million bottles were so manufactured. Within the limits of the quantity of ink available in the writing line and bearing in mind contamination of both pens and ink supply at the point of use, inks originally manufactured to similar formulas may react so as to be virtually indistinguishable. From the foregoing, it follows, simply and unequivocally, that under ordinary circumstances no ink writing is definitely identifiable with the pen which produced it, or the ink writing on any other document, or independent ink writings on the same document.

It is entirely possible to classify or group a questioned ink writing as similar in all characteristics to a particular brand of ink, a particular ink supply, the ink in a particular pen, or the ink in other ink writings. This grouping is accomplished by microscopic, photographic, and chemical tests. Inks of the same class are not necessarily identical and they should not be so styled.

While it is entirely proper, if he so finds, for the document examiner to report that two inks are "similar in all observable characteristics," he should not leave the rest of the story untold. What is left unsaid at times may be more important than what is said. Wittingly or unwittingly, the examiner should not upgrade the primary finding that two inks are similar and of the same class of constituents to the secondary conclusion that such similar inks are necessarily identical. Identical they may be in a given case, but that finding lies properly with the trier of fact, from his evaluation of the circumstance that the two inks are of the same class plus the other facts and circumstances of the entire case.

Differences in inks present quite a dissimilar problem which is susceptible of clear-cut solution. Ink differences are demonstrable and they frequently provide direct and positive evidence that a document was not all written with the same ink, has been altered,

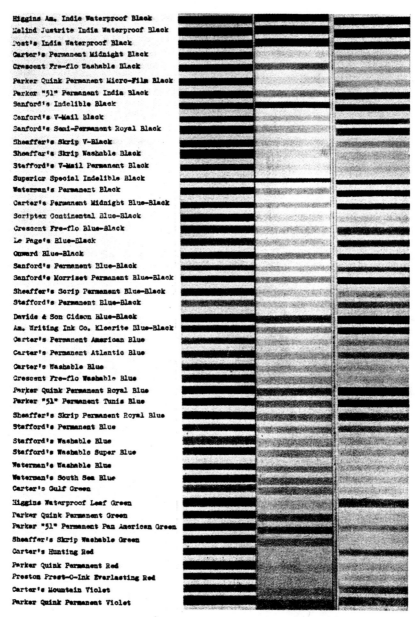

Figure 61. Forty-eight common inks. Compare unfiltered black and white rendition in Col. 1 with degrees of transparency to infrared shown in Col. 2. Col. 3 illustrates reactions to water (light blotting).

contains substitutions, was not all written at the same time and place, or was not written with the same pen and ink, as urged by its proponents. Writing inks may be differentiated by the same variety of methods which are used to classify similar inks—microscopic study of the ink line, color readings, color filters, ultraviolet and infrared viewing and photography, chemical reagents, paper chromatography, and paper electrophoresis. The latter three methods have the disadvantage of slightly altering the ink line at the testing points which may be objectionable if a single figure or letter is in issue.

Differences in comparative transparency to infrared radiation are themselves sufficient to differentiate many inks which appear similar in visible light. This is likewise true of many copying or "indelible" pencils.

The ascertainment of the age of ink in a writing line is frequently, in fact usually, indeterminate. The popular blue-black iron inks afford some basis for the estimation of age within very broad limits. When writing with a blue-black iron ink is first accomplished, the provisional blue color is quite evident. Thereafter the blue darkens, at first very rapidly and then very gradually through stages of an approximate violet, until it reaches a virtual black. Ultimately after many years, this iron ink reaches a brownish-black or a brown with suggestions of yellow tinges.

These progressive color changes are affected by a variety of conditions most of which cannot be hypothesized with any degree of certainty in a given case. Among these external conditions are: the purity or contamination of the ink mixture when written, the lightness or heaviness of the ink deposits in the writing line, the condition of the pen, the absorptive qualities of the writing paper, use or non-use of a blotter, handling, light, heat, air circulation, humidity, and the possible secondary application of foreign agents or forced "ageing."

A lightly written paragraph on cheap paper, lying exposed to daily sunlight atop a filing cabinet in a drafty storeroom would "age" much more rapidly than heavily written entries in a closed ledger reposed in a dark, cold, damp vault. A line of writing from a new bottle of newly manufactured ink would be less "aged" at the outset but would "age" more rapidly thereafter, than a line of writing from an old, unstoppered bottle of ink which had already been affected by oxidation before it left the bottle. It should be evident that the numerous unknowns which are part and parcel of virtually all ink writings restrict the examiner and thwart critical comparisons.

Writing in blue-black iron ink which is predominantly blue to the naked eye in daylight and is darkening rapidly may have been written as recently as seven or fourteen days. Writing in blue-black iron ink which is less blue to the naked eye but which is still predominantly blue under the microscope and is darkening perceptibly is relatively recent, probably within sixty to ninety days, and certainly within eighteen months. "Darkening" in these references means progression to dark blue-violet at normal room temperatures. A rapid darkening might be observable between color readings twenty-four to ninety-six hours apart. A perceptible darkening of a somewhat older ink might be observable between color readings taken thirty to one hundred and twenty days apart.

Some older studies have indicated rather guardedly that blue-black iron ink reaches its substantially neutral black, with perhaps a minimal violet tinge, in three to four years after which it remains black for many years. Studies of current blue-black iron inks indicate that many do not reach the substantially neutral black for a much longer period, perhaps five to six years. Writing in this class of ink which has turned brownish-black or brown is relatively old, perhaps twenty-five or a hundred years old. A blue-black iron ink signature disclosing pronounced darkening of the provisional blue, and purporting to have been written ten or twenty-five or a hundred years prior to its examination is obviously fraudulent. However, no reliable method has been devised to this time which permits critical estimations of the age of blue-black iron inks after the first violent changes in the provisional blue and before the appearance of the ultimate brown.

Questions relating to a series of entries or a series of writings sometimes provide comparative basis for age estimation, especially when the writings are on the same or similar paper and were subjected to common handling and storage. The examiner may be able to determine that of two or more writings alleged to be the same age, one is not as old as the remainder. Under the most favorable conditions, the estimation of the age of blue-black iron inks should be approached with the utmost conservatism, and with the knowledge that one who presumes to date a questioned document via ink tests should be prepared likewise to date similar documents which may be presented to him on cross-examination.

Carbon inks offer no basis for an estimation of age. The carbon black inks might be likened in this respect to pencil writings. Carbon is chemically inert and it does not undergo changes in the writing line which may be observed and catalogued.

Aniline dye inks, such as the popular washable blues, do not undergo progressive recordable changes and they too do not provide basis for an estimation of their age in the writing line. The impracticability of presently estimating the age of ball pen inks in the writing line has been commented upon previously in this chapter.

The inks with which typewriter ribbons are impregnated may be grouped or differentiated as to class of constituents. This grouping vs. differentiation is accomplished by comparative chemical tests of known and questioned typewriting lines. Typewriting ink differences may be vital to establish that what purports to be an integral part of a single typewriting operation was actually accomplished with a different typewriter ribbon than purportedly companion typewriting. As with carbon writing inks, no method has been developed to date by which the age of typewriting ink in the typewritten line may be accurately determined from the ink alone.

SYMPATHETIC INKS

Sympathetic or "invisible" inks are routinely encountered in many criminal and civil investigations. The criminal or subversive who dispatches secret messages through a suspected, possible, or actual censorship may at times pose complex problems because the variety of media which could conceivably be utilized is almost endless. However, most sympathetic inks or pseudo-inks react to light, heat, ultra-violet light, or iodine gases. The application of involved chemical or photographic techniques for those which do not so react is a job for the expert and his methods in this regard are not within the coverage of this present work. The field investigator may satisfactorily develop the majority of "invisible" inks through application of the following procedures:

(1) Examine the document in sunlight and under heavy reflected artificial illumination. Note particularly areas of the document which have no visible writing or printing. Do not neglect the reverse of the document. Are there depressions, indentations, or scratches which form a pattern? Does the document appear to have been damp or wet prior to your examination? Are the visible writing lines feathered or blurred, as from intersections with invisible writings? Does the document have a peculiar color or odor?

(2) Look through the document, first toward sunlight and thereafter to artificial lights. If a photographic printer or transmitted light box is available, examine the document by placing it on the outer glass and transmitting light through it.

(3) Examine the document under light rays directed to it at an oblique angle. Utilize sunlight by holding the document at eye level as you look toward the sunlight. Then use an artificial light source such as a "gooseneck" lamp or even a five-cell flashlight. Carefully scrutinize the document, while slowly changing the angle of illumination, beginning at approximately thirty-three degrees and increasing the angle gradually until the light rays are parallel to the document.

(4) Examine the document under filtered ultra-violet light.

(5) Heat the document in an oven provided with an opening for continuous viewing. An electric iron may be used but care is necessary. Paper chars easily. Whether an oven or an iron is used, those portions which will touch the document should be thoroughly cleaned to preclude contamination or sticking, and continued observation should be maintained to prevent scorching.

(6) Fume the document with iodine gases by activating iodine crystals. Devices commonly used for developing fingerprints on paper are among those suitable for this purpose.

The everyday use of sympathetic inks by laundries and dry cleaners deserves the consideration of the investigator. Articles of clothing which are germane to questions of identification should be carefully examined for both visible and invisible identifying markings. The sympathetic inks used by commercial laundries and dry cleaners are highly fluorescent and the identifying codes and markings of these agencies are usually of prominent size. Examination under ultra-violet light renders such markings readily discernible. The large scale use of fluorescent markings by laundries and dry cleaners provides a cover for secret writings and messages which should not be overlooked. What may appear to be innocent markings on a handkerchief or shirt, let us say, should be examined critically, when the circumstances warrant, to be certain that they are the routine commercial markings they purport to be.

The investigator himself frequently will find it necessary to mark or tag documents with invisible identification, in order to establish a continuity of evidential handling. There are available from commercial sources and suppliers of law enforcement equipment varieties of marking inks which fluoresce brightly when exposed to ultra violet light. Care in marking should be employed so that the paper or other surface is not perceptibly disturbed.

When a selection of color and marking surface is possible, it is preferable to mark documents or other items of neutral color and with non-reflecting surfaces. Glass rods, styli, or clean pens are among suitable marking instruments. Should fluorescent ink be unavailable commercially, a mixture of 19 parts benzene and one part anthracene or a mixture of 25 mg. anthracene and 10 ml. acetone to which is added 25 ml. of water will provide satisfactory results on most document surfaces. In an emergency field situation, one might utilize Murine, an eye cleansing solution which is available at any drug store and may be purchased without attracting attention. The writer, under emergent conditions, marked several small documents with Murine by using a wood shaving as the applicator. This incident occurred about seven years ago and the markings remain invisible under ordinary illumination and they are still strikingly fluorescent when exposed to ultra-violet light.

PAPER

The variety of legal proof which is adducible from the inherent and accidental properties of paper is almost endless. Obvious paper questions are presented when the genuineness of an entire document is challenged or a document is disputed as to its age. Less apparent paper issues exist which are relevant to the original source of a document, its manner of preparation, its course of handling, and its detailed history. Additionally, the properties of paper will frequently serve to establish the relationship of a document to a known document or other known evidence, and to demonstrate the association of a document with a known individual, time, place, or circumstance.

Ordinary writing paper may be broadly described as a thin sheet of matted vegetable fiber, usually wood pulp, plus a mineral filler, such as clay or titanium dioxide, and a sizing, such as rosin or starch, and synthetic dyestuffs. Fillers are used to improve color, opacity, surface regularity, and printability. Size is employed to make writing paper liquid resistant as contrasted with blotting paper which is unsized. Dyestuffs in writing paper provide quality of color, a variety of different colors, and uniformity within the same colors. These basic constituents together with the other physical components and properties injected by the manufacturing and distributing processes provide the ground lines for the examination and comparison of the inherent properties of writing paper.

Paper which comes into question may be only a single sheet or even a portion of a sheet. The testing of evidential paper usually must be confined to non-destructive testing, that is, tests which do not alter the evidential paper. Such tests include consideration of color, texture, gloss, finish, length, width, thickness, weight, formation, opacity, fiber composition, cutting markings, imperfections, and spectrophotometer examination. A single sheet of paper may be presumed to be somewhat less than completely representative of the manufacturing batch of which it is a part. For this reason, and because of the limited scope embodied in the tests indicated, they may not provide basis for a definite conclusion whether a questioned and known paper are of common origin in many cases.

When a number of sheets is available and when chemical and spectrographic testing may also be resorted to, additional data may be developed to assist in the classification of a paper's inherent properties. Through chemical and spectrographic tests, filler and size ingredients may be isolated, fiber composition may be analyzed, absorption may be rated, and inorganic materials may be determined.

It should be emphasized that a definite conclusion, however reached, as to the common origin of two papers only classifies such papers within the same manufacturing lot or group. The probative significance of such a conclusion should be accurately weighed in advance of a request for paper comparisons. All such requests should specifically state *whether* and to what degree and in what areas a given sheet of paper may be altered incident to examination and comparison.

Ordinarily, there are no accurately measurable characteristics through which it is possible to resolve definitely through paper analysis alone whether a given piece of paper is as old as it purports to be, say two years, five years, ten years, or fifty years old. It is not at all unusual, however, for the document examiner to establish the true age of a document, which is submitted to him as a "paper question," by other means, such as typewriting, printing or printed format, handwriting chronology of signers, foreign adherents to the document, indented writing outlines, writing and other off-sets, numbering machine impressions, rubber and metal stamped impressions, etc.

Watermarks in paper are highly useful in tracing the manufacturer and commercial distribution of watermarked paper. They frequently prove vital in establishing the authenticity or spuriousness of documents, legitimacy of which hinges irrevocably on the actual date of their execution.

Watermarks are registered by their owners with the United States Patent Office. These marks and the names and addresses of their owner-users may be found in *Paper Directory* and in *Lockwood's Directory of the Paper and Allied Trades.** The date

---

Paper Directory is published by Walden Sons and Mott., Inc., 93 Worth Street, New York, New York, and *Lockwood's Directory of the Paper and Allied Trades* is published by Bulkley, Dunton and Company, 295 Madison Avenue, New York, New York.

a watermark was first placed in use, and the dates of progressive changes in its design may be of controlling importance in dating an evidential document. These and other watermark data are ascertainable from the registered owners of watermarks.

The following case history offers a typical example of how watermark data alone can expose a fabricated document. The plaintiff in an important civil action alleged that the defendant breached his obligation of fidelity to his former employer, the plaintiff, by engaging in competition with the latter while still in his employ. At issue were substantial profits derived from the disputed competition. The defendant resisted the suit on several grounds including his contention that he had resigned and terminated his employment with the plaintiff prior to the time when he admittedly entered into competition against him. Such competition proceeded from a joint venture contract between the defendant and a third party which was executed on July 15, 1943. The defendant contended that he resigned from the plaintiff's employ on June 15, 1943, effective July 10, 1943, or five days prior to the joint venture contract.

In support of this allegation, the defendant brought into court a purported original carbon copy of a manuscript resignation. He testified that it was, in fact, a duplicate original made with the same impressions of the pen with which he prepared the original pen-written resignation. He testified further that he had mailed to the office of his then employer the original resignation and retained in his possession since June 15, 1943, the alleged carbon duplicate which he produced in evidence.

The purported resignation copy was submitted to Mr. George G. Swett, Examiner of Questioned Documents, Saint Louis, Missouri. Examiner Swett found that the copy bore the watermark "Cronicon U. S. A. Writing," which he determined to be owned and used by the Hammermill Paper Company, Erie, Pennsylvania. Through consultation with the excellent personnel and records of that manufacturer, Examiner Swett ascertained that paper watermarked "Cronicon" was produced by Hammermill from January 31, 1935, to April 1, 1951. The exclusive distributor was a national chain of retail merchandising establishments in the

WATERMARK NUMBER ONE

WATERMARK NUMBER TWO

QUESTIONED WATERMARK

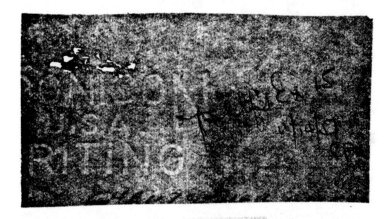

1 INCH

Figure 62. Questioned watermark contains characteristics of Watermark Number Two, incompatible with alleged date of questioned document.

lower price range. The first runs of this watermarked paper beginning January 31, 1935, bore a watermark design reading "Cronicon U. S. A." This watermark was utilized continuously until February 1, 1946, on *tablet* paper. The latter was converted to a higher grade *writing* paper in 1946. Incident to the augmentation of the paper stock, the watermark was changed to read "Cronicon U. S. A. Writing." The initial run of the latter paper and watermark was made on February 9, 1946. No further changes were made in the watermark until its discontinuance on April 1, 1951.

The alleged resignation copy which purported to have been written on and dated June 15, 1943, bore the watermark which was not produced until on and after February 9, 1946. More striking proof of spuriousness is difficult to envision. Apparently the proponent of the resignation "copy" was duly impressed. Following Examiner Swett's testimony, he recanted his perjurous allegations and acknowledged that he had fabricated the alleged original copy of the "resignation" some time during the year 1946. An interesting further commentary is that the defendant and proponent of this document did not concede the correctness of the paper's history as revealed through its watermark, until his counsel had made strenuous albeit unsuccessful objections to the testimony and demonstration of Examiner Swett.

The surface dimensions or thickness of an evidential document may affirm or disavow what is alleged by the presenter. A defendant, whose handwriting had been conclusively identified with a forged check endorsement, presented a receipt which purported to establish payment of the proceeds of the disputed check to the true payee thereof. The defendant acknowledged that she had endorsed and cashed the disputed check, although out of court she had previously denied the transaction with vigor. She further testified that she had mailed the proceeds of the check in the form of cash to the true payee, who had thereafter mailed her the receipt which she offered in support of her version of the transaction. The defendant also produced an envelope, duly postmarked, timely and geographically logical, which she asserted was the vehicle of transmission of the receipt.

Examination of the handwriting on the envelope confirmed

that it was in fact the writing of the true payee of the disputed
check. Analysis of the handwriting in the "receipt" disclosed
that it was a skillful imitation of the writing of the true payee.
But the most telling blow to the defendant's attempted exculpatory
statements was provided by the comparative dimensions of the
envelope and "receipt." The envelope measured three and one-
half inches by five and one-quarter inches. The "receipt" scaled
three and one-quarter inches by five and five-eighths inches. The
receipt had not been folded. This simple dimensional conflict in the
lengths of the envelope and "receipt" established conclusively in
itself that the "receipt" was not mailed or received in the envelope
as alleged by the defendant. As might have been anticipated, it
was subsequently ascertained that the envelope in question had
actually contained a letter from the payee to the defendant inquiring whether the latter had forwarded the very check in dispute.

In another case, a registered envelope was submitted which
had allegedly been rifled in transit of a large amount of currency.
Examination was conducted to determine whether the envelope
had been surreptitiously opened and resealed and, if so, whether
the point of rifling was indicated by physical irregularities of the
envelope. The envelope measured four and one-eighth inches by
nine and one-half inches. When mailed, it was said to have contained a brief communication of transmittal, and some twenty
items of currency which were listed in the handwriting of the
mailer on a piece of heavy cardboard, to which the currency was
attached. The cardboard scaled three and one-eighth inches by
nine and one-quarter inches. The envelope, piece of cardboard,
and communication were reported by the addressee as having been
received in his office without the related currency. The sender
alleged rifling in transit and alluded to the suspicious appearance of
two of the three sealing flaps of the envelope.

Laboratory examination of the envelope disclosed paper fiber
disturbances, characteristic of opening and resealing, in the sealing
flap areas. Secondary application of mucilage was evident also.
Of particular note was the further circumstance that the "added"
mucilage, obviously applied in the resealing operation, had caused
the inside portions of the envelope to adhere significantly about

Figure 63. Right panel reveals stamped impression on envelope, subsequent to opening and resealing. Compare with impression on left, recorded prior to opening and resealing.

one inch from the resealed end of the envelope. It followed that, after the resealing, only eight and one-half inches rather than the original nine and one-half inches were available to accommodate the piece of cardboard et al. Clearly one cannot inclose an unfolded nine and one-quarter inch piece of cardboard in an eight and one-half inch space. The cardboard was necessarily received by the addressee *before* the envelope was resealed and the rifling occurred *after* delivery.

In a recent case, the matching serrations of two "torn" pieces of paper established conclusively that they were part of one initial sheet, much to the amazement of the holders of the respective pieces who had professed no relationship or connection one with the other. An address, scribbled on a piece of paper hurriedly torn from a brown shopping bag, was definitely associated with the bag through the serrated edges of each section and proved to be the undoing of the "bag holder," a chief check thief and the "address holder," one of his subordinates specializing in uttering and passing stolen checks.

Carbon paper can prove to be the vital evidential link when multiple copies of key documents are known or suspected. In a notorious poison pen case, various victims had received identical carbon copies of numerous typewritten letters. An analysis of the mailing dates and format of certain of these multiple letters revealed that the poison pen prepared groups of copies at one time and thereafter mailed them a few at a time from her supply.

When the poison pen was apprehended, a careful search of her residence disclosed a cache of carbon paper and carbon copies of letters which she, displaying her guilt, attempted to conceal. The carbon copies were found to be identical with incriminating letters theretofore typewritten and mailed by the poison pen. Examination of the carbon paper via transmitted light, including carbon paper which was virtually "worn out" in its center sections, disclosed identical portions of incriminating typewritten messages in the marginal areas of the carbon paper.

In a major bookie raid, one of the defendants was seized in his living quarters as he was in the act of hiding a sheet headed "Canasta Points." This sheet listed various names and amounts of the usual bookie accounting type. The defendant insisted that this list was his personal method of maintaining his "canasta" records and he protested an utter lack of knowledge concerning an adjacent bookie headquarters with its betting paraphernalia and multitudinous telephones.

In the betting headquarters, an alert internal revenue agent-police team located a number of blank pads of paper with interleaved carbon sheets which seemed to correspond with the "Canasta Points" sheet of the self-styled canasta enthusiast who had "never even been in that room" and asserted "how would I know what was going on there?" On laboratory examination, one of the carbon sheets recovered from the betting headquarters was determined to be an identical carbon original of the names and other listings on the "Canasta Points" sheet. The identity of the original sheet and its carbon counterpart was demonstrated at the trial of the defendant by juxtaposing an enlarged photograph of the original "Canasta Points" sheet and an infrared projection in reverse of the impressions on the wax side of the carbon paper. Such

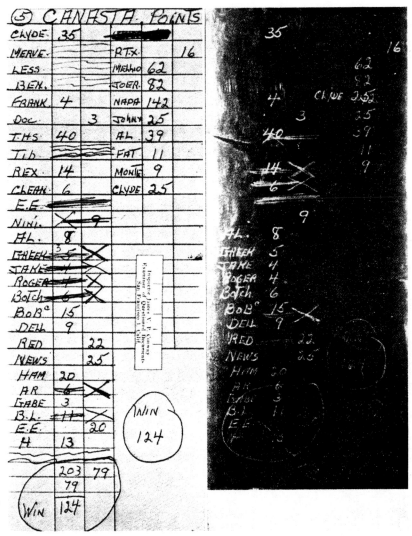

Figure 64. Left section illustrates suspected bookie sheet recovered incident to residence arrest. Right section shows infrared print of carbon paper recovered from bookie headquarters.

forceful proof of association between the defendant and the incriminating place and records was not rebutted and it serves to point up the value of proof via documentary demonstration.

A striking evidential association of another variety was developed in a second major poison pen investigation. The poison pen periodically consigned pages of her rather voluminous diary to her long suffering trash can. Some thirty or forty of these handwritten pages were recovered by a thinking, diligent investigator. Analysis of these pages revealed the poison pen intermittently confided to her diary the identical *thoughts* which she messaged anonymously to the victims of her vicious letter-writing activities.

Whether prospective and actual copies are physical carbons or other manner of duplicate originals, they should be assiduously sought by the investigator as prime and irrefutable linkage between their author and incriminating original evidential documents.

Writing impression duplicates on "second sheets" are cogent witnesses to otherwise unwitnessed acts. A potent example of this was developed in a recent major forgery investigation. A series of bank statements and related canceled checks of the depositors were stolen in transit to the respective depositor-addressees. These thefts were followed by the negotiation of a flood of forged checks drawn against the bank accounts of the depositors. The forgeries were skillful simulations of the writing of the various depositors. These forgeries were of a caliber which would deceive even the wariest of bank bookkeepers and a few deceived the depositors themselves, who were not immediately cognizant that the forgeries were being debited against their bank accounts. Patently, the forger was making efficient use of the canceled checks stolen with the bank statements as the models from which to perfect the simulated forgeries.

Several checks were forged against the account of one of the victims in amounts which included "Forty Three" and "Seventy Eight" dollars and bearing the date "March 9." In the home of a prime suspect an alert investigator noted what appeared to be indentations or depressions on the outer page of a writing tablet. Laboratory examination of this page by oblique illumination disclosed numerous impressed drawings of the name of the particular victim. Other impressions were developed to read "March 9," "Forty Three" and "Seventy Eight." All of these impressions

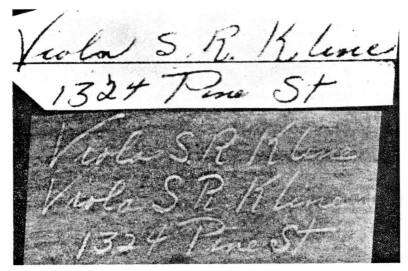

Figure 65. Indented writings in lower section provide positive link to forged endorsement above.

were strikingly imitative of the genuine writing of the depositor-victim. These writing impressions constituted no less than proof positive that the admitted owner of the tablet had had in her possession the stolen canceled checks from which she had practiced simulating the form of the depositor's handwriting in the precise particulars which thereafter appeared on forged checks. One cannot cross-examine or explain away such intimate duplicate originals of incriminating documents. The tablet owner ultimately executed a complete confession.

Blotting paper also should not be overlooked. Blotters record in mirror image a duplicate outline of original "blotted" writings. They can be examined readily by studying their reflections in a small hand mirror.

The time and effort required for this and similar avenues of inquiry are trivial. The results may be highly significant. The forger and the anonymous deceiver who blot their vicious handiwork create a silent witness in the blotter. True it may be destroyed or become obliterated before it is called upon to testify. But the diligent inquirer for the truth concerning evidential documents should leave no paper unturned in his search.

MISCELLANEOUS DOCUMENT PROBLEMS

OBLITERATIONS, ERASURES, ALTERATIONS, MARKINGS

Evidential documents are routinely encountered whose content has been suppressed, augmented, or altered. In the course of both legitimate and fraudulent handling, documents are subjected to physical, mechanical, and chemical agents which may either change or obstruct their true messages, or make important record in their true history.

The application of viewing and photographic techniques is first in order in these cases and handling of the document should be kept to the minimum. *Non-destructive testing is ever the prime objective.* Chemical techniques, while frequently applicable and necessary, are distinctly for secondary consideration as they alter a document, however minutely, and in a sense involve the very issue which is the basic problem in many of these matters.

Daily the check investigator is confronted with check endorsements which have been seriously obscured by stamped impressions, accumulated as the checks wended their way through commercial establishments, banks, clearing houses, and accounting offices. These overriding impressions may be red, green, blue, purple, or black and the underlying endorsements may be written with any of the numerous varieties of pencils, fluid, and ballpen inks. The paper stock of the checks also may be of virtually any hue.

A large percentage of these overstampings may be neutralized by appropriate color filters. Filters are used both for viewing and photography. A red filter will eliminate or subdue a red stamped impression, a blue filter will reduce or eliminate a blue stamped impression, a green filter will neutralize a green impression, and so forth. Infrared viewing and photography are helpful in some complicated instances when an endorsement has been covered up by a maze of overstamped impressions perhaps involving two or more colors.

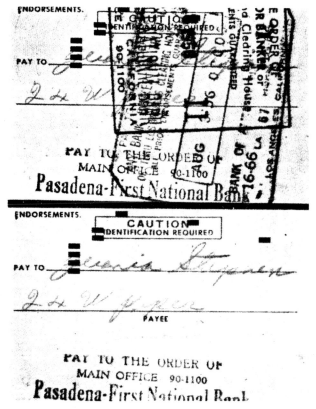

Figure 66. Endorsement obscured by bankstamps restored to legibility by filter photography.

Black and deep purple impressions present difficulties, especially if an ink endorsement underneath was written with a pale synthetic dye ink. It must be recognized also that it is not possible through color filtration to separate a written endorsement from a stamped impression if both are substantially the same color. Nevertheless, the experienced document examiner enjoys a high percentage of success in problems of this nature and he should be consulted for special photographic and viewing techniques, including infrared, ultra-violet, and X ray as applicable.

The check investigator should not be subservient to these overriding impressions which impede his examination of disputed writings, but should undertake to use routine filter techniques himself in the less complicated problems and seek specialized assistance when his own efforts are not productive. A simple and economical set of color filters for routine field examinations may be made from colored plastic sheets, available from the stationers or a plastic supply house. Several shades of red, blue, green, yellow, and amber can be obtained and individual sheets cut to about three by five inches. Sets of the various colors can then be bound at one end for ready usage. For viewing, the plastic filter sheet is interposed between the eye and the overstamped endorsement.

Occasionally, printing such as that in the return address of an envelope, or typewriting is intentionally obscured with writing ink or other obliterating strokes in order to impede recognition. The synthetic dye inks and many of the iron base inks are sufficiently transparent to infrared radiation so that photography of the printing or typewriting "through" such inks is possible. Carbon obliterating strokes are not amenable to the infrared technique. Carbon writing inks can frequently be dissolved and blotted off sufficiently to render readable printing or typewriting which is underneath.

In one case, a canvas money bag was recovered from the automobile of a suspect in a daring $50,000 robbery. The area of the bag which normally contained the identifying number was saturated with a heavy blue-black ink which entirely obliterated all traces of identifying markings. The saturation was so dense that it rendered opaque the affected area of the bag in what seemed to have been an obvious effort to prevent identification of the bag. Despite the opacity of the near black saturation to transmitted light, it proved relatively transparent to infrared radiation. The accompanying illustrations show the valueless bag as it appeared under visible illumination, as contrasted with the vital evidential link provided by the infrared photograph which revealed the obliterated number to be "P.O.10425." The latter was identified with the robbery loot and proved essential in the conviction of the number-conscious hoodlum.

In another case during World War II, the S. S. Henry Bergh ran aground off The Farrallones. At the hearing to evaluate the

OBLITERATED NUMBER ON CANVAS

CONTRAST FILTER—PROCESS PANCROMATIC FILM

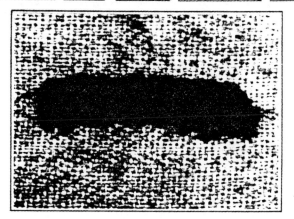

CORNING FILTER NO. 254—INFRARED FILM

Figure 67.

events leading up to the grounding and to assess responsibility, it became vital to ascertain the entries in the pertinent page of the Engine Room Bell Book. The latter had been written in pencil and incident to the ship's damage following the grounding, the entries in issue had been completely obscured by an agglomeration of oily sludge. The page was bathed in xylene which effec-

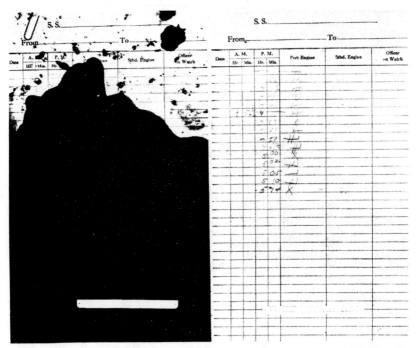

Figure 68. Record obliterated by oily sludge restored to legibility by xylene bath.

tively reduced the obliterating oil and rendered fully visible every detail of the original entries. The accompanying illustrations reflect how a useless page withholding the needed information was transformed by the proper technique to tell its authentic story.

It will be evident that the method of deciphering obliterated writings must be varied according to the constituents of the original writing and the composition and manner of its obliteration. Similarly, the successful restoration of erased writings hinges on the composition of the original writing media and the manner by which the writings were erased.

Iron base inks which have been chemically "erased" by commercial ink eradicator can usually be developed through ultra-violet radiation, chemical fuming, or chemical staining via aerosol or direct application. Difficulty is encountered when subsequent overwriting lies in the same paths or pen-tracks as the erased writing. Good results may be expected in restorative efforts involving iron base inks which have been subjected to chemical eradication provided appreciable disturbance to the paper in the affected area is not also present.

Conversely, synthetic dye inks which have been chemically eradicated or washed rarely respond to development attempts. Occasionally, the pen will have produced sufficient impressions in the paper to permit decipherment by oblique light examination.

Ink and pencil writing which has been subjected to abrasion by a rubber eraser, sandpaper, a knife, or other abrasive agent may be said to be susceptible to restoration in reverse proportion to the thoroughness injected into the eradication efforts. Heavy abrasion which has eliminated all visible traces of the original writing and seriously disturbed the paper fibers in the affected area usually defies restorative efforts.

None should expect the impossible when it is desired to decipher an erased writing. Neither should he pessimistically neglect restorative efforts because they are not successful in all cases. The investigator should insure that all problems involving evidential erasures are submitted to a qualified document examiner and he should resist unskilled restorative dabbling by the inexperienced, which not only may be unsuccessful but which may so damage the affected area as to eliminate completely any possibility of ultimate restoration.

The submitter of all document problems involving erasures and obliterations should specifically advise the document examiner at the time of submission whether the document may be subjected to chemical treatment, if non-destructive testing proves unsuccessful.

The presence of alterations and changes in a document's content escapes notice more frequently than is realized even by those who are concerned in the use of documents as evidence and proof. Many astute investigators and attorneys now routinely submit important documents to the document examiner for diagnosis in the manner of the patient who has an annual medical examination even when he believes he is in good physical condition. As with the patient, it is frequently determined through competent diagnosis that an important key document is not all that it purports to be, not all that its proponents say it is.

Every mark, every hole, every fold, every crease on a piece of paper testifies either pro or contra the origin and the history claimed for that document. Such minutiae proved to be irresistibly persuasive at the 1951 trial of a rather formidable defendant on the charge of using the United States Mails in a scheme to defraud. The defendant's activities involved the mailing of numerous letters over a four or five year period, and particularly a monthly mimeographed publication. The government established in its case that this publication consistently urged the purchase of allegedly valuable timberland to which the purchasers would receive unimpeachable title and likely profits. A series of victims testified that, relying on these representations respecting clear titles and probable profits, they had invested large sums and had received neither land nor profits.

While testifying in his own behalf, the defendant offered in evidence a mass of copies of his monthly publication, including what purported to be a five page issue of October 10, 1946. Thereafter, his counsel posed questions resulting in direct references to this particular issue. The first four pages of such document reiterated the misrepresentations charged to the defendant by the government. The fifth page of this document placed limitations on these statements, rendering them innocuous. Immediately the fifth page became vital to the basic issue of good faith versus fraud, "Send money—full satisfaction guaranteed" versus "Buy at your own risk." The trial's outcome hinged on the authenticity or otherwise of the fifth page.

The able prosecutor and the astute trial judge inquired as to the preparation and history of the defendant's five-page offering in a manner which was a model of thoroughness and objectivity. The prosecutor made no premature attack but developed every detail of the document's alleged origin and handling. The court indulged no prejudgment or partisanship but calmly and fairly insisted that all of the document's facets should be spread fully on the record. The approach of the prosecutor and judge was that if the document was in fact a five page issue of October 10, 1946, as urged by its proponent, the defendant, he should be required to elucidate fully so that the document's physical properties and condition might be weighed in the light of his urgings.

Under this skilled and perceptive approach, the defendant testified that: (a) the stencils for each of the document's five pages were prepared on the same typewriter, at the same time and place, in his presence (b) the five pages were mimeographed concurrently and assembled immediately thereafter (c) the five page assembly was stapled in the upper left hand corner as one document, copies were folded and mailed, and the document offered in evidence, after folding, had been placed in his files and had remained therein under his control from 1946 until 1951 when he produced it in court.

Analysis of the questioned document, at the direction of the court, disclosed that every representation made for it was demonstrably false: (1) The stencils for the first four pages were prepared while the typewriter was in stencil position while the stencil for page five was prepared while the typewriter was in ribbon position. (2) The paper stock of the first four pages was similar while the paper stock of the fifth page was different in weight and quality. (3) The typeface designs agreed throughout the five pages; however, letter "h" which appeared 170 times on the first four pages disclosed no damage. This letter which appeared 75 times on page five disclosed a broken serif on that page. A later issue dated October 26, 1946, disclosed letter "h" to be undamaged with all serifs intact. (4) The staple was brittle and tarnished from oxidation with the distinct exception of gleaming new breaks in each shoulder, which showed clearly that it had been pried open recently by hand and bent back into closed position. (5) Page four revealed *four holes* from the staple, the customary two holes from the prongs of the staple plus two inner terminal holes resulting from crimping in of the prong ends by the stapling machine, while page five revealed only the customary *two holes*. (6) Pages four to one revealed progressively decreasing depressions on their reverse sides from the pressure of the staple when these pages were folded, whereas page five revealed no such depression on its reverse. (7) The folds on pages one through four registered precisely as a unit, while the folds on page five diverged and were of different depth. (8) Pages one through three showed some migration on their reverses from opposing pages, whereas the reverse of page four showed no such off-set.

Can one possibly explain how he might punch holes through the reverse of a page four without also causing holes in page five if it were really there? Can one possibly explain how indentations could be made on the reverses of pages four through one without also causing indentations on page five if it were really there? Can one possibly explain how letter "h" was undamaged for four pages, became damaged for the fifth page, and then reverted to an undamaged condition sixteen days later on a subsequent three page document?

The would-be timber baron was convicted of mail fraud and thereafter convicted for perjury respecting his statements under oath about the preparation and history of the exculpatory fifth page. He did not testify at his perjury trial, but he did appeal his conviction on the principal grounds that the expert evidence respecting the fabricated fifth page was circumstantial and, therefore, less than the "direct and positive evidence of falsity of the defendant's sworn testimony" necessary to convict in perjury cases. The appellate court in upholding the conviction* restated its previous rule, which is of interest, "In the Federal cases in which documents have been used to establish perjury, the documents have, for practical purposes, directly established the falsity of the statement under oath." The latter is reported in 180 F 2d 781, CCA 9, Radomsky v. United States.

It is important to consider that in this trial and in many similar investigative and trial situations, the physical aspects of

---

*Barker v. United States, 9th C.C.A., #13181, 8-21-52.

the disputed document would lose much of and perhaps all of their significance if its proponent is not caused to take a definite position concerning all details of the document's preparation and history. The presenter of a document, be it authentic or spurious, should be timely caused to supply specific yardsticks by which his offering may be later weighed and measured.

CROSS-MARKS

Occasionally, disputes arise concerning documents alleged to have been executed by individuals who are unable to write and who sign by cross-mark. While one need not expect to find conclusive individuality in every cross-mark, it is true that many such markings are highly personalized. When a series of such marks is in question, sufficient individuality may be adducible to identify authentic marks and to exclude forgeries. Failing eyesight, physical infirmity, and general writing incapacity are frequently reflected in authentic marks which are not found in the fabrications of the forger. The reverse may also be true.

A case in point concerned three checks totaling over fifteen thousand dollars alleged to have been endorsed in mark by a wealthy old gentleman in his eighties. The latter died shortly after the checks were negotiated and it was developed that the proceeds were not in his possession at the time of death. A group of admittedly authentic and contemporaneous cross-marks was available for comparison with the three cross-marks in dispute.

The accompanying illustration tells the truth of this matter. Clearly, the tremulous old gentleman did not in the three separate questioned cross-marks cast aside his infirmities and at the same time change the direction of the strokes making up his cross-mark. The court hearing the issues did not have any difficulty in distinguishing the inconsistencies of the questioned cross-marks and rendered a verdict against their proponent. The latter elected not to appeal the verdict.

Cross-marks also may become vital in election disputes involving manually marked ballots. An important union strike vote became a national incident about fifteen years ago, largely because of the findings of document experts who were retained to

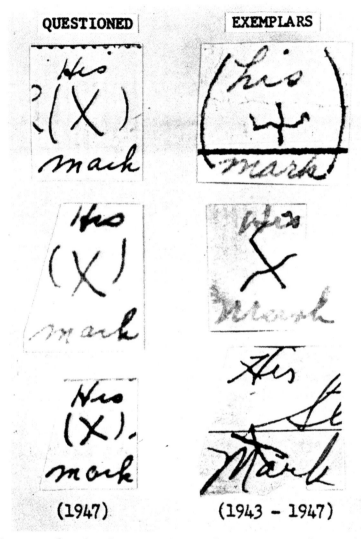

Figure 69. Questioned cross marks revealing spuriousness by superior pen control than demonstrated in exemplars.

examine the ballots. Their examinations disclosed large groups of ballots marked with a sameness which could only indicate fraud. In addition, hundreds of the ballots disclosed indentations which were obviously the result of mass marking by a few ballot stuffers.

In these cases, a careful study of the correct balloting procedure and the prescribed handling of the ballots, prior and subsequent to their marking, is prerequisite to examination of questioned ballots. Cutting, marking, smearing, folding, mark designs, marking instruments, indentations, application or adherence of foreign agents—all should be interpreted in the light of the manner in which the ballots should have been processed by the legitimate voter and thereafter by legitimate election officials.

A clear conflict between the physical properties of the voted ballot, and the proper balloting procedures, such as cross-mark indentations on one ballot from the mass marking of other ballots, is conclusive evidence of fraud which is easily demonstrated.

CHARRED AND WATERSOAKED DOCUMENTS

Charred and watersoaked documents are of prime interest to the arson and accident investigator, and they may arise in any type of criminal or civil inquiry. This class of evidential documents is vital to the registered owners of burned securities and to corporations and public agencies which must adjudicate claims bearing on obligations and securities which have been partially destroyed by fire or water. Insurance policies, wills, checks, notes, lease agreements, contracts, currency, bonds, stock certificates—the list of documents which may be accidentally or deliberately attacked by fire and water is as endless as the uses to which documents are put, and the prospective victims omit no man.

Burned papers which have been reduced to ashes are not decipherable. Necessity promotes progress and the incendiary attacks of World War II with their large scale destruction spurred the improvement of techniques for processing burned documents. However, there is no method which will restore the pulverized ashes of documents to their previously whole and readable state.

Charred documents, although completely blackened and carbonized, are usually amenable to decipherment when they have not been reduced to unmanageable small fragments. Results are contingent also on the type of original writing and the composition of the original paper. For example, the printed and typewritten portions of a charred stock certificate or the signature thereon in an iron base ink will respond to laboratory treatment more readily than the burned memorandum written in aniline ink on a commercial grade memo pad.

The foremost consideration which must be directed to charred documents is care in their handling. The laboratory specialist can accomplish nothing with ashes or minute carbon fragments. Each recovered item must be handled delicately to preserve it in the precise state of its initial recovery. Burned papers recovered in their pre-burning repository, for example a strong box, a steel filing cabinet, a small safe, a vault drawer, or a metal trunk should be transported to the document examiner, without being removed from such repository and without being handled therein. Movement within the repository should be prevented by light cushioning, using cotton or a similar soft protective material.

Efforts should never be made by the untrained to separate the individual units of bunches or groups of charred documents. All phases of treating, packing, and handling charred documents must be carried on under an absolute minimum of air circulation. Any document which has been subjected to intense heat hangs to potential decipherment and readability by a tenuous thread. A carelessly opened window, a thoughtlessly slammed door, or even an unguarded sneeze can tear asunder the fragile carbonized remnants of important documents.

Situations arise, especially in criminal investigations, when burned or partially burned documents, or a single document, are found in a stove, fireplace, a waste basket or other improvised incinerator, hastily contrived by the departing criminal, intent on destroying incriminating evidence. Special equipment may be unavailable to the investigator on the scene who must act promptly.

A piece of stiff cardboard, a section of glass, a cakeplate, or a dustpan may be pressed into service. Such an implement should be gently slipped underneath the charred papers. Thereafter, bearing the recovered papers, it should be placed into any box which can be covered. A hosiery, candy, writing paper, or even an open-end cereal box has been used successfully under emergent conditions. The box should be large enough to accommodate the papers and their supporting implement without disturbing the former in any way. If cotton or other soft cushioning material is unavailable, a hand towel may be used by suspending it immediately above the recovered papers, while they are carefully transported to the document examiner's laboratory.

Field investigations frequently require inventiveness and ingenuity because of unusual conditions and limitations both of time and facilities. The important responsibility for the investigator is to insure that reasonable, common sense methods of recovery and transportation are adopted to guarantee that charred documents are not separated, broken, crushed, pulverized, or otherwise altered in their course from initial recovery to the document examiner's laboratory for restorative treatment.

Watersoaked documents not infrequently are companion to charred documents, both being residual to a fire. Especially in industrial fires, records such as inventories, accounting data, research reports, and personnel records may be relatively unaffected by fire but receive extensive water damage. Drownings, shipwrecks, air crashes, and just plain negligence produce a quota of documents which have been rendered visually illegible by water. Some of these papers, when recovered, are adhered together after lengthy periods of immersion.

There is no magical formula which will restore all watersoaked documents to full and complete legibility. Success is met frequently, however, and it is proportionate to the constituents of the original writing agents. Printing, typewriting, pencil writing, and most ball pen writing are affected very little by water. Accordingly, documents whose original word content was accomplished by one or more of these writing media can be deciphered, provided the parent paper has not been seriously damaged. Iron base inks such as the popular blue-blacks are partially affected by water. The residual deposits, after immersion in water, of iron base inks are usually sufficient to permit decipherment of original writings, again assuming that the parent paper has not been seriously affected. Washable dye inks such as the popular blues are exactly what their names implies. They are wholly affected by water. Unless the pen with which they were applied made appreciable furrows or indentations in the paper, and unless the latter were not neutralized by the water action, writing accomplished with one of the washable dye inks cannot be restored to legibility after water soaking.

Watersoaked documents may be torn, crumpled, or otherwise additionally damaged, by accident or design. Extreme situations are encountered when an apparently incriminating document is extricated in a sodden and masticated state from the busy jaws of a desperate criminal. Many seemingly hopeless situations produce highly demonstrable evidence.

Several years ago a rather glib young man was in the act of negotiating a postal money order, ostensibly issued for eighty-eight dollars, when a policeman entered the particular place of business. The young man seemed to experience, suddenly and concurrently with the officer's arrival, an acute consciousness of guilt accompanied by hunger pangs. He departed posthaste, all the while munching animatedly on the money order which he had placed into his mouth. The policeman joined in hot pursuit and after a chase of about three blocks, he collared the young man with some definiteness, causing him to disgorge what was now a whitish ball of seemingly hopelessly entwined paper fibers. The sprinter of the first part averred that he was in a hurry to catch a streetcar and he could not understand why anyone should question his taste for paper, or for that matter, for blue postal money orders.

When referred for examination, the ball of paper had been permitted to dry for several days. It was quite brittle and decipherment seemed unlikely. Using stainless steel tweezers, the ball was carefully unwound onto glass slides. Drops of glycerin solution similar to that used to flatten photographic prints were applied progressively in order to soften the paper mass and permit separation of the intertwined fibers. The comingled strands were carefully scrutinized with about 10X magnification, to permit peeling in the proper direction and to avoid incipient tearing. Ultimately, over eighty-five percent of the postal money order was reassembled, including the complete serial numbers and data as to place and date of issuance.

Through reference to the parent records so identified, it was ascertained that this money order had in fact been issued for eight dollars. Handwriting comparisons of the application for the money order in the lower amount revealed that all the particulars of application were written by the erstwhile sprinter and paper chewer. The amount areas of the restored money order were chemically fumed (potassium thiocyanate crystals acidified with hydrochloric acid) and the words "Eighty-Eight" as well as the figures "88" were rendered legible and corresponded with the handwriting habits of the purchaser. This demonstrable evidence, coupled with the attempt of the forger to destroy the altered money order and to flee from the scene, were conclusive factors in his conviction for altering and uttering the instrument which he had vainly sought to silence.

Whatever the size, shape, or condition of a charred, water-soaked, or otherwise damaged document which is important to reveal the truth of a civil or criminal issue, the investigator will be on firm ground if he will: (a) preserve the document in the precise condition in which it is recovered, and (b) promptly consult a qualified document examiner to survey the available avenues of restoration and decipherment. Documents of the class under discussion frequently require a combination of visual, photographic, physical, and chemical techniques. Every problem is not soluble. Many are. And no problem is soluble unless the evidential documents are carefully preserved and presented to qualified personnel timely for appraisal.

LEFT-HAND WRITING

It is estimated that from perhaps three to five per cent of mature writers normally write with the left hand. The question is frequently posed whether the document examiner can detect left-hand writing. The correct answer is "yes and no."

Certainly, no qualified examiner would contend that he could invariably distinguish right-hand writing from left-hand writing on the basis of the internal indications of a writing alone. There are peculiarities of execution which the examiner recognizes as usually characteristic of left-hand writing. Most naturally left-handed writers cross their letter "t" from right to left. These writers inject

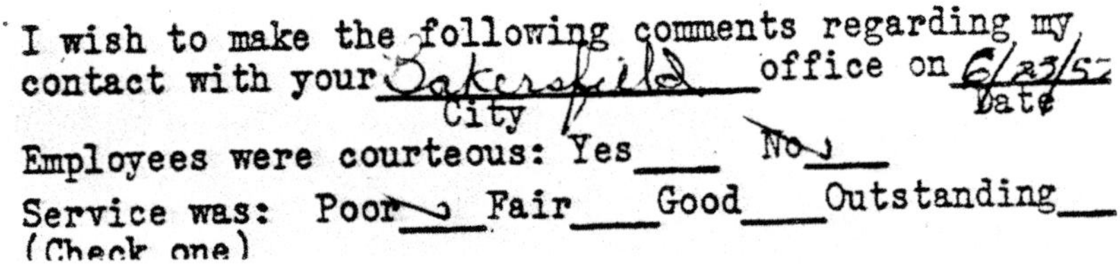

```
 I wish to make the following comments regarding my
 contact with your  Bakersfield      office on 6/23/5_
                    City                           Date
 Employees were courteous: Yes____ No___
 Service was:  Poor__ Fair___ Good___ Outstanding___
 (Check one)
```

Figure 70. Check marks by left-handed writer.

similar right-to-left movement in "i" dots and punctuation mark-ings in many instances. The "left-hand" direction of "t" crossings, "i" dots, periods and commas is usually quite evident to the experi-enced examiner, when any considerable quantity of writing is involved, and especially when a fountain pen has been used.

The left-hand writer who writes from above the writing line may reveal his contortions of movement by a pattern of smudges or smears as his hand progresses across the previously written page. Occasionally, accidental ink smears of a finger or fingers also will disclose the non-writing member and successively, therefore, the active writing hand.

The naturally right-handed writer who resorts to his left hand under abnormal writing conditions such as injury or decep-tion, may adopt awkward counter-clockwise ovals and circles, as in "a," "o," "d," "g," "A," and "O." Clumsy left-hand uncertainty may be apparent at the turns and upstrokes of the upper and lower loop letters, "b," "f," "g," "h," "j," "k," "l," "p," "q," "y," and "z." Irregularities of letter proportion and adherence to the writing line may be evident. This class of writer who abnormally writes with his left hand may inject gyrations of slant and movement which disclose the difficulty experienced by his hand and eyes as they seek to adjust to an unfamiliar writing coordination. Rele-vant considerations would obtain in respect to the naturally left-handed writer who under abnormal writing conditions, changes to his right hand.

It will suffice to understand that one should be able to dem-onstrate well a hypothesis of left-hand execution before he com-mits himself to that appraisal of a questioned writing.

Incident to the procurement of request exemplars, investigators not infrequently will be faced with deceptive efforts by suspects being interviewed who allege "I'm left-handed. I can't write with my right hand," or perhaps vice versa. It is advisable to observe closely these subjects to ascertain whether they grasp the writing instrument familiarly with the asserted writing member. Additionally, these subjects should be scrutinized for any evidences of incoordination between eye position and writing efforts, and any lack of facility in adjusting the writing paper to the alleged writing hand. Many subjects, while bent on deception, will unconsciously pick up the writing instrument with their normal writing hand and thereafter shift the instrument to their untrained hand. Similarly, they will from habit place the writing paper in its usual writing position from which it must be readjusted to conform to their awkward writing member. Unnatural head

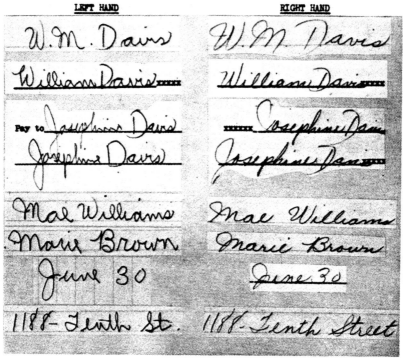

Figure 71. Ambidextrous writer, 25 years of age, high school education.

movements frequently ensue until the writer strikes an eye position which is consistent with his "new" writing hand.

Proof positive of deception of this sort is provided by exemplars prepared by the subject in the regular course of business. Such exemplars should be sought assiduously in every case wherein any doubt exists as to the natural writing hand of suspected writers. The systematic investigator who through intelligent observation and adequate regular-course-of-business exemplars gives the lie to clumsy, awkward-hand "exemplars" becomes in sound position to expose further lies on the part of deceptive subjects.

A contrasting problem is encountered in situations wherein the questioned handwriting was executed with the left or awkward writing hand, and the only available exemplars were written with the writer's right or normal writing hand. While God endowed man with two hands, He provided him with but a single mental system. The deceiver who resorts to his untrained writing hand incident to fraud, extortion, or other vicious anonymity, must rely on the same intellect, training, and experience which will guide his usual writing member. As a consequence, there is a common origin but a different implementation which must be surmounted by the individual who attempts to camouflage his identity by writing with his left or untrained writing hand.

Certainly some writers can and do succeed in so obscuring their writing habits that definite identifications are precluded. Success at deception via the left or awkward hand is more apt to be achieved when the quantity of questioned writing is limited. Conversely, this author has observed many cases wherein left or awkward-hand writings were effectively identified through right or normal-hand exemplars. Success or failure in these endeavors is proportionate to the capability of the writer, and the quality and quantity of the writings which are in issue.

THE DOCUMENT EXAMINER

The practised examination of questioned documents, like many other applied sciences we take for granted today, is the obvious and necessary outgrowth of the vastly increased incidence of the instruments with which it concerns itself. Unlike many of its companion sciences of especial interest to the field of law enforcement, the examination of questioned documents was forced to prove itself through a difficult and, in many respects, unreasonable early existence. The brands of its beginnings and early struggles illuminate somewhat the present estate and future paths of the scientific examination of evidential documents and the subject will be touched upon briefly for that reason.

Surrounded as we are today by a relatively high and ever improving standard of literacy, it is not too readily recalled by all those who should do so occasionally, that such was not always our lot. In the colonial era and in the early days of this great Republic, many contracts and formal acts of high import were bound by a handshake, or a simple verbal pronouncement. When these acts were challenged and became the subjects of court contests, not infrequently they were decided by some jurors, and even an occasional judge, who could read and write but little, if at all.

Our dedicated forefathers were smiled on by Providence and their efforts were rewarded, gradually by some criteria and incredibly rapidly by others, with the high standard of literacy by which we are now blessed. Our increased educational opportunities, our ever extending population, our industrial expansion, the commercial, governmental, and social refinements concomitant to the better life in the United States, and the development of the written word leading to almost a mania for documentation have produced documents, good and bad, much faster than first the law, and later the law enforcement profession, became equipped to adjudge their authenticity and spuriousness.

Several weighty and almost insurmountable obstructions to the proof of the truth respecting disputed documents were inherited from old English law. Chief of these were the holdings that (a) writings were inadmissible as standards of comparison to prove or disprove genuineness or authorship, unless they happened to be in evidence priorly for some other purpose and (b) the reasons for the conclusion of the document expert, then usually referred to simply as a handwriting expert, were objectionable and inadmissible.

Throughout the first century of our Independence, one or both of these tenets of exclusion were embraced by virtually all the courts in this country, the state courts of Massachusetts and Connecticut being notable exceptions. These impediments persisted when, between 1865 and 1870, following the Civil War, what seems to have been the first major questioned document case litigated in the United States, the Sylvia Ann Howland will case, was tried at New Bedford, Massachusetts.

Enlightenment gradually superseded these relics of ignorance. Provisions of law such as Section 1731, Title 28, United States Code, originally enacted in substance on February 26, 1913, are now common to all the states, and insure the admissibility of exemplar matter, to wit:

"The admitted or proved handwriting of any person shall be admissible, for purposes of comparison, to determine genuineness of other handwriting attributed to such person."

Slowly but surely, case law firmly established that if an expert's conclusions were relevant and admissible, his reasons were not only likewise relevant and admissible, but highly indispensable for an intelligent decision by jury, trial judge, and reviewer. The general acceptance and endorsement of reasons in expert testimony was the natural forerunner for a second important development. This was the use of illustrative photographs and demonstrative charts in support of the expert's conclusions and reasons.

These improvements in the handling of questioned document cases in our courts were achieved gradually and they are tributes to the technical skill, the intellectual integrity, the vision, and the dedicated perseverance of several pioneers in particular. Deserving prime mention is the late Albert S. Osborn of New York whose *Questioned Documents* was published in 1910. This was the first thoroughgoing treatise respecting questioned documents which stressed the reasoning, and the demonstration in support of the expert's conclusions, rather than the expert's "opinion." Osborn's later *The Problem of Proof*, in 1927, provided the inquiring lawyer with a core of specific data for application to the questioned document problem in litigation.

Concurrently with the pioneering efforts of Osborn and other document examiners, the late renowned dean of Northwestern University Law School, John H. Wigmore, by his constructive criticisms of the restrictive rules of evidence* promoted their revision and by his encouragement of the efforts of forensic scientists spurred their development of improved techniques.

Occasionally to this day, some adolescent with a law degree will object that opposing counsel is "cross-examining his own witness" when the latter is requested to explain the impressive reasons for his conclusions. Or the lawyer knowingly opposing the truth will object to the introduction of a group of telling exemplars with "One signature should be enough. The rest can only be cumulative." Or an uninformed judge will disallow effective photographic enlargements because "I do not see what they can add— I have previously admitted the original documents." However, because of the accomplishments of Osborn, Wigmore, and others, substantially in the sixty years from 1875 to 1935, the document examiner of today rather uniformly enjoys at least the legal opportunity of promoting justice by examining adequate exemplars, and providing his conclusions, his reasons, and photographic demonstrations in support thereof, so that the trier of fact, be it court, or jury, can make its own, not credulous, but reasoned determination.

It will be seen that in the days when inadequate exemplars were the rule, through the period when the presentation of reasons was precluded or seriously impeded, and during the slow transition to reasoned verbal and photographic demonstrations, there

---

.*Wigmore on Evidence, 1904, 1923, 1940.

were scant grounds to distinguish the skilled document examiner from the incompetent examiner. Bank clerks, penmanship instructors, college professors, government agents—almost anyone might step forward with an "opinion" on an important document. Hiding behind bare "opinions" usually involving insufficient exemplars, giving no reasons, and presenting no photographic demonstration, it is not surprising that some incompetents and charlatans became recognized as document "experts." The more inadequate some of these individuals were, the more dogmatic were their empiricisms. Intermittently they were successful, even against able and honest opposition. Occasionally their conclusions were correct. But the restrictive court procedures under which they were suffered to testify, retarded the development of any considerable number of able examiners, and sheltered the tenure of the dubious "expert," right or wrong.

Because of the difficult conditions surrounding the introduction of questioned document facts in our courts, some of which conditions prevailed to a degree through the nineteen twenties, the status of the document examiner was not attractive, professionally or financially. It is not difficult to understand, therefore, why only a very limited number of objective individuals had theretofore undertaken serious, extended studies of the subject. Document testimony was assigned in many of the older legal decisions as weak, and occasionally it was severely criticized by the bench and bar. Certainly some of it was weak. Did not its very critics see to that? For so long as document testimony stemmed from inadequate exemplars and was denied a reasoned exposition and demonstration, document testimony could not be more than weak.

But with the advent of adequate exemplars, adequate reasons for conclusions, and adequate photographic demonstrations, the document examiner was given the tools to raise this class of evidence from its lowly estate. The improved legal atmosphere of the nineteen twenties and nineteen thirties, coupled with the rising tide of documents in general use, gave the document examiner a new look and a new outlook. He had before him a compelling incentive for proficiency.

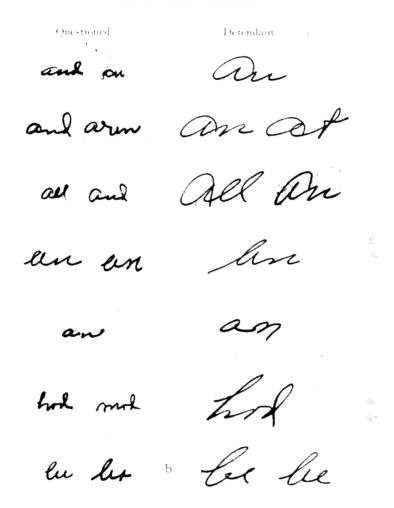

Figure 72. Study of letters *a* and *b*. Observe five separate individualities in *a*. This illustration and four following represent about one fifth of demonstration made in notorious poison pen case.

More and more lawyers were coming to the realization with the courts that deficient reasons and deficient demonstrations in document cases indicated either deficient evidence, a deficient expert, or both. By 1930, a small but effective group of private specialists had initiated concerted research in all phases of questioned document problems. Occasionally, an advocate will endeavor to cast the shadow of the dark past on effective document testimony of today. References to pre-1930 legal decisions must be viewed in the light of the legal and technical progress made in the intervening years. Both laboratory and courtroom conditions which are routinely accepted today simply did not exist twenty-five years ago.

The public as a whole was introduced to the "new" document examiner in the sensational trial of Bruno Richard Hauptmann at Flemington, New Jersey, in 1934. Fourteen letters were directed to the famous parents of the kidnapped Lindberg baby, the first of these letters being left at the scene from which the baby was abducted. The other letters contained follow-up ransom demands and instructions. Eight document examiners* positively identified Hauptmann's handwriting with the series of letters. These experts conclusively demonstrated Hauptmann's authorship by a vivid photographic illustration of his handwriting individualities as they appeared in the kidnap letters and in Hauptmann's exemplars. Hauptmann's own estimate of the value of the testimony adduced by these eight document examiners was tellingly reported after his conviction by the *New York World-Telegram* of February 20, 1936, to wit, "Dot handwriting is the worstest thing against me."

Concurrent with legal and technical advancements in problems exclusively associated with questioned documents, and public cognizance thereof, companion progress was being achieved in forensic chemistry, microscopy, photography, and the so-called police sciences. What was undoubtedly the first comprehensive scientific police laboratory in this country was established in 1930 as the Scientific Crime Detection Laboratory, a division of Northwestern University Law School. In this project, document examiners and all those dedicated to enlightened law enforcement owe much to the late Dean Wigmore and to the first Director of this Laboratory, the late Colonel Calvin Hooker Goddard. Techniques

---

*Harry E. Cassidy, Richmond, Virginia; Albert D. Osborn, New York, New York; Albert S. Osborn, New York, New York; J. Clark Sellers, Los Angeles, California; Dr. Wilmer Souder, Washington, D. C.; Elbridge W. Stein, New York, New York; John F. Tyrrell, Milwaukee, Wisconsin; and Herbert J. Walter, Chicago, Illinois.

and methods in document examination were researched at the Scientific Crime Detection Laboratory* from the standpoint and needs of law enforcement.

Not the least of the Northwestern Laboratory's accomplishments was the publication via the *American Journal of Police Science* of papers illustrating document problems and their solution. The *American Journal of Police Science* was combined with the *Journal of the American Institute of Criminal Law and Criminology* in 1932 as the *Journal of Criminal Law, Criminology and Police Science*. Through the intervening years, this Journal has published numerous authoritative articles by leading document examiners in a significant contribution to the better understanding of evidential document questions.

The Federal Government provided some effective impetus to the passage from the dark ages of guesswork respecting evidential documents to the enlightened application of scientific principles, research, and experience to the many questioned document problems arising in Federal matters. The Treasury Department established the first Federal position of document examiner in 1921. From that beginning, the Treasury Department has progressed to a modern laboratory and trained staff of examiners to provide authoritative counsel concerning the evidential documents relevant to the jurisdiction of the Treasury Department. One has only to envision the millions of Government checks and bonds in circulation to appreciate a few of the document problems peculiar to the Treasury Department.

Pioneering research was also conducted by the National Bureau of Standards of the Department of Commerce beginning in the nineteen twenties. The Bureau of Standards thereafter participated in the introduction of the scientific examination of questioned documents in the Federal Bureau of Investigation of the Department of Justice in about 1933. From a fledgling beginning of less than twenty-five years ago, it is interesting to note that the work of the Document Section, Technical Laboratory, of the Federal Bureau of Investigation has increased until in Fiscal Year 1955, document examinations constituted the largest individual cat-

*Chicago Police Department Crime Detection Laboratory since 1938.

Questioned   Defendant

Figure 73. Letters *c* and *d*. Observe particularly the proportion variations in *d* depending on its use as initial or terminal letter.

egory of scientific examinations conducted by the Federal Bureau of Investigation's Laboratory. The face value of some 23,500 bogus checks alone, which were submitted to the Document Section for examination in Fiscal Year 1955, are reported to have totalled over $3,350,000. Fraudulent checks examined by the Document

Section in Fiscal Years 1953 through 1955 represented the staggering total face value of almost ten million dollars.

The Post Office Department, which shepherds billions of documents over every highway and byway and into every city and hamlet, established a laboratory program through its Inspection Service in 1939. Over fifty-five thousand documents were analyzed in Postal Inspection Service laboratories during Fiscal Year 1956. Currently, the Postal Inspection Service is the only civilian Federal Agency which operates outside of the seat of Government a system of laboratories* primarily devoted to the investigation and analysis of evidential documents.

World War II emphasized to the military services the need for procuring and training document examiners to cope effectively with the many evidential documents born of military operations, intelligence, and personnel. Document Sections in the military laboratories at Camp Gordon, Georgia; Frankfurt, Germany; and Tokyo, Japan have resulted. The Veterans Administration established a single position of document examiner in 1939, from which has developed the laboratory facilities of the Identification and Detection Division of that Agency, handling the many evidential documents arising out of veterans' affairs. For some years the United States Secret Service has utilized document specialists in its Protective Research Division, handling documents pertinent to the protection and security of the President.

As the employment by the Federal Government of document specialists has expanded from the single examiner in 1921 to over fifty examiners in the various federal agencies today, the United States Civil Service Commission adopted detailed standards and specifications** covering the federal positions primarily concerned with the scientific analysis of writings and documents. The necessity for a variety of levels of qualifications and responsibility was recognized. The lowest federal levels embrace the trainee who has no responsibility or authority for independent

---

*Field Identification Laboratories of the Postal Inspection Service are located in Cincinnati, Ohio, Saint Louis, Missouri, Chicago, Illinois, and San Francisco, California.

**Document Examining Series and Document Analysis Series of the United States Civil Service Commission.

conclusions and whose qualifications might simply be:

1. Ability to acquire a knowledge of handwriting classifications, individualities, and the styles of writing commonly employed.

2. Ability to acquire a knowledge of the principles and techniques of examining and evaluating handwriting individualities.

3. Ability to acquire a knowledge of the principles and techniques of examining and evaluating typewriting individualities and mechanical impressions.

4. Evidence of ability to use instruments, equipment, and apparatus necessary in the examination of handwriting, typewriting, and mechanical impressions.

5. Evidence of ability to evaluate the individualities of handwriting, typewriting, and mechanical impressions.

The highest federal classification levels cover the document examiner who is charged with complete personal responsibility for his methods and independent conclusions in complex cases. His qualifications should include:

1. Comprehensive and detailed knowledge of the statutes, regulations, and policies of the employing agency; thorough knowledge of the classes of documents handled within the jurisdiction of the employing agency.

2. Outstanding ability to express facts and the results of examinations clearly, concisely, and objectively, orally and in writing.

3. Thorough knowledge of the history of handwriting, the development of handwriting, handwriting execution, the systems of writing employed in the United States, the principles and techniques of examining and evaluating handwriting individualities, typewriting individualities, and the characteristics of mechanical impressions.

4. Thorough knowledge of the volitional and non-volitional factors, for example, age, physical illness, intoxication, mental disease, deception, and fraud, causing variations in handwriting; thorough knowledge of the effects of foreign handwriting systems on English language handwriting.

5. Keen, accurate, and highly developed powers of rapid and intelligent observation, sustained concentration, and deductive reasoning in questioned document problems; thorough knowledge of the nomenclature and technical terms used in document examination.

6. Outstanding ability to assume individual responsibility for the results, findings, and conclusions of examinations; demonstrated outstanding ability in a minimum of five thousand separate examinations to recognize, detect, and identify individualities, abnormalcies, inadvertencies, errors, simulations, etc., in handwritings, typewritings, and mechanical impressions, to evaluate the inferences drawn from such examinations, and to draw therefrom correct and accurate conclusions regarding identity or non-identity.

7. Thorough knowledge of criminal methods and the psychology of criminals with particular application to the fabrication, forgery, and alteration of documents.

8. Thorough knowledge of the rules of evidence and court rulings relevant thereto in the field of questioned documents; thorough knowledge of practices and proceedings of federal, state, and military courts, and judicial and quasi-judicial bodies as they affect the expert witness.

9. Outstanding skill in the composition and presentation of photographic charts and other demonstrative exhibits; demonstrated ability in a minimum of one hundred separate trials before a variety of courts to speak convincingly before a jury or court, under direct and cross-examination, authoritatively and impartially, and to explain technical procedures, and inferences and conclusions from document evidence.

10. Thorough knowledge of the operation of scientific instruments and apparatus designed in the fields of metrology, microscopy, and photography, including ultra-violet and infrared examining and photographic techniques, and their special application to document examinations.

11. Demonstrated ability to plan, direct, and conduct original research projects, independently and with trained assistants;

demonstrated ability to train and supervise document examiners and laboratory technicians.

12. Knowledge of the principal chemical and physical characteristics of paper, ink, and other writing media; knowledge of the basic ingredients of the most commonly used writing inks and the chemical agents necessary to classify them and to restore

Questioned   Defendant

Figure 74. *o* and *to* combinations.

them to legibility; knowledge of paper manufacturing processes, sealing, fastening, binding, printing, photoengraving, and other graphic arts; ability to conduct and interpret the results of tests necessary to determine the age, kind, quality, or authenticity of writing media.

The qualifications which have been cited relate to the general practitioner in the document field, it being understood that the casework requirements of individual laboratories can and do necessitate the telescoping or expanding of specialization in particular areas of document work. The training and development of document examiners, both in public and private service, has necessarily consisted in large part of training under qualified practicing examiners. Other avenues of effective training have not been available. The very nature of many document problems, particularly those relating to the identification of handwriting, necessitates instruction on a case basis in addition to the theoretical basis. The recognition and interpretation of individualities in documents must be experienced for an extended period under critical supervision to be truly learned.

There are recognized limitations in the development of curricula at the college level for the foundation in the embryonic document examiner of qualifications corresponding to those previously cited herein. In addition, there has been a dearth of qualified instructors. Some confusion also has resulted from misplaced emphasis on the peripheral document problems at the expense of the central questions involving handwriting and typewriting. Nevertheless, a considerable contribution is today being recorded and the future prospects seem bright for increased preparation of students at the graduate and undergraduate levels for subsequent internship in laboratories dedicated to the scientific examination and interpretation of documents.

Several leading universities have sponsored short courses designed to inform the prosecutor, the investigator, and the student of government in the recognition and handling of questioned document problems. This class of instruction makes no pretension of equipping its enrollees as document examiners but it does promote very effectively their development of evidential facts from documents, independently and via consultation with document examiners.

Since its organization in 1942 and informally prior thereto, the members of the American Society of Questioned Document Examiners have assiduously explored the improvement of techniques for examining and demonstrating document evidence. This Society has been a pillar of strength in the private practice of document examination in this country. Unfortunately the Society's membership is small, it has included no document examiners in the public service, and the results of its aggregate researches have not been widely circulated. However, the American Society of Questioned Document Examiners has significantly contributed to scientific document examination in law enforcement through the acceptance by its individual members of civil and criminal cases from public agencies, cooperative assistance to examiners in the public service, and the extension of guest participation in the annual seminars of the Society.

The International Association for Identification for many years has included scientific presentations of document problems in its annual conference agenda and in its monthly publication. While the International Association for Identification lacks homogeneity from the standpoint of the document examiner, its programs and membership have been instrumental in focusing attention on the dual necessity for the scientific approach to evidential documents and for the elevation of qualifications and standards for personnel who are functionally concerned with document examinations in law enforcement.

The American Academy of Forensic Sciences, which was organized in 1948, through its Questioned Document Section and collaboration of the latter with the other sections of the Academy, is proving to be an effective medium through which the scientific interpretation of evidential documents is being stimulated and advanced. The Academy's Questioned Document Section is making an auspicious beginning and its prognosis is good. Like that of any new effort, its full impact is some years ahead.

A growing number of state bureaus of investigation and identification, state police departments, county sheriff's offices, and city police departments has established the position of document examiner, in realization of the fact that more investigations will turn on the "scrap of paper" than on any other category of physical evidence. Training programs, in-service and in cooperation with academic institutions, to promote document consciousness and utilization are definitely on the increase.

Much progress has been made and is now transpiring. But the transition from the age of guesswork respecting evidential documents to the universal application of scientific principles to evidential documents is by no means complete or even fully understood throughout law enforcement circles. The day to day necessity for skilled document interpretations has far outstripped the number of qualified examiners. Entire states and some of the important, some of the most important, cities in the United States do not have a single qualified document expert. In some major areas of federal law enforcement and in altogether too many state and local departments of enforcement, the surface has barely been scratched in questioned document case development. In addition, an astonishing ignorance exists in some quarters as to just what a document examiner is, should be, or can do.

In many departments of enforcement which operate identification and detection laboratories, document examinations represent the largest single category of scientific examinations. Clearly, staff personnel should be best equipped to handle their most recurrent type of examination. It is distinctly not a sound practice to assign a photographer, a chemist, a criminalist, a fingerprint technician, a general identification specialist, a check investigator, or what have you, to positions in which the most numerous tasks are outside the assignee's training, *unless professional training and supervision are thereafter provided.*

Every bureau chief, every department head, every chief of police, every sheriff, every investigator, every lawyer, and every judge has the responsibility of satisfying himself concerning the qualifications of the document examiner he engages or must consider. The discharge of this responsibility should not be a cursory or vague operation. The document examiner's qualifications should be weighed in the light of the specific problems under inquiry.

Whether the document examiner is an employee or a private consultant, use of his services constitutes his endorsement, and is tantamount to a guarantee of his qualifications. Good faith and simple justice require that an unqualified examiner should not be permitted the sponsorship of any agency or individual. Simple efficiency and an awareness of the needs of our day require that efforts be directed to the effective utilization of fully qualified examiners, and to the training of additional qualified personnel.

Of passing pertinence is the nonsense one hears occasionally that document examination can be "picked up in a year or so." When one inquires as to who is supervising one of these "picking up" processes, he usually finds that it is the "picker upper" himself. Further inquiry may reveal that it is more or less, usually less, understood that the novice will confine his efforts for the first year or so to "opinions in simple cases." Additional probing not infrequently discloses that the beginner himself decides whether a given case is a "simple case."

The truism should be omnipresent that to the unqualified, all cases are of equal complexity and equally beyond understanding. When one does not understand a language "cat" and "antidisestablishmentarianism" are qually without meaning. One cannot adhere to limitations he does not recognize. He cannot recognize limitations he has not learned. The technical ability required to analyze a five dollar forgery may exceed that necessary to the interpretation of a five million dollar contract. Only a qualified document examiner is in completely capable position to evaluate the performance and progress of the trainee or would-be examiner. But there are certain basic considerations which anyone can apply to the document examiner whose services concern him.

Document examinations present tangible problems. Their proper solution proceeds from reasoning and should never represent an intrinsical play on credulity. Cognizance must be taken that the chief classes of document problems arising in law enforcement are the detection of forged signatures and writings, the identification of writings of all classes, and classification and identification of typewriting.

Obviously, these specific areas must be within the firm grasp

Figure 75. Terminal *s* and additional facets of *t*.

of the truly qualified examiner. When handwritings are in issue, it should be established when, where, and under whom, their examiner studied handwriting execution, and the relative frequency of handwriting individualities. Is this examiner a self-taught or self-made examiner or have his efforts withstood the light of professional supervision and evaluation, and if so, for what period and by whom? What is the scope of the examiner's study of the available literature dealing with handwriting and documents?

What is the examiner's estimate and comprehension of *Questioned Documents* by Osborn? *Handwriting Movement* by Freeman? *Forged, Anonymous, and Suspect Documents* by Quirke? *Ames on Forgery? Documents and their Scientific Examination* by Mitchell? *Disputed Handwriting* by Hagan? *Bibliotics* by Frazer? What experiments has the examiner undertaken? Does he rate Frazer's nebulae on a par with Osborn's sound principles?

It is essential that it be ascertained whether an individual holding himself out as a document examiner has ever borne the functional responsibility of interpreting handwriting and typewriting individualities, alterations, and forgery problems, or whether he is simply a "jack of all trades" with no specialized training and experience. It should be specifically established whether a would-be examiner is relying on irrelevant qualifications, perhaps in chemistry, physics, education, or law, to feign qualifications in specific document questions which have not an answer in chemistry, physics, education, or law.

What are the examiner's professional attainments? Is he a member of any of the professional societies? Has he prepared or published any technical papers? Are such papers in point with the subject matter concerning which the examiner proffers his services? It should be constantly borne in mind that the examiner's training and experience should be pinpointed in the light of the particular case or cases in which his conclusions are to be considered or are in prospect. Do his training and experience fit the problem of which he assumes to speak with authority?

Conclusions in document cases vary in their certainty, proportionate to the quantity and the quality of the exemplified individualities on which they are based. Evidence in documents varies from that producing the lowest presumption to that which inspires the highest moral certainty. Forgeries vary in their skill from that which fairly shrieks its spuriousness to that about which no examiner could be certain. The experienced, qualified examiner so understands. But the unqualified examiner presumes to answer all questions. Proper questioning of an examiner and evaluation of his record will reveal whether he purports to do that which no man can do.

There are those who seem to think that an examiner, at some mysterious point in his deliberations, emerges into an "opinion" and that "opinions" in all cases occupy the same niche. Evidence and proof are not any more or any less synonomous as applied to document evidence, than when applied to any other class of evidence. Evidence adducible from handwriting, from typewriting, from ink, from paper, from documents sometimes clearly establishes the truth, sometimes it tends to establish the truth, and sometimes it is simply inconclusive. The examiner who always has a definite "yes" or "no" to every problem defies reason and experience. It is not an imposing task to elicit from a document examiner whether he espouses reasoning or credulity. No examiner merits belief without understanding, and his entire attitude should clearly reveal dedication to reasons and reasoning.

In obvious conflict with reasons and reasoning is the examiner who purports to be able to answer document questions consistently based on a cursory examination of a few minutes duration. There is an occasional case respecting which the solution is obvious from perhaps a five minutes' study. An example would be the sort of handwriting problem wherein the suspected writer does not possess the requisite skill which is demonstrated in a forged endorsement, or vice versa. The vast majority of problems encountered in document examinations merits careful study for hours, and even days. Special photographs, measurements, and microscopic studies are the rule rather than the exception.

The qualified examiner does not dispense snap-judgments. When "curbstone" advice is necessary, it will usually be necessary for the examiner to qualify his statements with the provision that they are subject to confirmation by a thorough study of the evidence. If the problem is in that rare category which is susceptible to a quick, on-the-spot solution, the examiner will point out why such is the case. Those in administrative or client relationship to document examiners should appreciate that those who render, those who receive, and those who expect five-minute "opinions" consistently in document cases are indulging guesswork. Guess-

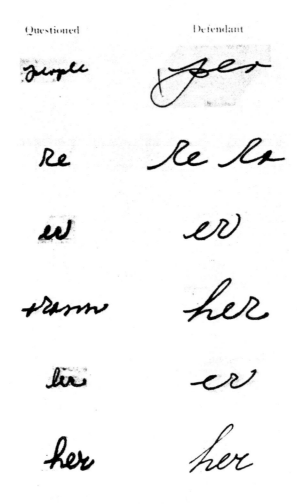

Figure 76. Six individualities in letter *r*.

work serves neither the cause of science nor of justice and it is not justified by expediency, or the temporal exigencies of a fast moving investigation. Possible error is too high a price for speed.

It is not only proper but it is advisable when one is dealing with an unfamiliar document examiner for the first time, or otherwise in a very important case, to request a complete exposition of the basis of the examiner's conclusions, as a part of the investigative phase of the case. The examiner's conclusions, his reasons, and his photographic illustrations are not apt to convince juror or judge, or the partisans on the opposite side of the case, if they are found wanting in the measure of convincingness by those who have retained the examiner. This procedure is likewise appropriate for administrative officials with document examiners on their staffs. The official who protests his incapacity to evaluate a reasoned exposition by a document examiner on his own staff, is saying that he is incapable of performing the duties he expects judges and jurors to discharge in the cases in which he has an interest. No responsible official or attorney should sponsor the conclusions of a document examiner whose reasons do not first convince him.

In considering the selection or endorsement of a document examiner, additional considerations of pertinence concern the impressions he has made on those who previously retained him, counsel who have opposed him, and the courts before which he has appeared. Does he emphasize himself or the evidence? Is the examiner known for always agreeing with those who have retained him? Has he illustrated his objectivity by way of conclusions adverse to his clients, and conclusions pointing out that no definite answer was possible in certain cases due to inadequacies in the evidence? Does the examiner research new and old document problems in association with other examiners or is he a lone operator who "knows" all the answers? Those who utilize the services of document examiners and those who must evaluate the conclusions of document examiners serve well the causes of both science and justice when their appraisals are searching.

The author has been asked frequently about the advisability of small and large law enforcement agencies recruiting and developing their own document examiners. The optimum method of training is a recurring topic. Fully cognizant that disparate conditions prevail in different agencies, the following general criteria are suggested for serious consideration.

The initial factor concerns, of course, the simple necessity for the services of a document specialist. How many cases arise per month in which your department currently needs the services of a document examiner? More pointedly, how many cases are denied the needed services of a document examiner because none is readily available? Are you expending fees covering one or two or a few cases a year which are the equivalent of the annual salary of an examiner who could handle several hundred cases? What is the potential case volume of your department in the foreseeable future?

Case volume is of prime importance because document examination, properly conducted, is a specialized, full-time assignment. It is not a part-time chore for the fingerprint technician, photographer, chemist, or general criminalist. One of the melancholy pictures in law enforcement today sees the fingerprint technician, photographer, chemist, or criminalist with little or no training in document examinations, who is pushed or pushes himself into document work and has no prospect of supervised case volume to repair reasonably his deficiencies through experience. Document examinations vary greatly in their complexities and requirements, temporally and otherwise, but an average case volume of twenty-five cases per month is probably advisable before any department establishes the position of document examiner.

A desirable arrangement in some cities is for an enforcement agency to retain a qualified examiner or firm of examiners in private practice on an annual basis. This sort of arrangement can provide qualified service on a permanent basis if consistent with the case volume of the employing agency. If the volume increases, arrangements can be considered for the training of staff examiners for the enforcement agency, under the aegis of the private examiner who is qualified and who is familiar with the specific needs of the employing agency. Another advantageous procedure in many local situations is the utilization of state facilities. A state identification laboratory, with appropriate support from various local departments, usually generates a volume of case work which is much more conducive to a high standard of proficiency than the requirements of the local departments individually.

At whatever level of law enforcement the position of document examiner is established, it will usually be necessary to train existing or specifically recruited personnel. The selection of a trainee examiner should never be haphazard. Errors in training will not necessarily nullify a trainee. An error in the selection of the trainee will negative any and all training. Mr. George G. Swett, Examiner of Questioned Documents, Saint Louis, Missouri, aptly stated some time ago: "The document examiner must be judged upon his ability to search, to reason, to interpret properly, and to report accurately . . . What is needed in a laboratory is a well trained fact finder who operates within the limits of his science . . . Although the examiner of questioned documents of today is much more than a 'handwriting expert' the determination of facts through the comparison of handwritings remains his major function."

Examiner Swett's observations are appropriate in reviewing the basic requirements of the trainee. He should have a sound educational background. Chemistry, physics, mathematics, statistics, psychology, philosophy, photography, law, advanced penmanship, criminalistics—all will help the trainee but none is indispensable at the outset of his training and none or all will necessarily guarantee his success. In assessing an applicant's educational background, a prima facie acceptance of completed courses may satisfy the personnel officer but it does not represent an adequate appraisal for the efficient administrator. The applicant's educational performances by courses should be carefully evaluated, and in the light of his activities subsequent thereto, with the view to gaining a correct insight into his real and not imagined or desired aptitudes.

Psychological tests and searching interviews of the prospective trainee are recommended to determine whether he is argumentative, impatient, opinionated, egotistical, or given to shallow reasoning. His basic judgment and common sense should be explored searchingly. The manner in which the applicant has acquitted himself in the more difficult situations of his own experience and his responses to test situations will frequently confirm the applicant's orderly thought processes or expose deficiencies in common sense.

Training should not be dissipated on the evasive or intellectually dishonest applicant who resolves all doubtful issues in his own favor through untruths, half truths, or deliberate omissions. Tendencies to sophistry are irreconcilable with the frame of mind which is essential to the search for the truth in documents or anything else. Such disqualifying proclivities should not escape the initial scrutiny to which the would-be examiner is subjected. Scientific integrity in evidential matters can hardly be expected from examiners of dubious moral or intellectual fiber.

Always assuming the applicant's deep interest in document examination, an initial requirement is his proficiency in recognizing, adjudging, and differentiating minutiae of sizes, shapes, and designs. Visual acuity by commonly accepted criteria is insufficient. The prospective trainee should be carefully tested for his aptitude in distinguishing and memorizing inconspicuous variations and spatial relationships in lines, angles, curves, circles, typewritten characters, fingerprint patterns, and handwritten letter conformations. One who stumbles in differentiating geometric configurations, who cannot accurately count the ridges in a fingerprint pattern, who cannot distinguish two different typeface styles, or who cannot readily fit together a "jigsaw" puzzle is not a likely prospect for success in the field of document examination.

The aspirant for training must have the ability to express himself with precision, orally and in writing. This qualification should never be unduly compromised. The examiner's first duty is to discover the facts. Thereafter, his value is measured by his ability to explain and establish these facts in the minds of others. A distinct asset is the somewhat indefinable quality of inspiring confidence and belief through forceful verbal and written presentations. These abilities can be developed in the trainee, but the applicant should be appraised carefully for his capacity to respond to such training. Any serious deficiencies in these particulars are obvious disqualifying grounds.

The capacity to accept responsibility, current and potential and accumulative, is another requisite for the successful document examiner. Admittedly this talent has no constant common denominator in the human equation. As a necessary ingredient of the document examiner in a strictly personal sense, its manifestations must be viewed critically. Without the inherent capability to embrace grave responsibility, the trainee will never develop beyond mediocrity.

The qualified document examiner must routinely accept individual responsibility for his findings and conclusions, as revealed by the evidence. He is not responsible for the existence of evidence but he must not flinch in the face of its correct interpretation. His findings on the evidence in many cases will affect personal liberties, personal reputations, extensive properties. They will not always be pleasing to his clients or administrative superiors. They may be very controversial at times, perhaps publicly controversial. If the document examiner is imbued with any predisposition to expedient findings, his objectivity is prejudiced. If he is unable to shoulder the pressure of personal findings and personal conclusions, better that he labor in some less demanding field.

The opposite extreme of reckless encroachment on responsibilities not properly within one's own province likewise must be guarded against. The examiner's proper acceptance of his own responsibility embodies no arrogation of the discrete areas of, for example, the field investigator, the attorney, judge, and jury. Another consideration is the mental apprehension of error. If one's fear of error exceeds that salutary fear which season's one's judgment to that overwhelming fear which destroys one's judgment, better that he seek a situation wherein another makes the difficult decisions.

There is no room in the efficient document laboratory for the "yes" man, the "no" man, the "I hesitate" man, the "I know everything" man, or the "this pressure is killing me" man. But the door opens wide for the mentally alert young man with keen, accurate, and highly developed powers of rapid and intelligent observation. Diligent cataloguing of observations, sustained concentration, deductive reasoning, and honest, clear reporting are rewarding to, if demanding of, the true fact finder. He invites the challenge of the cases which seem to defy solution. Such are high among the basic attitudes and aptitudes to be sought in the prospective document examiner trainee.

The needs of different agencies, the receptivity of individual trainees, and the effectiveness of the training presentation will tend to regulate the advisable emphasis and extensiveness of the various training phases for the aspiring document examiner. It would be presumptuous to attempt to delineate each and every step which would be requisite to the needs of every agency, or the order in which the various training phases should be undertaken. Nevertheless, there are certain basic data which should be within the knowledge of the general practitioner in the document examination field, subject to elaboration to fit case requirements. The development of these data require studies of and case assignments in:

1. Statutes, regulations, policies, procedures, and objectives governing the employing agency.

2. Specific classes of documents and document problems confronting the employing agency.

3. Typeface designs utilized by the several typewriter manufacturers.

4. Individualities of typefaces and typewriter operation which identify the individual typewriter.

5. History of handwriting and development of American handwriting.

6. Handwriting systems in the United States.

7. Foreign handwriting systems which influence handwriting encountered in the United States.

8. Handwriting movement and execution as applied to cursive script, manuscript writing, block printing, numerals, and punctuation.

9. The characteristics of traced and simulated signatures and writings.

10. Various volitional and non-volitional factors affecting handwriting variations and execution, for example, intentional deception, nervousness, fatigue, illness, excitement, intoxication, missing spectacles, advanced age, undue hurry, muscular strain, unusual writing implements, abnormal writing position, etc.

11. Effective methods of procuring exemplars.

12. Mathematics of handwriting probabilities.

13. The laboratory report and its verbal exposition.

14. Chemical and mechanical erasures and alterations.

15. Development of erased and obliterated writings.

16. Photographic copying of documents by reflected, trans-

mitted, and oblique visible light, and by infrared and ultra-violet.

17. Composition of photographic charts illustrating differences and agreements in handwriting, typewriting, etc.

18. Differentiation of writing inks and classification of writing inks; sympathetic inks; characteristics of typewriter ribbons.

19. Printing and duplicating processes; adhesives, sealing, and binding; cutting and fastening processes.

20. Differentiation of writing papers and the classification of writing papers.

21. Differentiation of writing instruments and the classification of writing instruments.

22. Sequence of crossed lines, sequence of written and type-written lines and stamped impressions, sequence of writings and folds and creases.

23. The development of latent fingerprints on documents.

24. Court procedures—qualifying the document expert, the development of the expert's conclusions, reasons, and demonstration on direct examination, and the expert's responses on cross-examination.

25. Questioned Document law.

There is considerable practical merit to assigning typewriting classification and identification early in the training program. Such procedure is a medium of demonstrating to both the trainee and his instructor the former's ability to distinguish inconspicuous agreements and differences, as well as the trainee's thoroughness, patience, objectivity, and courage of conviction. The trainee's confidence can be opportunely developed by enabling him to gain early proficiency in typewriting examinations wherein, unlike handwriting examinations, the trainee can be provided with rather readily understandable criteria of individualities.

Throughout the trainee's internship on case assignments he should invariably be caused to commit the reasons for his conclusions to writing in somewhat detailed fashion. The reasons for his conclusions provide a greater insight to the trainee's ability than do the conclusions themselves. His reasoning should be closely scrutinized, case by case, to detect deficiencies. The complexity of case assignments should be augmented systematically by the instructing examiner, who should maintain a detailed record of the correctness of the trainee's conclusions and reasoning.

The trainee who does not consistently demonstrate the accuracy of his conclusions and the reasons therefor while under the supervision and guidance of an instructing examiner clearly is not prepared to render reports or to dispense advice on his own responsibility. Experience in a minimum of perhaps two hundred separate cases involving handwriting examinations wherein the trainee has demonstrated accuracy is recommended before the trainee is considered for independent conclusions involving handwriting. An apt trainee might be considered for independent conclusions in typewriting examinations after perhaps one hundred separate typewriting examinations wherein he has demonstrated unbroken accuracy.

It should be universally recognized by everyone that no mysterious transformation will automatically encompass the trainee when he is permitted to function on his own responsibility and is saluted with the cliche "expert." The day he first "qualifies" in court will not suddenly confer any qualifications whatsoever on the new examiner. He must have previously acquired his qualifications through study, experimentation, research, and supervised case experience or he remains unqualified, irrespective of the endorsement he may have been granted by a less than discerning court.

A wise rule for every administrator under whose auspices examiners are trained is to require the instructing document examiners to assume the responsibility of determining when, if ever, a trainee should be permitted to report independent conclusions for authoritative acceptance. The instructor who recommends independent responsibilities for the trainee should report in detail the trainee's accomplishments supporting such recommendation.

How many separate cases has the trainee handled with accurate conclusions and reasons? What sorts of errors has he made? What specific type of problems have his case experiences involved? In what varieties of casework does the trainee require further instruction and experience? In what varieties of problems does the trainee particularly excel? Are there case classifications he should not be assigned and, if so, why? Has the trainee been imbued with the realization that there will ever be certain complex cases in which he should consult with experienced examiners, and with specialists in other fields, such as chemistry, before approaching a final judgment? *Has a system been established to maintain a continuing evaluation of the trainee's performance after he is advanced to examiner status, or will he be the "undertaker" as well as the "doctor" as soon as he begins to function independently of his instructors?*

Law enforcement department heads need not hesitate to bestow their seal of approval on the examiner who has truly acquired expertness. Conversely, no administrator should take lightly the responsibility of assuring himself that his department does not guarantee nonexistent qualifications. In any doubtful situations or as a matter of routine practice, the counsel of document examiners in private practice or examiners employed by other public agencies might well be solicited in respect to budding trainees. In the training of a document examiner as in most other endeavors, thoroughness is the forerunner of efficiency. The cause of justice is served best by a positive program producing and utilizing competent specialists, consistently aware of and operating within the limits of their science.

EXPERT DOCUMENT TESTIMONY

The function of the questioned document expert in court is to present his conclusions, the reasons therefor and usually photographic visual aids in support thereof, so that the trier of fact, whether court or jury, may make its own reasoned determination of the truth of the matter on trial. To discharge this function, the expert must embrace unreservedly the proposition that the ultimate finding is the province of the court and jury. The expert should not undertake to arrogate to himself the function of either. His efforts should remain elucidatory on the basis of the evidential documents he has analyzed, and in the light of his specialized training and experience. The expert should shoulder fully his responsibility of forcefully and effectively demonstrating the true evidential facts, so that the court and jury are led through the cogency of his reasons and illustrations to adopt his conclusions as their own.

The so-called opinion of an expert, standing alone, is of limited significance and properly open to question. It tends to focus attention on the expert rather than on the evidence, on credulity rather than on reasoning. It places the most partisan and least qualified on the same plane as the most conscientious and best qualified. Conversely, when the expert's conclusion is independently supported by reasons, drawn from the evidence, explained and illustrated, his testimony amounts to a demonstration.

The indiscriminate use of the word "opinion" in reference to expert testimony concerning documents tends to mislead many who are unversed in the rules of evidence. As a matter of fact, "opinion" seems to confuse many who should be conversant with the relevant legal technicalities and practical realities. Every document examiner has heard from the lips of investigators and attorneys, presumably schooled in the law, "You don't need to examine these documents thoroughly. I don't want you to spend a lot of time on them. All I need is your 'opinion.'"

It seems probable that this and similar statements, which are by no means uncommon, are not founded on stupidity, negligence, or dishonorable intent but are rather the outgrowth of the history of expert testimony combined with the meaning of the word "opinion" to the man in the street. Some of the responsibility for less than laudatory appraisals of opinion evidence undoubtedly stems from expert witnesses who have well served the detractors of opinion evidence by presenting bare opinions, without reinforcement in reasons and illustrations. Certainly some of the inaccurate understanding of opinion evidence rests with attorneys opposing the facts, who ardently pursue the catch-phrase "opinion." Their objective is to divert attention from the evidence where it belongs, to the expert and to supersede his reasons and illustrations in a barrage of "opinion," "just an opinion," "only an opinion," "merely an opinion." Such attorneys hide behind the legalism which they well understand, *and which they well understand that jurors do not understand,* that the expert witness does not testify from "direct knowledge of facts."

The document expert's testimony proceeds from knowledge acquired by his analysis of tangible evidence. Unlike the subjects of many other classes of expert and lay testimony, evidential documents are before the court and jury for their own inspection and evaluation. Is it reasonable to conclude, from behind a veil of defensive legalisms or otherwise, that the qualified document expert cannot adduce and demonstrate facts from a knowledge of such tangible evidence? Properly presented expert evidence concerning documents is demonstrable, verbally and pictorially. Can as much or more be said of the recollections of the lay witness, even the truthful, non-exaggerating, non-evasive, observant one, who does testify from "direct knowledge of facts"?

Perhaps from the standpoint of legalistic etymology, the classification "opinion" may be sound as applied to expert document evidence. But jurors who are called upon to decide these matters are not and cannot be expected to be students of legal semantics. Neither can they be expected to know that the cliche "opinion" is intimately associated with the dark past when the document expert in our courts was not permitted to explain and illustrate the reasons for his "opinions." Neither can jurors be expected to expunge from their thinking, as they enter the jury box, their day-to-day understanding of an "opinion" as somewhat less than a firm conviction.

Document examiners, attorneys, and judges should face up to the development that there is a difference between "expert evidence" concerning documents which interprets and illustrates a firm conviction on the evidence, which the court and jury can independently observe, and "opinion evidence" which expresses a summary of general belief without a reasoned and illustrated reinforcement from within the evidence itself.

Document examiners have the obligation of presenting reasoned conclusions on the evidence and supporting them when possible by an effective photographic demonstration. When a photographic or other visual aid exposition is not possible, it should be explained why such is the case. And when the examiner's conclusions are equivalent to less than firm convictions, he should specifically so represent, giving the reasons why his conclusions embody qualifications or limitations.

Both document examiners and attorneys might well avoid the jury-misleading word "opinion." Based on numerous discussions with jurors and others concerned, this writer is convinced that "expert evidence" and "conclusion" convey much more accurately to the average juror what the qualified document expert on the witness stand today signifies, than do "opinion evidence" and "opinion." The jury instructions of some judges succumb to this legalistic doubletalk by stressing the word "opinion" and tending inevitably thereby to separate the expert's conclusions from his reasons and demonstrative exhibits. Those courts serve well the cause of justice who emphasize in jury instructions that expert testimony in sum total should be weighed in the scales of its aggregate reasonableness and convincingness. No advocate should ask for more.

Prerequisite to testimony on the part of the document expert, it is essential that his testimonial capacity be clearly established. His expertness should be subjected to specific preliminary examination in the procedure referred to as qualifying the witness.

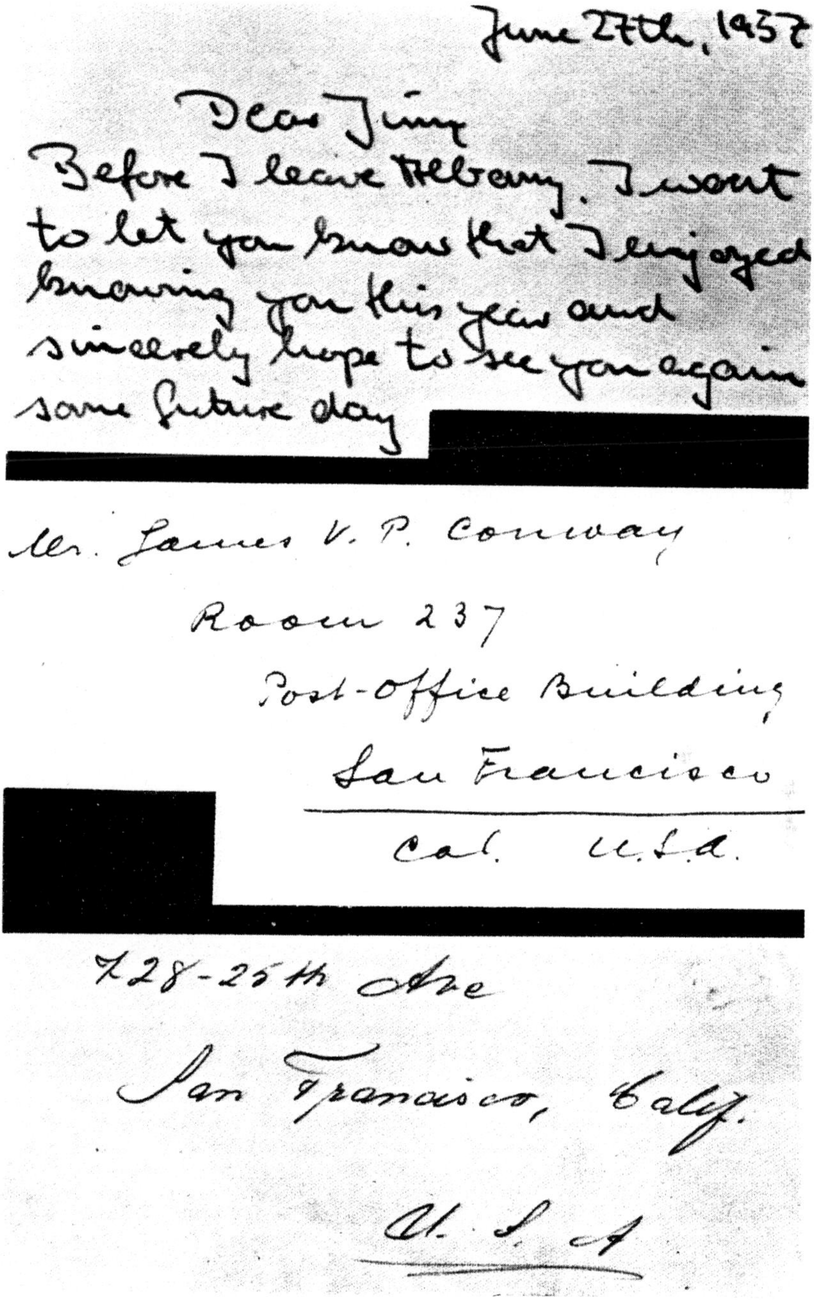

June 27th, 1957

Dear Jim

Before I leave Albany. I want to let you know that I enjoyed knowing you this year and sincerely hope to see you again some future day

Mr. James V. P. Conway

Room 237

Post-Office Building

San Francisco

Cal. U.S.A.

728-25th Ave

San Francisco, Calif.

U.S.A

Figure 77. Writing by German, Dutch, and Swedish nationals. Compare with Figures 11, 12, 13, and 78.

Stated simply, this procedure consists of a series of questions which are propounded to the expert witness to elicit by his answers whether he has special knowledge and skills. The series of qualifying questions is further designed to show that the expert's qualifications are beyond those of the average juror and are needed to assist the court and jury in evaluating relevant evidence, specifically within the expert's field of special knowledge and skill. Too frequently, this preliminary phase of expert testimony receives less than thorough consideration by counsel and the witness. Of infinitely greater cause for concern are the casual and ultra-liberal evaluations made by some judges of a proffered expert witness' qualifications.

The bench, the bar, and the officialdom of law enforcement complain occasionally about deficiencies in expert testimony of all classes. Many of these complaints are not without merit. All deserve the serious consideration of the expert witness. Like his neighbors, he is not only what he is, he is also what others think he is.

The cornerstone of a few deficiencies, at least, can be laid at the feet of the bench, the bar, and law enforcement officers. Attorneys engage the services of witnesses whom searching inquiry, never made, would find wanting. Courts permit witnesses to testify as experts simply because one of the parties to a court contest so called the witnesses to testify, and their answers to a few "qualifying" questions seem to indicate a modicum of special knowledge and skill. Police departments, city, county, state, and federal agencies permit personnel to testify in court as "experts" who have neither requisite training nor experience. Investigators and prosecutors and defense lawyers shop around to a variety of specialists hoping to find one who will succumb to a prosecution or defense theory, depending on the shopper.

Would-be experts also contribute to deficiencies. There seems to be an irrational push on the part of many inexperienced specialists to mount the witness stand as "experts" about the time they draw their first pay check. Although it does not require a superabundance of intelligence and integrity to suspect when and where one should fear to tread, the brash young trainee, newly wandering outside academic halls, may be entitled to at least partial forgiveness for his unbalanced desire to testify, ready or not. The pressures of professional ambition and financial advancements are admittedly severe. In some quarters—notably those so-called personnel and budget offices with which society has become afflicted—professional accomplishments are frequently measured by whether and how often the specialist has traipsed to court. But the fact stands clear that the courts have every right to presume that public agencies are in position to guarantee the specific qualifications of their employees who are permitted to present them-

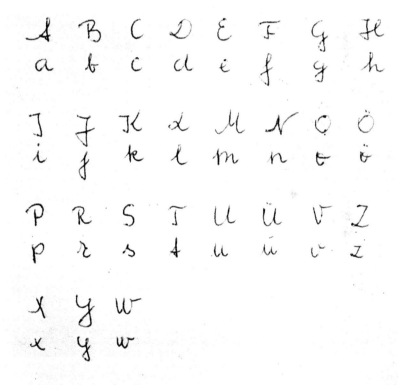

Figure 78. Writing by Hungarian. Compare with Figures 11, 12, 13, and 77.

selves in court as expert witnesses. The heads of law enforcement departments, other public agencies, and universities should maintain ordered houses in this regard so that their responsibilities to themselves, the courts, and the public are efficiently discharged.

The circumstance that an expert should not be sponsored in a particular field of knowledge should not be lost sight of in the partisanship of pressing, pre-trial preparation. Attorneys and judges share the responsibility with the witness and such other sponsors as he may have for misleading and erroneous testimony which emanates from the non-expert who is nevertheless presented as and adjudged to be qualified.

It is considered essential, therefore, that the expert witness' qualifications should be explored in some considerable detail not only to establish his testamonial capacity but additionally, because the extent and nature of the witness' qualifications have a direct relevancy to the soundness of his conclusions and reasoning. Further, a record should be made so that in the event of an appeal, the reviewing court will have an accurate description of the witness' qualifications or lack of them.

A favorite device of attorneys opposing a witness whom they know to be well qualified is to agree to stipulate to his qualifications. The acceptance of such a stipulation is probably in order in non-jury cases which are not likely to be appealed, and when the witness is known to the court from prior appearances. It is distinctly inadvisable for an attorney to accept such a stipulation when it prevents the court and the jury from becoming acquainted with the witness' qualifications and excludes them from the case record.

The following list of questions illustrates a simple method of developing the document expert's qualifications in a case involving handwriting. This list is not intended to be all-inclusive or adaptable without revision to every expert witness in his special field. It does incorporate basis for consideration of the important problem of qualifying the document witness.

1. What is your name?
2. What is your business, profession or occupation?
3. Where is your office located?

4. You understand, do you not, that under the law it is necessary for me to ask you a series of questions so that the Court and Jury may be acquainted with your background and experience in the field of evidential documents?

5. Do you operate a scientific laboratory devoted to the analysis of handwriting, the detection of forgery, and related matters having to do with questioned and disputed documents?

6. Of what do your laboratory facilities consist?

7. Describe your duties in your assignment with the X Department.

8. Do you devote all of your time to the examination of questioned and disputed document cases in your official position?

9. How long have you been so engaged?

10. What, if any, special training and study did you undertake preparatory to your taking up duties as a questioned document examiner?

11. I assume you have studied under or in association with practicing specialists in the questioned document field, is that correct?

12. I will ask you to mention the names of your instructors.

13. How many questioned and known documents have you independently studied in your capacity as a questioned document examiner?

14. In approximately how many separate cases have you rendered formal written reports as a questioned document examiner?

15. Is the identification of handwriting the most important phase of your work?

16. Just how is handwriting identified?

17. Is it always possible to identify a given handwriting with the person who actually wrote it?

18. I take it that it is not possible to answer with a definite "yes" or "no" every one of the cases which is submitted to your laboratory, is that correct?

19. And I assume further that when there is any limitation to the definiteness of your laboratory findings, you so report, is that correct?

20. Are you a member of any scientific organizations of questioned document examiners and other forensic scientists?

21. Have you conducted any research projects having to do with the analysis of questioned documents?

22. Have you written any technical papers or books dealing with questioned documents and related subjects?

23. Have you heretofore testified in any courts of record as a questioned document expert and, if so, please mention some of the courts and jurisdictions in which you have so testified?

24. Approximately how many times have you testified as a questioned document expert?

25. You previously testified that you have examined some thousands of cases. From your preceding answer, obviously you testify in only a small percentage of the cases which you examine. Just why is that?

Should the case in which the expert is called to testify relate to typewriting, ink, paper, chemical alterations, etc., specific questions should be injected to develop the witness' conversance with the exact problem which is before the court. Less than adequate expositions are made to courts and juries occasionally by witnesses who may be truly expert in one field but who invade areas, closely related or otherwise, in which they are less than expert. A witness of integrity, of course, does not solicit or encourage these situations and when, through force of necessity, he finds himself therein, he makes his position and his limitations clear to the court.

There are other witnesses, perhaps more imbued with enthusiasm or pedantry than they are lacking in professional integrity, who do not hesitate to encroach on unfamiliar terrain. One may see the general criminalist having little or no background in handwriting identification presume to testify on handwriting questions. Or one may encounter the document examiner having little or no foundation in paper chemistry presume to testify on intricate paper chemistry questions. While it is perhaps true that such witnesses possess some knowledge in these areas, in which they have not highly specialized, beyond that of the average man in the street, the witness' specializations should not be inaccurately posed. The witness' training and experience should be recorded in the light

QUESTIONED

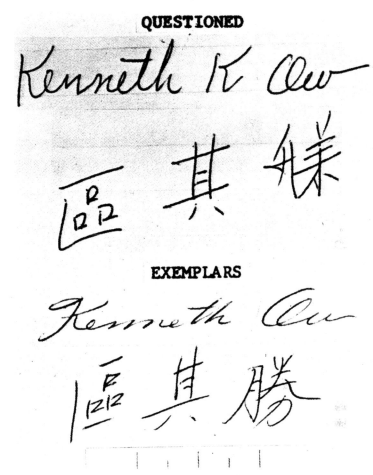

EXEMPLARS

Figure 79. Interesting case involving simulation of signatures in English and Chinese. Simulator failed similarly in execution and conformation of both English and Chinese signatures.

of the precise problem of which he assumes to speak, so that the court and jury may accurately and fairly assess his conclusions and reasoning.

The expert should ever remember that having been determined to be qualified by the trial judge, he has the obligation of confirming that judicial underwriting of his qualifications by wholehearted dedication to the truth as revealed by the evidence.

Misguided partisanship in the interests of the party sponsoring his court appearance traduces the court's judgment as well as the witness' reasoning. Advocacy by the expert rarely escapes the jury. It is not only professionally improper, it prejudices success in convincing the jury of the validity of the witness' reasoning. Advocacy on the part of the expert certainly will not do other than lower the value of the expert's testimony in the eyes of the court, experienced in separating evidence from partisanship.

It does not follow that the expert witness should not cooperate fully with the attorney who has called him to testify. Cooperation in bringing out the evidence, all of it, is an integral part of witness participation. All aspects of the case should be discussed thoroughly by counsel and expert pre-trial to the end that the witness' conclusions, reasons, and illustrative exhibits are presented to the best advantage. Some attorneys specialize in walking pre-trial conferences en route from their offices to the courtroom in the minutes preceding the trial. This is scarcely a recommended procedure in the interests of thoroughness. If expert evidence is relevant as an aid to the court and jury in assessing the truth of a court contest, it merits the thoughtful intercooperation of expert and attorney, in advance of as well as during the former's testimony.

Much fumbling around by both attorney and witness will be avoided if they jointly come to an agreement on the manner in which direct examination of the witness will be conducted. The following list of questions outlines a method of post-qualifying direct examination in a simple case involving the genuineness of a check endorsement.

1. Prior to coming to court to testify, have you examined certain documents which are involved in this trial?

2. At whose request was your examination conducted?

3. When and where did you make your examination?

4. I hand you Government Exhibit One which has been identified as a Treasury check payable to Jane Doe and ask you if it is one of the documents which you have examined?

5. I hand you Government Exhibit Two consisting of five separate pages which have been identified as containing the hand-

writing of Jane Doe, and ask you if you have also examined this Exhibit?

6. For what purpose did you examine Government Exhibits One and Two?

7. Describe the manner and method of your examination of Government Exhibits One and Two.

8. As a result of your examination, did you arrive at a conclusion whether the endorsement "Jane Doe" on Government Exhibit One was written by Jane Doe whose admitted handwriting appears in Government Exhibit Two?

9. What is your conclusion?

10. In the course of your work in this case did you prepare any photographs to illustrate the basis of your conclusion?

11. Please produce these photographs and explain how they were made and what they represent.

12. These photographs, which have been marked Government Exhibits Three, Four, and Five are true and correct photographic reproductions of the endorsement on Government Exhibit One and six signatures of Jane Doe from Government Exhibit Two, is that correct?

13. I will now ask you to explain to the Court and Jury, using Government Exhibits One through Five for purposes of illustration as necessary, the reasons for your conclusion that the endorsement on Government Exhibit One and the handwriting of Jane Doe in Government Exhibit Two were written by one and the same person.

This brief list of questions obviously is not intended to fit every situation, especially the more complicated testimony required when large volumes of exhibits are involved. It does embody the fundamental considerations which should be studied by the attorney and witness in preparing direct examination.

There are attorneys, possibly influenced by out-of-date court decisions, who seem to think that the witness should be dropped immediately after he has stated his conclusions. These attorneys apparently feel that asking their witness for the basis of his conclusions constitutes cross-examination. If the witness' conclusions are relevant, his reasons are doubly pertinent. They should be fully exposed on direct examination. They are the most significant assistance which the witness can contribute to the deliberations of the court and jury. When the reasons of the expert witness are not heard on direct examination, the odds are that they will never be heard. The astute opposing counsel will ask no questions of the qualified expert, and certainly he will ask few or none when the expert has been subjected to an abbreviated direct examination. Why should an attorney emphasize his opposition's case by cross-examining the witness who obviously should know far more about the evidential documents than the attorney?

Expert testimony should be presented, whenever possible, following examination of original documents. It is well known that originals are not always available for examination. This is especially true of official records of the various instrumentalities of government. Intermittently, officials from their ivory towers loftily refuse to release an original document which is relevant to important litigation, or the original of an important disputed document may be in the hands of the opposition. Documents of importance become lost, strayed, and stolen. In these days of microfilming, original documents are routinely destroyed which thereafter may assume vital importance in civil and criminal cases. For one reason or another, the document examiner is continually confronted with issues wherein his examination is limited to photostatic or photographic copies, particularly the former.

Considerable confusion seems to exist respecting the technical propriety of an expert conclusion based on an examination of a photostatic copy of the original. This recurring question, which is of some considerable importance in law enforcement circles, should involve no confused thinking on the part of the qualified document examiner. For too many years he has bowed to the presumed dictates of outmoded principles concerning the examination of photostats. There are many cases in which the document examiner can arrive at sound and reliable conclusions from photostatic copies today. There are also many cases in which photostatic copies are grossly inadequate to a sound conclusion. It is no different with original documents. They do not all embody basis for definite conclusions.

When Osborn stated in *Questioned Documents* in 1910 "The principal objection to the 'photostat' photograph is that by this process nearly all intermediate tones are lost," he was referring to the photostats of that date. In the intervening fifty odd years, and more particularly within the past fifteen years, the quality of photostatic reproductions and photographs of all classes has been significantly improved. Photostats need not "lose" all intermediate tones. Correctly made, they are not excessively contrasty and without detail as they were fifty years ago. Photostat paper of this age retains tonal gradations sufficient to reproduce definitively many original documents.

Recently, this writer participated in a discussion of this question with some twenty of the leading document examiners in the United States. There was unanimous agreement that the examination of photostats, properly prepared, in many cases will provide the basis for the definite determination of disputed document questions and is proper foundation for expert testimony. Contrasty photostats or those with other defects in preparation are not adequate to determine intricate questions of line quality today any more than they were fifty years ago, when no other could be made.

Consideration must also be directed to the proposition whether it can be reliably accepted that a photostat is a correct overall reproduction of its original. Photostats made prior to the date when their originals came into question support the general assumption of reliability. If they were made in the regular course of business by a county recorder, bank, government office, or other party having no conceivable connection with or interest in the matter in dispute, their general reliability is further enhanced. When these or similar conditions have been met, and the photostats themselves disclose that they are of definitive quality and do not limit consideration of the question in dispute, certainly an examiner can adduce basis for sound conclusions.

Quite a different situation would be presented by a photostat which was prepared after the controversy arose concerning its original, and which was produced by a party in interest. It would assume still less reliability if it was excessively contrasty or otherwise inadequately prepared. The shadow of unreliability would grow if a reasonable hypothesis of "composition" was in order. It is well known that parts of two or more original documents can be photostated or photographed in composite form to simulate a single original document.

Telltale indications of tracing or simulation on a photostat or photograph alert the examiner immediately to the fact that an ultimate conclusion is not warranted in advance of an examination of the original document. The defense advocate who protests that the handwriting of no man can be identified from a photostatic copy speaks error. The civil litigant who argues that all photostats are as reliable as their originals likewise engages inaccuracy. The document examiner need not apologize for what he can see and evaluate. He should not speculate about what he cannot see and cannot evaluate. In brief, the examination of photostats and photographs requires analytical reasoning, experience, and objectivity as does every document problem.

Occasionally, the effectiveness of expert testimony is seriously impeded by the failure of an attorney to recognize timely that all the documents which the expert has examined will not be admitted into evidence, or that documents additional to those which the expert has considered in his examination have become material to his testimony. In criminal cases, the investigating officer can be of great assistance in endeavoring to foresee any change in the documents which are relevant to the examiner's testimony. It is a very discouraging experience for an examiner, who arrives at a trial with a forceful photographic demonstration, which took days and perhaps weeks to assemble, to find on his arrival that his work has been negatived because he unknowingly included documents which have become immaterial or excluded documents which have become pertinent. To forestall these situations, it is advisable for the examiner to describe with particularity in his written reports the documents on which he bases his conclusions and proposes to found his testimony. The examiner should take steps to insure that the attorney who calls him to testify is furnished a copy of such report to obviate any misapprehension during pre-trial preparations.

In cases in which large volumes of documents are involved, the investigator, attorney, and examiner should ordinarily participate jointly in the selection of representative documents which most effectively illustrate the evidential facts. In mass forgeries, for example, it is customary for prosecutors to charge formally only a percentage, sometimes a very small percentage, of the total forged instruments. The selection of forgeries to be cited in an indictment or information should be made by the prosecutor after a careful evaluation of *all* pertinent evidence. Selections which ignore the effective presentation of expert testimony do not serve the cause of efficient and complete prosecutions. Not all forgeries or handwriting identifications are equally demonstrable. The document expert can be of material assistance during the pre-trial consultations in delineating those documents which will be most amenable to demonstration in the event of a trial contest.

The choice of exemplars which are to be introduced at a trial likewise should be a consultative effort involving the investigator, attorney, and examiner, when there is a variety of exemplars permitting some selection for trial purposes. It can be confusing to introduce handwriting exemplars which are related intimately to other issues of the case on trial. A handwritten statement by a defendant which contains untrue, self-serving declarations by him, should be avoided for exemplar purposes unless it is to be introduced for other purposes. Such statements may in the eyes of a jury tend to bind the prosecution to the self-serving statements of the defendant rather than to the handwriting individualities of the defendant. Attorneys can make limited offers and judges can instruct juries as to exactly what they may consider, but it is wiser not to attempt to "unring bells."

Exemplars which can only be identified ex visu scriptionis by a witness who has seen the person write should likewise be avoided. This mode of proof, while sufficient in law in most jurisdictions, has no excuse for existence in this age. This rule of law is the product of the dark past. It was probably necessary in the seventeenth or eighteenth centuries but it does not serve the cause of justice today. The premise that an untrained witness can reliably identify a writing by virtue of having seen the individual in question write, as little as one or two instances and perhaps on remote occasions when the act of writing was incidental, would be laughed at any place but in the courtroom. There will be an occasional temptation to gain evidential stature via this mode of proof for an exemplar which the attorney and expert witness are satisfied is reliable. It would be well to recognize, however, that the continued used of this faulty mode of proof keeps open the door for the opposition's introduction of unreliable and misleading "exemplars" by the same method.

It is always advisable, when possible, to introduce some regular-course-of-business exemplars as well as request exemplars of the individual whose handwriting is to be identified. There are several practical and technical advantages to the inclusion in the evidence of such exemplars which were prepared informally and prior to the date of the questioned documents with which they are to be linked. Such exemplars cannot be reasonably attacked as unfair, imitative of the questioned documents, the result of improper influence, or the product of duress. Further, such exemplars are bound to carry the message of fairness and thoroughness to the court and jury. Additionally, they provide the document expert with an ally should he be asked to dispense snap judgments during cross-examination.

It is a favorite device of some cross-examiners to present the document expert with two or three bits of writing and to ask the witness whether they were written by the same person, perhaps the defendant. Obviously, the question as it is familiarly presented has not the slightest resemblance to the basis of the witness' direct examination. Some courtroom tragedians adopt great surprise when the expert does not immediately emote a definite conclusion from a thirty second, unmagnified glance at unidentified writings, perhaps prepared fraudulently during the trial, after the expert's direct examination, and with the express object of misleading him. The poor light of the average courtroom lends itself well to such "drama."

Opposing counsel should, of course, object to the injection of unidentified documents which have not been shown to be of any pertinence and which have not been admitted or proved to be in the handwriting of any of the principals in the case. At best this sort of cross-examination gives rise to proof of purely collateral issues which could lengthen a trial ad infinitum on collateral issues and tend to muddle rather than clarify the issues on trial.

If the expert is directed by the court to conduct an examination of writings which are presented on cross-examination, the expert should undertake to make a proper examination, using such time and technical equipment as are essential, in view of the nature of the problem. The expert should request that several exemplars of the known writer or writers be supplied, that at least one of these be from regular-course-of-business writings, preceding the date of the questioned document, and that information and cooperation concerning the cross-examination writings be comparable to that which was supplied in respect to the exemplars used for the witness' direct testimony. The probability is that the witness will not be successful in converting the issue presented on cross-examination to correspond fairly with the subject of his direct testimony. But he should make the effort so to do, and he should unmask any unreasonable requests for just what they are. The examiner would well remember that he will be in much stronger position to resist unfair exemplars on cross-examination, when he has founded his direct testimony on some exemplars which were prepared informally, in the regular course of events, prior to the dates of the questioned documents.

Similarly, the examiner will be in more favorable light when he is presented a question which has no definite answer or conclusion, if he has previously shunned the impression of knowing all the answers to all questions. Every inexperienced examiner has undoubtedly been tortured at times because the more he examines certain documents, the more indecisive his feelings concerning them become. There is a natural tendency for the inexperienced to feel that he is overlooking something, or misinterpreting some phase of a problem which he has not solved with definiteness. Sometimes in haste or desperation at failing to reach a clear-cut solution, the inexperienced examiner will express a conclusion which he has not really settled on in his own mind and cannot support with reasons which satisfy even himself.

It is well for every examiner to recall that it is not uncommon for even the most highly skilled examiner to have less than a definite conclusion to certain complex problems. This is a normal and reasonable situation. Not all documents embody basis for definite answers. When one is less than certain after a thorough study of a document problem, it is no part of weakness to so report. If an unreasonable question presented on cross-examination does not admit of a definite conclusion, the examiner should not hesitate to give his best judgment of the factors which lend themselves to reasonable solution, but he should also point out any "loaded" elements of such questions. No examiner will err, on cross-examination or otherwise, if he makes certain that all his conclusions are deliberately supported by valid reasons, and that he expresses no conclusions unless they represent firm personal convictions.

Document problems which do not admit of a definite conclusion in and of themselves present a distinct dilemma to the attorney when they form a part of his case in chief. Should he offer the limited or qualified testimony of the document expert and run the risk of its being misinterpreted? Or should he present no expert testimony at all, when it is less than conclusive in character, and run the risk that the jury will infer that such testimony, had it been offered, would have been adverse to his case?

This is not a problem which lends itself to generalities but there are certain basic considerations which deserve mention. When a case involving documents can be decided independently of the results of a scientific analysis which has produced less than a definite conclusion, it is probably proper in most instances to present no expert document testimony. But if the nature of the case leaves the court and jury in inevitable speculation as to why expert testimony has not been presented, it would appear necessary to offer such testimony, whether it is limited or qualified.

When the attorney has decided to present the qualified conclusions of the document expert, he should plan carefully with the expert the manner of his direct examination. Questions should be propounded to show clearly: (a) that all questioned and disputed document cases do not admit of a definite conclusion, (b) the reasons why the documents in the case at issue do not admit of a definite conclusion, (c) the detailed reasons which tend to support but do not definitely support the particular conclusion, and (d) *that the document expert has considered nothing but the evidential documents in reaching his qualified or limited conclusion.* Thereafter, counsel should argue that the testimony of the expert is by its very nature reasonable and unbiased, *and that it is cumulative to all the other evidence in the case.*

The document examiner who is called to testify to a qualified conclusion may be importuned by an enthusiastic advocate to indulge in obtuse language which tends to camouflage the limitations of the examiner's conclusion. The document expert should embrace no obligation to puff the evidence, to lead any court or jury to believe his conclusion is more than it really is. If the evidential documents lack adequacy for a definite finding, it is the expert's responsibility to say so. He should indulge in no language which obscures his real conclusions. Circumlocution such as "similar in all observable characteristics" is incomplete. It fails to meet the proposition whether the evidence embodies individualities in adequate kind and number in itself to support a firm conclusion and, if so, what that conclusion is, and what the individualities are which support it.

A word or two need be said concerning the question: "Do not document experts frequently disagree?" The number of basic disagreements between competent experts who have examined the same material is negligible in proportion to the volume of document examinations being accomplished. For those who are interested in percentages, such disagreements are estimated at a small fraction of one percent of the evidential document cases submitted for formal analysis by competent personnel. For example, in one series of some six thousand cases, basic disagreements between competent examiners averaged approximately one tenth of one percent.

Opposing testimony among two or more document experts

is rare. The instances which do occur, however, are a source of grave concern to every thinking examiner. What causes those disagreements which do develop? One or more of the following: (a) inadequate or non-representative exemplars, (b) misinformation supplied by other witnesses which is so intimately linked to the evidential documents as to influence their evaluation, (c) less than a high order of skill in analyzing a given document problem, (d) honest divergence of judgment in assessing an intricate pecularity or series of characteristics, for example, the tremor of infirmity versus the tremor of fraudulent simulation, and (e) dishonesty.

One point in connection with disagreements should be maintained in ordered perspective. Expert testimony in the hundreds of cases in which there are no disagreements should not be besmirched by the circumstance that in some few cases, disagreements among experts have occurred. Additionally, in those isolated cases wherein disagreements are encountered, the following considerations are pertinent: Is the so-called disagreement a basic divergence in conclusions or does it relate rather to the degree of certainty respecting the same conclusion? Have all the experts examined the identical documents and been supplied the same external information and, if not, what significance have the documents and data which were not commonly considered? Are the experts equally qualified and experienced in the specific problem in issue? Did the experts perform examinations of equal thoroughness? Which expert presents the more convincing reasons for his conclusions?

Especially in connection with criminal matters, one frequently is asked whether a case should be tried on the testimony of the document expert alone. In this author's view, such question poses a misconception of the real issue and evades the underlying question which should be resolved in deciding whether a charge should be filed or a case should be tried. A case should not be set in motion any more or any less readily on the testimony of a document expert, than it should on the testimony of a doctor, a lawyer, or an Indian chief. The consideration which should be decided in advance of a decision to try each case is whether the

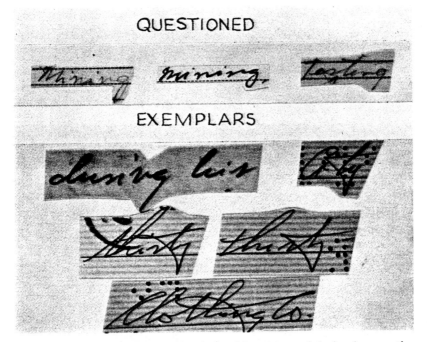

Figure 80. Striking individuality in rapid writing of jurist—interruption of movement following *i* to inject *i* dot.

testimony of the document expert in the particular case is convincing in and of itself. Only when the answer is a clear-cut, resolute "yes" should a case be founded on document testimony alone. An attorney has available to him the means of resolving this question. Pre-trial demonstrations by the prospective expert witness should be the rule rather than the exception in cases wherein the document evidence is the principal or only evidence.

Virtually every attorney opposing the facts and who is without evidence to rebut effective document testimony will lament with all due melancholy that the examination of questioned documents is not an exact science. One would almost be led to infer momentarily that everything should be disregarded which is not per se "an exact science." Fortunately, for lawyers, judges, defendants and litigants, mechanics, professors, generals, butchers, bakers, candlestick makers, and inexact mathematicians, our civilization and the administration of justice are firmly entrenched in reason, and they do not debar all human endeavor embodying less than built-in, incontrovertible, infallible exactitude.

The simple truths are: the testimony of the document expert should be accepted when it convinces; the testimony of the document expert should be rejected when it fails to convince. It should be accepted for what it is worth, no more and no less.

And should the document expert taste error in this mortal sphere—reasonable, honest, non-disqualifying error—pray let us extend him the repechage. No master should subordinate the work and testimony of the document examiner or anyone else save convincingness and reasonableness, honor and justice.

BIBLIOGRAPHY

The following books and articles are recommended study and reference material for those who would pursue the interpretation and exposition of evidential documents. Many of the listed works themselves have extensive bibliographies to which attention is also specifically directed.

Ames, D. T.: *Ames on Forgery*, New York, Ames-Rollinson, 1900.

Black, D. A.: *Decipherment of Charred Documents*, JCC, Vol. 38, 1948.

Brown, C. and Kirk, P. L.: *Paper Electrophoresis in the Identification of Writing Inks*, JCC, Vol. 45, 1954.
Horizontal Paper Chromatography in the Identification of Ball Point Pen Inks, JCC, Vol. 45, 1954.

Business Equipment Publishing Co.: *The Typewriter, History and Encyclopedia*, New York, 1923.

Casey, J. P.: *Pulp and Paper*, 2 vol., New York, Interscience, 1952.

Chabot, C. and Twistleton, E.: *The Handwriting of Junius*, London, Murray, 1871.

Clark, W.: *Photography by Infrared*, 2nd ed., New York, Wiley, 1946.

Conway, J. V. P.: *The Identification of Handprinting*, JCC, Vol. 45, 1955.

Davis, R.: *Methods of Deciphering Charred Records*, Scientific Paper No. 454, U. S. Bureau of Standards, 1922.

Freeman, F.: *The Teaching of Handwriting*, Boston, Houghton-Mifflin, 1914.

Graff, J. H.: *A Color Atlas of Fiber Identification*, Appleton, Wisc., Inst. of Paper Chemistry, 1940.
Fiber Analysis, Pulp and Paper Microscopy, Appleton, Wisc., Inst. of Paper Chemistry, 1942.

Grant, J.: *Books and Documents*, London, Grafton, 1937.

Gross, H.: *Criminal Investigation*, 3rd ed., London, Sweet-Maxwell, 1934.

Hilton, O.: *Scientific Examination of Questioned Documents*, Chicago, Callaghan, 1956.
A Systematic Method for Identifying the Make and Age Model of a Typewriter from Its Work, JCC, Vol. 41, 1951.

Hunter, D.: *Papermaking Through Eighteen Centuries*, New York, Rudge, 1930.

Kirk, P. L.: *Crime Investigation*, New York, Interscience, 1953.

Lehner, S.: *The Manufacture of Ink*, 3rd rev., London, Scott-Greenwood, 1926.

Lucas, A.: *Forensic Chemistry and Scientific Criminal Investigation*, 4th ed., London, Arnold, 1945.

Mason, W. A.: *A History of the Art of Writing*, New York, Macmillan, 1920.

Mitchell, C. A.: *Documents and Their Scientific Examination*, London, Griffin, 1922.

Mitchell, C. A. and Hepworth, T. C.: *Inks, Their Composition and Manufacture*, 4th ed., London, Griffin, 1937.

O'Hara, C. E. and Osterburg, J. W.: *An Introduction to Criminalistics*, New York, Macmillan, 1952.

O'Neill, M. E.: *The Restoration of Obliterated Ink Writing*, JCC, Vol. 27, 1936.

Osborn, A. S.: *Questioned Documents*, 2nd ed., Albany, N. Y., Boyd, 1929. *The Problem of Proof*, Newark, N. J., Essex, 1926.

Osborn, A. S. and Osborn, A. D.: *Questioned Document Problems*, Albany, N. Y., Boyd, 1944.

Quirke, A. J.: *Forged Anonymous and Suspect Documents*, London, Routledge, 1930.

Radley, J. A. and Grant, J.: *Fluorescence Analysis in Ultra Violet Light*, New York, Van Nostrand, 1933.

Rhodes, H. T. F.: *The Craft of Forgery*, London, Murray, 1934. *Forensic Chemistry*, New York, Chem. Pub., 1940.

Roberts, S. H.: *Eradication, Erasure and Obliteration*, J. Chem. Ed., Vol. 22, 1945.

Saudek, R.: *Experiments with Handwriting*, London, Allen-Unwin, 1928.

Scott, C.: *Photographic Evidence*, Kansas City, Mo., Vernon, 1942.

Stevenson, J. N., Editor: *The Manufacture of Pulp and Paper*, 3 vol., New York, McGraw-Hill, 1937-38-39.

Waters, C. E.: *Inks*, Circular C426, U. S. Bureau of Standards, 1940.

Williams, T. I.: *An Introduction to Chromatography*, London, Blackie, 1948.

INDEX